ƒP

THE MYTH OF THE FIRST THREE YEARS

A New Understanding of
Early Brain Development and Lifelong Learning

John T. Bruer

THE FREE PRESS

The Free Press
A Division of Simon & Schuster
1230 Avenue of the Americas
New York, NY 10020

The Free Press and colophon are trademarks
of Simon & Schuster Inc.

Manufactured in the United States of America

Designed by MM Design 2000, Inc.

10 9 8 7 6 5 4 3 2 1

Library of Congress Cataloging-In-Publication Data

Bruer, John T., 1949-
        The myth of the first three years a new understanding of early
Brain development and lifelong learning / John T. Bruer.
        p. cm.
Includes bibliographical references and index.
1. Learning, Psychology of.   2. Educational psychology.
3. Pediatric neuropsychology.   I. Title.
BF318.B79   1999   99-34934
155.4'13—dc21   CIP

ISBN: 0-7432-4260-2

For information regarding special discounts for bulk purchases, please contact Simon &
Schuster Special Sales at 1-800-456-6798 or business@simonandschuster.com

FOR LILI

CONTENTS

ACKNOWLEDGMENTS

O ver the past two years, many people have helped me with this project. Although I had been following research in cognition and neuroscience, my colleague Susan Fitzpatrick first suggested that I start thinking about what that research might really mean for child development. Since then, she has regularly and cheerfully explained numerous topics in neuroscience to me and reviewed draft chapters. Susan's suggestion and urging resulted in a lecture I delivered at Carnegie-Mellon University in November 1996. Howard Gardner read an article I had written based on the lecture and encouraged me to publish it. It appeared as "Education and the Brain: A Bridge Too Far" in the November issue of *Educational Researcher*.

Responses to the article prompted me to expand the article into a book on brain science and early childhood development. Mike Rose and Steve Pinker commented on early versions of the book proposal. Together, they urged me to try to think like a writer and write like a thinker. During the research and writing, Pat Goldman-Rakic, Bill Greenough, and Jeff Lichtman cheerfully answered e-mail questions about synapses, critical periods, and enriched environments and read draft chapters. Numerous other writers and scientists also willingly responded to e-mail inquiries from a person that some of them had never met or even heard of before. I thank them all for their help. Steve Sherblom and Mindy Bier made several valuable suggestions that make the book more reader-friendly than it otherwise might have been.

Susan Arellano helped me refine my early proposal and presented it to the editorial board of The Free Press. Philip Rappaport, my editor at The Free Press, has done a superb job keeping me on task and on schedule.

Thanks to my son Matthew for reminding me how the metric system works and for checking in at my study periodically with much appreciated mineral water and chocolate. Thanks to my son Jake for reminding me how my bibliographic management software works and for coming to my technological rescue on numerous occasions. Finally, thanks to my wife Lili for giving me the day-by-day support and encouragement I needed to see the project through.

I hope the final product is commensurate with the help, encouragement, and support all these people have given me.

St. Louis
May 31, 1999

THE MYTH OF THE
FIRST THREE YEARS

CHAPTER 1

THROUGH THE PRISM
OF THE FIRST THREE YEARS

One afternoon in early fall of 1996, the phone on my desk rang. The call was from a journalist who was writing an article for a national parenting magazine. She was doing a story for her readers based on the then recently released Carnegie Corporation report *Years of Promise*. She told me that I was on the media list for the report—a list of interested or knowledgeable people, sent out in the report's press kit, who would be willing to speak to journalists. My name appeared on the list because for the previous decade I had been funding and writing about applications of modern psychology to education and school reform.

She asked me, "Based on neuroscience, what can we tell parents about choosing a preschool for their children?" When I answered, "Based on neuroscience, absolutely nothing," I heard a gasp on the other end of the line. The journalist politely suggested that I must have been living under a rock for the past four years. She told me that there was a wealth of new neuroscience out there that suggested otherwise.

I did not think I had been living under a rock. And I did not offer my answer casually. For the four previous years, along with almost everyone else, I had been hearing murmurs about how new breakthroughs in neuroscience—our new, emerging understanding of how the brain worked and developed—were about to revolutionize how we think about children, childcare, and parenting. I had read the occasional articles, features, and editorials that had been published in major American newspapers. The headlines did get one's attention: "To Shape a Life, We Must Begin Before a Child is 3," "Building a Better Brain: A Child's First Three Years Provide Parents Once-in-Lifetime Opportunity to Dramatically Increase Intelligence," and "Youngest Kids Need Help, U.S. Told: Federal Government Urged to Focus on Their 1st Three Years." The articles under the headlines said that new brain research could now tell us how and when to build better brains in our children. The first three years—the years from birth to 3—we were told, are the critical years for building better brains.

In early 1996, I read Sharon Begley's February 19 *Newsweek* article, "Your Child's Brain." Although I was glad to see that brain science was getting cover-story attention, some of the claims and statements in the article, especially those offered by childcare advocates who were not brain scientists, seemed farfetched. But that is not unusual in popular articles about science and research.

In spring 1996, because I was on the media list, I saw an advance copy of the aforementioned Carnegie Corporation report, *Years of Promise*, which briefly touched on what the new brain science might mean for educational practice. The report's discussion of the brain science was so fleeting that I dismissed the neuroscience as rhetorical window dressing to increase interest in educational policy and reform. About that time, during a visit to the MacArthur Foundation, I read an editorial in the *Chicago Tribune* titled "The IQ Gap Begins at Birth for the Poor." In this piece, as in others I was now collecting in my file cabinet, the writer claimed that applying the new brain science offered "the quickest, kindest, most promising way to break" the cycle of poverty and ignorance among the nation's poor and to "raise the IQs of low-scoring children (who are disproportionately black). . . ."

However, the more I read, the more puzzled I became. For the previous eighteen years, at three private foundations, I had been following research and awarding grants in education, cognitive psychology, and neuroscience. All during that time, I was wondering when I would begin to see credible research that linked brain science with problems and issues in child development and education. I was puzzled because, despite what the headlines proclaimed and the articles stated, I had not yet seen any such research.

In late spring 1996, I had received an invitation to attend a July workshop in Denver, Colorado, sponsored by the Education Commission of the States and the Charles A. Dana Foundation. The workshop's title was "Bridging the Gap Between Neuroscience and Education." Based on the reputations of the sponsoring organizations, I thought that the workshop would offer an ideal opportunity for me to learn about the new brain research and its implications. Unfortunately, I had a scheduling conflict and could not go, but my colleague, Dr. Susan Fitzpatrick, a neuroscientist, attended in my place.

When she returned from Denver and briefed me about the meeting, I had expected to hear about new research linking brain development, child development, and education. Instead, she began her briefing with a one-word description of the workshop: "Bizarre." She told me, and my subsequent reading of the workshop report confirmed, that there was little neuroscience presented in Denver and certainly none that I had not previously known about. There were, however, Susan told me, wide-ranging policy discussions, bordering on the nonsensical, in which early childhood advocates appealed to what might be most charitably described as a "folk" understanding of brain development to support their favorite policy recommendations. Reflecting on the Denver meeting and its report, it seemed as if there was, in fact, no new brain science involved in the policy and media discussions of child development. What seemed to be happening was that selected pieces of rather old brain science were being used, and often misinterpreted, to support preexisting views about child development and early childhood policy.

Thus, my response to the journalist's call reflected my conviction, based on what I had read and heard up to that point, that there was no new brain science that could tell parents anything about choosing a preschool. Her call, however, did change how I thought about the issue. If claims about brain science were confined to rhetorical flourishes in policy documents like *Years of Promise* or to the editorial page of the *Chicago Tribune*, it was probably relatively harmless. It might even draw attention to some important issues that policymakers and newspaper readers might otherwise ignore. However, it struck me as a very different matter if people were taking the brain science seriously as a basis for policy and legislation and if parents were asking what the new brain science meant for raising their children and choosing schools. Following that call, I was no longer comfortable being merely puzzled or bemused about what I read in the newspapers. I wanted to understand what was going on and to consider more carefully what the brain science might actually mean for children, parents, and policy.

The White House Conference

My job as a foundation officer responsible for funding research in mind, brain, and education, plus some strategic letters from colleagues, earned me an invitation to the April 17, 1997, White House Conference on Early Childhood Development and Learning: What New Research on the Brain Tells Us About Our Youngest Children. For those interested in children and education, the conference was an exciting development. It promised to focus the nation's interest, even if only for a few days, on science, children, and related, highly significant social issues. What better occasion could there be to understand the growing enthusiasm for what brain science meant for parenting and policy?

Mrs. Clinton opened the conference. She emphasized the significance of our new understanding of the brain. Brain science confirms what parents have instinctively known, "that the song a father sings to his child in the morning, or a story that a mother reads to her child before bed, help lay the foundation for a child's life, in turn, for our nation's future." Unlike fifteen years ago, when we thought babies' brains were virtually complete at birth, she told us, we now know brains are a work in progress. This means, Mrs. Clinton said, that everything we do with a child has some kind of potential physical influence on that rapidly forming brain. Children's earliest experiences determine how their brains are wired. The first three years are critically important because so much is happening in the baby's brain. "These experiences," Mrs. Clinton said, "can determine whether children will grow up to be peaceful or violent citizens, focused or undisciplined workers, attentive or detached parents themselves." She did caution that the early years are not the only years that matter and that brain science also tells us that some parts of the brain, in her words the "neurological circuitry for many emotions," remain a work in progress until children are at least 15 years old.

Mrs. Clinton introduced the president, who outlined several initiatives that his administration was undertaking on behalf of mothers, families, and the nation's youngest citizens. The president in turn introduced the chairman for the morning session, Dr. David A. Hamburg, then president of the Carnegie Corporation of New York. It was Hamburg who three years earlier had initially called attention to the "quiet crisis" afflicting young children, a crisis addressed in the Carnegie Corporation's report *Starting Points*. That report, in Hamburg's words, "focused on the strong evidence from research on brain and behavior development, indicating the long term effects of early experience." *Starting Points*, he said, also noted the wide gap between scientific research and public knowledge, between what we know and what we are doing with that knowledge. The White House Conference represented a major step in an attempt to close that gap.

Dr. Donald Cohen, director of the Yale Child Study Center, spoke next. The Yale Center has been a leader in the areas of early childhood research and education. Mrs. Clinton had worked with the Child Study Center while she was a law student at Yale. In his talk, Cohen also mentioned that, while at Yale, both he and Mrs. Clinton had been students of Sally Provence, one of the pioneers in the study of early childhood deprivation. He proceeded to speak about the effects of early experience on children's behavior and development, stressing parents' active role in brain development and the importance of social and emotional relations in child development: "When parents and caregivers take care of a child they're doing a lot more than just feeding or bathing or comforting. They're helping the child's brain to develop, shaping his temperament and teaching the child about the world." These early experiences are enduring because they lay down the pattern for all future development. The correct experiences enable the child to use "his intellectual potential to its limits." Although, he cautioned, we should never write children off, it can be difficult to change long-lasting, maladaptive patterns later in life.

Oddly, only one neuroscientist spoke at the White House Conference, Dr. Carla Shatz of the University of California at Berkeley. She spoke for eight minutes (as did most of the other experts). Drawing on her own studies of the visual system, she summarized what neuroscientists know about early brain development. She explained that there are two major periods in brain development. During the first period, which starts before birth, the brain's gross wiring is laid out under genetic control. It is as if the brain were laying out the major trunk lines of a telephone system. Then, also prior to birth, a second phase begins. Spontaneous brain activity—neural firing that is not caused by sensory stimulation—starts. One can think of it, she explained, as "autodialing" among telephones. This activity among the brain's neural cells begins to construct its fine wiring. Following birth, sensory experience takes the place of the spontaneous, automatic dialing to complete the wiring process. During the fine-wiring phase, the neural connections, or synapses, that are used become permanent and the others wither away. Neuroscientists believe, Shatz explained, that relying on neural activity for fine-tuning results in brains that are more complex and sensitive than if they were hard-wired at birth. This complexity and sensitivity has survival value. As Shatz said, "If after all, things were just hard-wired—if everything in the brain were just strictly programmed genetically by molecules that wired everything up, A to B, C to D, and so on—then we wouldn't be nearly as adaptable as we are as organisms."

She also summarized a classic piece of neuroscientific research that figures prominently in the early childhood literature. Adults who suffer from cataracts for extended periods, say five years, can have surgery to fix the damaged eye's optics. The surgery restores adults' vision. Yet, children born with cataracts, if operated on at age 5 years, remain blind in the afflicted eye. Five years of abnormal visual experience early in life has different and more serious consequences than five years of abnormal visual experience late in life. David Hubel and Torsten Wiesel, who won the Nobel Prize in 1981, developed animal models, using cats and monkeys, in an attempt to figure out why adults and young children fare so differently following surgical treatment for cataracts. They found, among other things, that if kittens were deprived of visual input to one eye early in development, the kittens remained permanently blind in that eye. It is this research, Shatz said, that underscores the importance of early experience for brain development. Brain science tells us, she concluded, that there are "early periods of development, windows of opportunity or critical periods, as scientists call them, during which time experience is essential for brain wiring." Shatz's brilliant, highly accessible presentation was the only brain science presented at the White House Conference.

Dr. Patricia Kuhl, from the University of Washington, spoke about her work on infants' speech perception. Babies are born with the ability to discriminate the sounds found in all human languages, Kuhl told us. In her research, she has found that by six months of age infants have already focused on the particular sounds that their native language uses. Simply listening to adult speech alters infants' perceptual systems. This early perceptual learning makes the infant responsive to its linguistic environment but also renders the infant vulnerable, almost hostage, to that environment. She emphasized how important it is for parents to be sure that their infants can hear, see, and process stimuli present in the environment. She carefully noted that research cannot yet tell us how much talking it takes—thirty minutes a day or two hours a day—to support this kind of development and learning. She discouraged parents from trying to accelerate the normal course of language development: "We don't recommend flash cards to try to teach words to three-monthers." She advised doing what comes naturally: "Nature has provided a perfect fit between the parents' desire to communicate with the child and the child's ability to soak this information up." Kuhl's presentation marked the end of the scientific presentations at the conference.

The balance of the White House presentations addressed policy issues. All these presentations had a similar structure. If the experts mentioned brain science at all, and more than a few did not, it was early in their allotted eight minutes. They invoked the new brain science to give a prefatory, high-level justification for better prenatal, postpartum, and pediatric care; family planning; welfare reform; parent education; and high-quality day care and early childhood education.

Toward the end of the afternoon session, Rob Reiner spoke in his capacity as founder of the Rob Reiner Foundation and mastermind of the I Am Your Child campaign. I Am Your Child is a national public education campaign on early child development. Reiner spoke for around forty minutes on his efforts to educate the public about the far-reaching implications of the new brain science. He described his role as creating the public will to get the country to change how we think and "to look through the prism of zero to three in terms of problem solving at every level of society." According to Reiner, "If we want to have a real significant impact, not only on children's success in school and later on in life, healthy relationships, but also an impact on reduction in crime, teen pregnancy, drug abuse, child abuse, welfare, homelessness, and a variety of other social ills, we are going to have to address the first three years of life. There is no getting around it. All roads lead to Rome."

At the day's end, I left the East Room and caught a cab to National Airport, no less puzzled about the relevance of brain science to early childhood than when I had arrived.

I remained puzzled because at the conference I heard numerous wide-ranging policy recommendations based on the new brain science. Yet, I had heard relatively little brain research, none of which I could comfortably describe as new, and none that pro-vided a clear link between blind kittens and welfare reform. In fairness, and as David Hamburg had said, in a one-day confer-ence only a limited and highly selected body of material could be presented. Nonetheless, as I rode to the airport, my initial im-pression was that the only substantive link between Carla Shatz's morning presentation and Reiner's afternoon talk had been lunch with Mrs. Clinton.

Could it be true, as Reiner suggested, that if we understood the new brain science and acted on it we could solve social prob-lems ranging from infant mortality to unemployment to low in-telligence to urban violence? Could it be true, as he said, that what we know about brain development during the first three years of life was "the key to problem solving at every level of society?"

Based on what I had heard at the conference, my answer to both questions was "Highly unlikely." There were too many gap-ing holes, breathtaking leaps of faith, and monumental extrapo-lations in the arguments the participants made in their attempt to link problems like teenage pregnancy, drug addiction, and home-lessness with brain science.

Of course, one possibility was that a gifted, enthusiastic spokesman like Reiner might have used the occasion of a White House conference to get the message out forcefully and dramat-ically, engaging in a touch of hyperbole along the way.

Further post–White House reading suggested otherwise. Reiner's enthusiasm about the critical, wide-ranging implica-tions of brain development during the first three years was not confined to his White House remarks. It was also the central mes-sage in his national awareness campaign. In launching I Am Your Child, Reiner said, "A child born today will be three years old as we enter the new millennium. We know that these years last for-ever—they directly impact the adult that the child will become. As a country, we need to focus attention on these critical years so that our children truly reach their potential and to ensure that they grow to be healthy adults."

On July 21, 1998, as the brain and early childhood message

moved from the White House to levels of local government, Reiner addressed the National Association of Counties. He told them, "Whether or not a child becomes a toxic or non-toxic member of society is largely determined by what happens to the child in terms of his experiences with his parents and primary caregivers in those first three years."

Where did these ideas about brain and early childhood come from?

The Three Neurobiological Strands

Although Reiner is a superb spokesman for the campaign, neither the message nor the science that supposedly supports it is his creation. The source of the message and the science are two prominent policy documents, *Starting Points* and *Rethinking the Brain*. On numerous occasions, Reiner has cited *Starting Points* as the document that substantiated many of his beliefs about early childhood and that provided the impetus for him to move forward with the I Am Your Child campaign.

Starting Points has a structure exactly like the White House Conference. The report's discussion of brain science is confined to only 2 pages that appear early in the 132-page report, in a section entitled "The Critical Importance of the First Three Years." These few paragraphs on the brain, which cite three research papers and an unpublished speech, serve as a short prelude to the more extensive presentation of social and behavioral science and the discussion of policy issues.

Rethinking the Brain, released in conjunction with the White House Conference, extends and elaborates the brain science assumed to be fundamental to a science of early childhood. *Rethinking* addresses a professional audience and attempts to explain how the new brain science establishes the critical importance of the early years of life. *Rethinking* was written to summarize the research that was to be the scientific foundation for I Am Your Child.

Three recurrent neuroscientific themes or strands run through these documents, as they do through most of the popular literature on the brain and early child development. These three strands pick out significant, but not particularly new, findings from the field of developmental neurobiology—the science of brain development—as the basis for rethinking the relation between brain science and child development.

First, brain scientists have known for over two decades that the brain grows and changes during the early months and years following birth. Over the past twenty-five years, in a variety of species, neuroscientists have observed that starting shortly before or after birth (depending on the species), the brain is the site of a fit of "biological exuberance." Infant brains produce trillions more synapses—the connections between nerve cells—than are found in mature, adult brains. As *Rethinking* put it, the 2-year-old's brain has about twice as many synapses as her pediatrician's. During this early developmental period, brain connections form at a rate that far exceeds the rate at which connections are lost. In humans, this fit of exuberance—the period when synapse formation outstrips synapse elimination—seems to be confined to the first three years of life. *Rethinking* appropriately cites the research of Pasko Rakic at Yale University and Peter Huttenlocher at the University of Chicago as evidence for this developmental phenomenon.

The second neurobiological strand is the one Carla Shatz spoke about at the White House Conference. Neuroscientists know that there are critical periods in brain development. There are times during which the brain requires certain kinds of stimulation if it is to develop normally. Critical periods, then, are time windows during development, when, given the right kinds of stimuli, normal brain circuitry develops. The wrong kind or total lack of stimulation during these periods results in abnormal brain development. Once the windows close, the opportunity to wire certain kinds of neural pathways, if not totally eliminated, diminishes substantially. The development of the visual system is everyone's favorite example of a critical period. The birth-to-3 literature cites the work of David Hubel and Torsten Wiesel and their blind kittens in discussions of critical periods.

The third neurobiological strand that figures prominently in the brain and early childhood literature is that of enriched, or complex, environments. Animal studies over the past four decades, mostly on rats, have found that animals raised in complex, enriched environments have more synapses in certain parts of their brains than animals raised under more austere conditions. The birth-to-3 literature extrapolates this rodent finding to human infants. Some of the best research on the effects of rearing conditions on rodent brains is that of William Greenough and his colleagues at the University of Illinois.

Brain and early childhood articles, including *Starting Points* and *Rethinking the Brain,* weave these three strands together to formulate an argument that the first three years of life are uniquely important for optimal brain development. This argument is intended to support Reiner's assertion about the fundamental importance of looking through the prism of birth to 3 if we are to understand and solve problems at every level of society.

Most simply stated, the argument is this: During the first three years of life in humans, there is a period of rapid synapse formation that connects nerve cells into functioning circuits. This time of rapid synapse formation is *the* critical period in brain development. Although the brain continues to develop after this time, it does so by losing or eliminating synapses, not by forming new ones. It is during this critical period when enriched environments and increased stimulation can have the greatest effect on brain development. Thus, the first three years provide policymakers, caregivers, and parents a unique, biologically delimited window of opportunity, during which the right experiences and early childhood programs can help children build better brains.

Enthusiasts for this argument will, no doubt, accuse me of vastly oversimplifying their position. And I have, a bit, although you can find a statement of the argument almost identical to the one above in *Starting Smart: How Early Experiences Affect Brain Development,* a document presented on the Ounce of Prevention Fund Web site. For now, I would respond to this charge by pointing out that in the following chapters we will examine the argument and its premises much more fully and carefully as we try to understand what neuroscience does say and what its implica-

3 strands:
- biological exuberance
- critical period
- complex environments

tions might be for child development. I would also respond that, although the argument's champions might on occasion present more sophisticated, elaborated, and qualified versions, my simple, unvarnished statement captures the message that nonexpert parents, caregivers, and educators have taken away from the brain and early childhood literature.

The Promise of Brain-Based Policy, Education, and Parenting

For those who accept this three-stranded argument, looking through the prism of birth to 3 offers a vision no less global and far-reaching than the one Reiner articulated at the White House.

According to *Starting Points*, once we appreciate what brain science tells us about the critical importance of the first three years of life, it becomes evident that we should invest in better family planning, parenting education, and pre- and postnatal health services. We should guarantee high-quality childcare choices for all parents and use federal funds, if necessary, to assure that all parents have access to high-quality childcare. We should strengthen the Family and Medical Leave Act to provide several months, if not an entire year, of paid work leave for new mothers. We should improve salary and benefits for childcare workers, provide home-visiting services for first-time mothers, expand infant nutrition programs, take steps to reduce injuries to young children, and enact legislation to control firearms. Why? Because all of these things, and no doubt numerous others we could think of, have an impact on children's brains during the first three critical years.

If the first three years are so critically important, then as *Time* magazine reported, "There is an urgent need . . . for preschool programs to boost the brain power of youngsters born into impoverished rural and inner-city households." Why? Because, as some early childhood advocates argue, impoverished parents, preoccupied with the daily struggle to provide basic necessities for their children, may not have the resources, information, or time they need to provide stimulating experiences that foster brain growth. Following this argument, one solution would be more and better programs like Head Start.

Boosting brainpower in disadvantaged children was one of Head Start's primary, original objectives. A perennial criticism of Head Start has been that any cognitive gains its participants make, as measured by improved IQ scores, fade over the years and disappear. But, Head Start advocates argue, the new brain science offers a defense of the program and an explanation for why the early gains fade. Children enter Head Start at age 3, after the critical first three years of brain development are over. Thus, the Head Start experiences occur too late in life to fundamentally and permanently rewire children's brains. Therefore, the brain-based policy solution is to provide programs like Head Start for children during the first three critical years, when their brains can be fundamentally and permanently rewired. The science of early brain development, in this way, provides not only a ready defense of an existing program, but an argument for an expanded one. Congress no doubt considered this argument favorably when in 1994 they created Early Head Start as part of the Head Start reauthorization package. Early Head Start provides education and childcare on the Head Start model to children from birth to age 3.

Viewed through the prism of birth to 3, bad early childhood experiences—especially, it seems, among the nation's inner-city poor—cause permanent and detrimental brain changes. These brain-damaged individuals have a lifelong propensity for violence and criminal behavior. In *Inside the Brain*, science writer Ron Kotulak explained, "The first three years of a child's life are critically important to brain development. Unfortunately, for a growing number of children, the period from birth to age 3 has become a mental wasteland that can sustain only the gnarled roots of violent behavior. Society needs to focus on this period if it is to do something about the increasing rates of violent and criminal acts."

If we understood the new brain science, he goes on, we would also understand that children born to mothers without a high school education, 22 percent of all births in the United

States, are at special risk. Kotulak explains why: "These women often do not know how to promote stimulation—talk, toys, physical activity—to their infants, which can lead to stunting of the brain during the crucial first three years of life."

An editorial in the *Chicago Tribune* expanded on the theme that too few synapses beget too few synapses: "In the first year, the communications network within the brain develops at a breathtaking pace. But if the neural synapses, the bridges of that communications network, aren't exercised, they wither. That withering impoverishes the mind and, ultimately, nourishes the cycle of poverty." Impoverished minds result in impoverished citizens. Too few synapses, and our unwillingness to do something about it, explain why our citizens have behavioral problems, fail in school, are unable to a hold a job, and tend to engage in violent behavior. Too few synapses in the parents—a result of their own impoverished childhoods—further diminishes the brainpower of their offspring.

To use brain science to solve social problems like these would, of course, require that we have state institutions to assure that all children receive what we believe to be optimal developmental experiences, where "we" refers to society, not necessarily to parents or families. Dr. Bruce Perry, a child psychiatrist at the Baylor College of Medicine, has been highly vocal in spelling out his view of what the new brain science means for breaking the cycle of violence. Perry observed that we could solve these social problems but that it would require us to "transform our culture." According to Perry, "We need to change our child rearing practices, we need to change the malignant and destructive view that children are the property of their biological parents. Human beings evolved not as individuals, but as communities. . . . Children *belong* to the community, they are *entrusted* to parents." Needless to say, such a transformation would have far-reaching effects on our social, legal, and educational institutions. It would truly transform how we would think about families, children, and parents.

Looking through the prism of birth to 3 also has implications for formal education and school instruction. Frank Newman, president of the Education Commission of the States, said, "I don't think there is any question that these revelations [about early brain development] have a major impact on education policy and child rearing." Enriched school environments should help make the most of each child's mental capacities, but, echoing the Head Start argument, the new brain research indicates that formal schooling begins too late. "From the standpoint of brain development, children start school relatively late in life. Long before youngsters master the ABCs, their brains have passed many developmental milestones. Yet, education policy has not addressed how children learn before they arrive at school. Nor has policy focused on helping parents enrich the home environment so that their children will be ready to learn when they reach school age. Now research in brain development suggests it is time to rethink many educational policies, including those related to early childhood and special education." As one widely circulated quotation put it, we have to act and act early because "by the time a child starts first grade, the most critical of his learning years are past."

Of course, we would expect that looking through the prism of birth to 3 would also have some far-reaching implications for parenting. Popular articles do offer advice to parents. What is surprising, though, is that when we move from the global level of Early Head Start and eradicating urban violence, to the level of how to raise Jack and/or Jill, the advice to parents seems far less dramatic and revolutionary. Often the brain-based advice offered to parents is oddly vague, contradictory, and what one might call "middle-class traditional."

What should parents do to build better brains? What matters most during those early years? Instead of specific advice and a few new insights, parents are told that everything matters in those early years—loving, holding, talking, reading, and exploring the environment. During the critical years, when experiences can permanently rewire the brain, we should engage children in culturally valued activities. Early, but not later, exposure to music, art, or chess can, parents are told, change the fine anatomy of the child's brain forever. Parents should make use of the windows of developmental opportunity nature has provided, applying a full-court developmental press every minute during the birth-to-3 developmental season. Failure to exert full-court pressure can have long-term consequences. Parents must begin to realize that "if they, or their baby sitter, or day care provider isn't speaking articulately to baby, SAT scores may be at stake." The implications are sufficiently dire to make most middle-class parents take notice. The advice provided is sufficiently vague to leave parents deeply uncertain and profoundly anxious about what they should do differently and about what does matter—other than everything—during the early years.

Not only is the advice vague, but it is also contradictory. Brain-based parenting advice has the same character as the advice one gets from reading books on nutrition and diet that you can find in most airport bookstores. You want to live to be 100? You should have a glass of red wine every day, but avoid alcohol.

Here is one example sure to leave parents confused. The major theme in brain-based advice to parents is the importance of early stimulation during the critical years to facilitate optimal brain development. Those are the years during which parents, if they provide the right kind of stimulation, can build better brains. It is during those years that they and their baby-sitters can improve or damage future SAT scores. One would think that the science-based parenting advice surrounding such a central theme would be pretty clear-cut. It isn't.

Parents are sometimes told that it is time to throw out Dr. Benjamin Spock and his old advice to new parents, "Trust your common sense." Why? Because we now know that "for the majority of fathers and mothers, doing the things that maximize a child's potential is not intuitive." If so, parents need expert help. To fully exploit nature's windows of opportunity, an article in the *Chicago Tribune* cited this expert advice: "People often ask Dr. Harry Chugani how much mental stimulation a baby should receive. Chugani, a pediatric neurologist at Wayne State University in Detroit, said no precise answer can be given, but generally 'as much as you can.'"

On the other hand, parents are also told that although *opti-*

mal stimulation is good, *too much* stimulation is bad. The amount of talking, reading, and singing must be carefully matched to the child's developmental level, personality, and mood. According to child psychiatrist Stanley Greenspan, as quoted in *Newsweek,* "Only 20 to 30 percent of parents know how to do this instinctively." Its not just a matter of the more and the earlier the stimulation the better!

Yet other popular articles in *Newsweek, Time,* and *Working Mother* tell parents that the implications of brain science are not that radical and that the new discoveries reaffirm Dr. Spock's endorsement of common sense. Parents are told that science is, in fact, reaffirming what our parents and grandparents knew instinctively. In Sandra Blakeslee's *New York Times* article on the White House Conference, parents were told that although talking to babies is important, "the curriculum that most benefits babies is simply common sense."

Parent might well ask, "So, what is it I should do?" or "What's all the fuss about anyway?"

One place a bewildered parent might look for answers to these questions is the I Am Your Child Web site, the official site for the Reiner Foundation's national awareness campaign. The Web site and campaign are generously funded by fifteen major foundations and corporations, including the MacArthur Foundation, the AT&T Foundation, Johnson & Johnson, the Carnegie Corporation, the Dana Foundation, the Commonwealth Fund, the Robert Wood Johnson Foundation, and the Heinz Foundation. If we were to find a clear, concise brain-based message for parents, we would expect to find it there.

Once at the Web site, under the heading "The First Years Last Forever," a parent would find five paragraphs on brain development, in which brain science is presented in a very general, but accurate, way. A parent would read that an infant's brain has 100 billion nerve cells that grow and connect to form the circuits that control our senses, movement, and emotions. Early childhood experiences "help to determine brain structure, thus shaping the way people learn, think, and behave for the rest of their lives."

There is another section called "Brain Facts," which informs parents about early synapse formation, how experience shapes brain circuitry, and how critical periods or "prime times" occur during brain development. A parent would also read that the kind of care a child receives during these critical periods can effect development and that warm, responsive care is good for the brain.

I Am Your Child presents ten guidelines that parents can use to promote children's healthy development. Among these guidelines are: Be warm, loving, and responsive; talk, read, and sing to baby; use discipline to teach; be selective about TV watching; choose quality day care. There is nothing controversial on the list, but there is nothing on the list that would prompt the average parent to say, "Wow, I never heard that before!" Parents could find the same guiding principles in parenting books and advice columns published thirty years ago.

There are video clips on the Web site in which experts offer advice to parents. The experts include T. Berry Brazelton, Barbara Bowman, C. Everett Koop, and Bruce Perry. For the most part, these experts have substantial followings and deserved reputations in child development and public health, but none, with the possible exception of Perry, would consider himself or herself an expert in developmental neurobiology.

The site provides a list of links to other parenting Web sites and a bibliography of the parenting and child development literature that cites works published between 1980 and 1997. Among the authors are the "the usual suspects"—Brazelton, James Comer, Alvin Poussaint, Penelope Leach, to name a few. The I Am Your Child bibliography cites only one book on brain development, Kotulak's *Inside the Brain.*

If parents go to the site thinking that they will find new insights into parenting practices, derived from brain research, that will optimize brain, intellectual, and social development, they will be disappointed. After visiting the site and its associated links, many parents might still be wondering what all the fuss is about.

A parent who reads the I Am Your Child guidelines carefully, however, might notice that the guidelines emphasize the importance of a secure relationship, or secure attachment, between caregiver and child and what such a relationship means for a child's social and emotional development. This connection appears under the first guideline "Be warm, loving, and responsive" and links responsive care and secure relationships to research on attachment theory (a theory we will examine more closely in the next chapter). I Am Your Child states that research on attachment shows that children who receive warm and responsive care and who are securely attached to their caregivers cope with difficult times more easily when they are older. Securely attached infants are more likely to develop a healthy response to stressful situations, and this response is, the Web site suggests, the result of optimal early brain development. According to some attachment theorists, secure attachments are formed, or fail to form, during the first three years of life. This is why parents should provide warm, loving care, respond to baby's cues and clues, establish routines, establish a close tie to your child by talking, singing, and reading, and look for childcare that does all of the above.

The importance and lifelong consequences of attachment form the central message of I Am Your Child. It is no accident that the site's page introducing advice for parents carries the banner "The First Years Last Forever" and that the final words of advice are "the first years truly last forever." This same message is implicit in *Starting Points* and developed in some detail in *Rethinking the Brain*. It is this theoretical viewpoint that is at the basis of Reiner's conviction that all roads lead to Rome and that we should view children and the world through the prism of the first three years. This is why, as Reiner told the county government representatives to applause, "justice begins in the high chair, not the electric chair."

However, a thoughtful parent reading the Web site might also notice something else. There are some general statements about brain development, followed by ten rather traditional parenting guidelines, guidelines that for the most part emphasize social and emotional development. But just what is the connection, for example, between the 100 billion nerve cells, developing healthy brain circuitry, and selective TV watching? Does someone know that *Sesame Street* is better for the brain than *Rugrats* or *The Simpsons*? Do we know that one hour of television is good for the brain, two hours bad, and no television whatever the best of all? The short answer: no.

I Am Your Child suggests that there is a connection between brain science and the parenting advice, but like *Starting Points* and the White House Conference, it is not all that clear or specific about what that connection is. There is talk about the brain, followed by some hand waving, followed by advice to parents. None of this instills much confidence in the claim that the new brain science is about to revolutionize parenting and childcare.

Further Grounds for Skepticism: What Neuroscientists Say

There are additional reasons why we should be skeptical about the benefits of viewing the world through the prism of the first three years. Neuroscientists, as opposed to early childhood advocates, have a somewhat different view concerning the possible implications of early synapse formation, critical periods, and enriched environments for early childhood.

According to the brain and early childhood literature, early stimulation somehow affects early synapse and brain circuit formation. It implies that parents and caretakers can influence this process and that we know in some detail what kinds of early experiences would result in the desired brain circuits and in optimal brain development.

Neuroscientists, even neuroscientists who have been involved in discussions of early brain development, have a different view. In a September 1992 *Scientific American* article, Carla Shatz noted that if we observe children's behavior, it is evident that children who are grossly neglected—left in their cribs for the first year of life—develop motor skills abnormally slowly. From this observation, it is reasonable to infer, she says, that children do require a normal environment for normal development. Children need normal tactile, linguistic, and visual stimulation to develop normally. However, she continues, "Based in part on such observations, some people favor enriched environments for young children, in the hopes of enhancing development. Yet current studies provide no clear evidence that such extra stimulation is helpful. . . . Much research remains to be done before anyone can conclusively determine the types of sensory input that encourage the formation of particular neural connections in newborns." Apart from eliminating gross neglect, neuroscience cannot currently tell us much about whether we can, let alone how to, influence brain development during the early stage of exuberant synapse formation. If so, we should not be surprised that brain-based parenting advice is vague and contradictory.

The brain and early childhood literature suggests that the first three years of life is the critical period for brain development. It's a time when the young brain's learning power is almost limitless. As Hillary Clinton describes it, "The computer comes with so much memory capacity that for the first three years it can store more information than an army of humans could possibly input. By the end of three or four years, however, the pace of learning slows. The computer will continue to accept new information, but at a decreasing rate. . . . But it is clear that by the time most children begin preschool, the architecture of the brain has essentially been constructed. From that time until adolescence, the brain remains a relatively eager learner with occasional 'growth spurts,' but it will never again attain the incredible pace of learning that occurs in the first few years." After this critical period, as Harvard child psychiatrist Felton Earls told Ron Kotulak, "A kind of irreversibility sets in. There is this shaping process that goes on early, and then at the end of this process, be that age 2, 3 or 4, you have essentially designed a brain that probably is not going to change very much more."

This interpretation of critical periods assumes that the brain learns best and is unusually plastic only during the early, superdense years. It also assumes that the experiences we have during those years are particularly powerful and have long-term, irreversible consequences.

Again, neuroscientists see it a little differently. In a review on child development and neuroscience, Charles Nelson and Floyd

Bloom deftly summarize our emerging understanding of how molecular and cellular events contribute to brain development. Most important, they also discuss some genuinely new findings in neuroscience—what happens in the brain when adults learn new motor skills and the rapidity with which the adult brain can reorganize after loss of sensory input from an amputated limb. The new findings Nelson and Bloom allude to suggest that the brain retains its ability to reorganize itself in response to experience or injury throughout life. They conclude, ". . . it may be useful to question the simplistic view that the brain becomes unbendable and increasingly difficult to modify beyond the first few years of life. Although clearly much of brain development occurs late in gestation through the first years of postnatal life, the brain is far from set in its trajectory, even at the completion of adolescence." If so, we should be wary of claims that parents have only a single, biologically delimited, once-in-a-lifetime opportunity to help their children build better brains.

Although not in a scientific journal, the neuroscientist Arnold Scheibel, who, with his wife Marian Diamond, has studied the effects of enriched environments on brain development, arrived at a similar conclusion. In an article he wrote on the implications of the new brain science for education, Scheibel expressed reservations about popular claims that the brain's ability to learn varies during development and that teaching should be keyed to those critical periods when the brain is most receptive. "Those who subscribe to this view," he wrote, "might be left with the feeling that if we miss a critical window of opportunity between ages 3 and 6, or between 8 and 10, we have failed in our responsibilities, and the students we have missed are destined for linguistic or cognitive mediocrity. But I believe this is an inaccurate conclusion drawn from improperly interpreted structural and functional data." Scheibel goes on to argue that the brain remains a "superbly attuned learning instrument for virtually all of life." If so, we should be wary of the claim that by the time a child starts first grade the most critical of his learning years are past.

Finally, the brain and early childhood literature tends to misinterpret the significance of research on the effects of enriched environments on brain development. The policy and popular articles assume that if early experiences during the critical period sculpt the brain for life, then rich, complex early experiences will sculpt rich, complex brains for life: "Research bears out that an enriched environment can boost the number of synapses that children form." Based on a conviction that the early years are the most crucial learning years, these articles argue that early enrichment is particularly powerful: "In an environment rich in all sorts of learning experiences, the growth of synapses—the connections between nerve cells in the brain that relay information—is more lush, and this complex circuitry enlarges brain capacity. Infants who are not held and touched, whose playfulness and curiosity are not encouraged, form fewer of these critical connections."

Neuroscientists who have done research on the effects of enriched environments on brain structure take a different view. In 1997, William Greenough, one of the most prominent researchers in this area, wrote a short piece for the *APA Monitor*, a publication of the American Psychological Association. He stated that despite the claims of children's education organizations and articles in the popular press on how early childhood experiences can enhance children's cognitive development between the ages of 0 and 3, the neuroscience used to support these claims is not new. Furthermore, he continued, careful examination of the evidence does not support a selective focus on the first three years. Experience plays a major role in brain development, but claims that it plays a more important role in the first three years than at other times need to be assessed carefully. He emphasizes that his own, oft-cited research on animals raised in complex environments indicates that the brain continues to be plastic—modifiable by experience—throughout later development and into adulthood. According to Greenough, the existing neuroscientific and behavioral evidence do not support an exclusive focus on birth to 3 to the relative exclusion of older age groups. If so, we should be wary of claims that the only, or the most important, time to provide enrichment is the early years.

At this early point in our exploration of brain science and child development, what these neuroscientists are saying should serve to heighten our skepticism about what we read in the papers and see on the Internet. Their comments should at least prompt us to take a more careful, critical look at brain science and the merits of viewing the world through the prism of the first three years. Of course, by themselves the neuroscientists' assertions bear no more weight than do those of the most fervent birth-to-3 brain advocate. However, the neuroscientists have reasons for saying what they do, reasons that derive from their weighing and consideration of the existing scientific evidence. So, rather than merely listing authorities and assertions pro and con, it is time that we look carefully at that evidence. After we review the evidence in the subsequent chapters, we will see that we do not have a revolutionary, brain-based action agenda for child development. What we have instead is the Myth of the First Three Years. And, looking through this mythical lens gives us a highly distorted view of children, parents, and early childhood policy.

Some might ask, "Why should we care whether what we have is a research-based agenda or a myth? We need better programs and policies for children and current programs are underfunded. Any argument that would lead to improved opportunities and outcomes for children is a good argument." One could take this position and many well-intentioned early childhood advocates do take this view. It's the hard-nosed but often realistic view that everyone knows that policy arguments are merely exercises in political rhetoric. Sophisticated citizens (usually those making the arguments) know this and the argument is intended only to sway the emotions of the unsophisticated. On this view, science, as such, and the evidence it might bring to a policy discussion, do not matter. Science is just another rhetorical tool that happens to elicit a strong emotional response in the public, like God, the sanctity of motherhood, the innocence of childhood, and the flag. Some might then say, "It's a myth and I know it. But by God, given what I want to do, it's a useful myth." If this is the stance we wish to take, then we should also admit that our arguments about what to do for children and families and why we should do it carry the same weight as the blustery, staged debates from the left and right that entertain us over dinner on *Firing Line*. On this view, although science and scientists might have a place at the policy-setting table, others at the table do not take the science seriously if it conflicts with their policy goals.

On the other hand, if we do take the science seriously, then we have to care if we are acting on a science-based agenda or a myth. What a science-based policy argument should do is add some evidence and factual basis, beyond our own biases, prejudices, and ideological tastes, for what the preferable policy might be. Science should inform us of what the optimal strategies might be to reach a policy objective. What the science can add to the policy debate are insights about the causes, mechanisms, and leverage points that we could most effectively exploit to reach our goal. If the science is wrong, misleading, or misinterpreted, then we are trying to achieve our policy, and parenting, goals by pushing the wrong, ineffective, or nonexistent buttons. We are wasting time and resources attempting to bring about change via causes, mechanisms, and leverage points that do not exist.

The brain and early childhood literature appeals to neuroscience to argue for the unique importance of the first three years of life. According to that literature, seeing the world through the prism of birth to 3 is the key to improving opportunities and outcomes for children, families, and the nation. If this view is accurate, then Early Head Start, removing children from violent inner-city neighborhoods, and applying a full-court developmental press are good ideas. But what if, as our current grounds for skepticism at least suggest, brain science does not support that key claim? We might want to find other and better reasons to invest $4 billion in Early Head Start or to consider other ways, using other leverage points, to expend that money to help young children. We might be reluctant to transform our culture and change our views about who children belong to. We might question the prudence of decreasing expenditures for adult education or special education on the grounds that a person's intellectual and emotional course is firmly set during the early years. We might be reluctant to tell parents to apply full-court pressure during the early years and to suggest to parents that early learning problems will leave their children at a permanent disadvantage.

Being critical of the Myth does not mean being critical of making the world better for children. It signals, instead, a commitment to look at the science of early brain development seriously in the hope that we can identify the most efficient leverage points with which to push parenting practices and early childhood policy in the desired direction.

Myths often have interesting histories. The Myth of the First Three Years is no exception. The Myth's popularity and its beguiling, intuitive appeal is rooted in our cultural beliefs about children and childhood, our fascination with the mind-brain, and our perennial need to find reassuring answers to troubling questions. That history is the subject of the next chapter.

After we review the Myth's history, we will examine each of the Myth's three biological strands, reviewing the science and the conclusions we can and cannot draw from this research for child development. In Chapter 3, we will explore what neuroscientists know about rapid synapse development in the early years of life. Chapter 4 discusses our current neurobiological understanding of critical periods and what critical periods mean for childcare and development. Chapter 5 presents the research on enriched environments and examines what it implies for early childhood education and lifelong learning. Based on this review of what we know about early childhood and brain development, Chapter 6 attempts to answer the question "What is a parent, or any of us who are interested in children, brain science, and policy, to do?"

CHAPTER 2

THE STARTING POINTS

W hen my wife and I brought our firstborn son home from the hospital, his Chinese grandmother was there to help us novice parents through those initial trying weeks. Within minutes of seeing her first grandson, Grandmother noticed something highly unusual and disturbing. Most of us have two, nonintersecting lines that cross our palms, one beginning from each side of the hand. Our son had a single line that ran completely across his right palm. Grandmother interpreted this as indicating that our infant would, one day, kill someone.

Several months later, we were lucky to hire Gilda, a Filipino English teacher, to help us care for our son. She saw the single line on Jake's right palm and told us that our son was destined to become a powerful CEO. Gilda's was a slightly different interpretation, but one consistent with an apparent Oriental belief that the single right palm line indicated future power over human lives.

When Jake, now 12 years old and a child of the computer age, first heard these predictions, he gave a wry smile and said, "Who knows. Maybe I'll end up doing both. But a lot things are still going to happen between now and then." Jake, based on his beliefs of what determines a child's future, readily dismissed his grandmother's and Gilda's cultural-specific, one-palm-line theories. Grandmother and Gilda are infant determinists. Jake is not.

1. infant determinism
2. psych processes generalize broadly
3. human action motivated for sensory pleasure

Infant Determinism: As the Twig Is Bent

The starting point for the Myth of the First Three Years is not new brain science of the 1990s or even old brain science of the 1960s. The starting point was in Europe, three centuries ago, long before there was a science of the brain, where for historical and cultural reasons our progenitors came to believe that the early years of life held the same power over children's destinies as the single palm line. That belief persists and still has great appeal in our culture, as we saw in the fundamental message of I Am Your Child, "the first years last forever." Like Grandmother and Gilda, many of us still tend to be infant determinists. We just have a different theory.

In a recent book, the developmental psychologist Jerome Kagan characterizes infant determinism as one of three seductive ideas that influence how we think about human development and behavior in both our folk theories and scientific theories. According to Kagan, the other two seductive ideas are the belief that psychological processes generalize broadly—the belief for example that rat intelligence as measured in a laboratory maze tells us something specific and useful about human problem-solving ability—and the belief that most human action is motivated by a desire for sensory pleasure.

The infant determinist thesis holds that early experience—experience that occurs during the early, critical period of development—leaves an indelible, irreversible mark on the mind-brain-psyche for life. The Myth of the First Three Years is but the most recent and the most highly brain-based version of the determinist thesis.

Kagan traces the origins of the Myth to early eighteenth-century Europe. The wives of the successful bourgeois merchants and artisans no longer had to devote the greater part of the day to "gathering." Successful, urbanized families had been freed from the agricultural and domestic hard labor required for family survival. Mother no longer had to turn over the responsibility for postweaning childcare and socialization to older siblings or to other older children in their communal group, as is the practice in traditional and agricultural societies. The social role of these women had changed. They had become comfortable middle-class wives, who assumed, or were given, the role of shaping the futures of their infants. Successful infants would reflect well on the family and assure the family's future economic status. Rather than horoscopes or palm lines, urbanized Europeans and their American counterparts came to believe that a mother's care and love of an infant and her interaction with it were the most powerful and biologically natural forces in shaping the life of the child. These forces were so powerful that once infancy had passed, no future experiences could reverse or change the course the mother set for her infant in those early years. Of course, if a mother's care was natural and woman's status was defined in terms of this natural role, not caring for your children, or having other adults take care of them for you, was considered unnatural and detracted from the woman's status. Three centuries later this cultural mind-set of what we believe to be natural and what unnatural—a mind-set that easily confuses biological forces with cultural practices—continues to ensnare parents, particularly mothers, in a web of conflict and guilt. We still tend to believe that mothers have profound power, but only if they fulfill their "natural" obligations to their infants.

Although these beliefs developed in early eighteenth-century Europe and were legitimized in the writings of philosophers like Rousseau, infant determinism became immensely popular in early twentieth-century America. Kagan relates how one 1914 expert warned parents against taking their infants to any kind of public performance. Even if the child was well behaved or slept through the concert, this experience would leave an indelible developmental scar, for which the parents would pay dearly twenty to forty years later. Infant determinism in one guise or another was incorporated into all textbooks on developmental psychology. It became "scientific" to say that infants needed as much predictability and social interaction as mothers or caregivers could possibly provide.

Also, in a deterministic vein, psychoanalytic theory emphasized the lifelong effects of the mother's interaction with her infant. According to Freud, this relationship "is unique, without parallel, established unalterably for a whole lifetime as the first and strongest love-object and the prototype of all later love-relations."

Over the last four decades, versions of infant determinism have donned a more scientific or medical face, as child psychiatry became a focus of intellectual interest and as researchers became interested in the study of personality development. John Bowlby and Erik Erikson were major figures in this movement. They both argued that the first hours, weeks, and months of life had a profound influence on all of a child's subsequent development.

In the early 1950s, Bowlby formulated attachment theory. Although trained as a psychoanalyst, he developed his theory based on ideas from animal behavior, evolutionary biology, information processing, and psychology. Attachment theory attempts to explain how the predictable presence of responsive, loving attachment figures during infancy is the sine qua non of lifelong mental health. Bowlby's theory, as elaborated in the 1960s and 1970s by Mary Ainsworth, continues to have a considerable impact on how researchers think about parent-infant relationships and on the message these researchers transmit to parents and caregivers.

The importance of an early loving bond between mother and infant also entered into assumptions about animal research. In the 1950s and 1960s, Harry Harlow at the University of Wisconsin studied the effects of social deprivation, including lack of a responsive mother, on infant rhesus monkeys. Harlow's experiments, some published in scientific articles with titles like "The Nature of Love" and "Love in Infant Monkeys," showed that monkeys suffered lasting adverse effects if social-maternal deprivation occurred early in their lives. Deprived adult monkeys suffered few, if any, adverse effects from isolation. This suggested that there was a critical period early in monkey life where loving care was essential for long-term, healthy development.

Harlow and his colleagues viewed the monkey experiments as a model for primates in general, including humans.

In the 1960s, psychologists such as Benjamin S. Bloom and Joseph McVicker Hunt further popularized the notion of critical periods in child development. During these periods, the right experiences would protect children forever from future hardships and misfortunes, not unlike how polio vaccine protects children from that disease for life. The wrong experiences, on the other hand, would blunt the development of children's potential and if severe enough would result in mental illness. In his influential 1964 book *Stability and Change in Human Characteristics*, Bloom argued that there was a critical period in a child's life during which an enriched environment could permanently raise a child's intelligence. To support his theoretical views, he cited the work of Freud, Erikson, Bowlby, and other child psychiatrists, as well as some of the then emerging work on the effects of sensory deprivation on monkeys.

In the mid-1970s, a group of medical, psychological, and educational experts joined in a major collaborative study, sponsored by the National Institutes of Health, called the Clinical Infant Development Project. This study examined the development of healthy infants raised in "multi-risk" families, families where poverty, mental illness, marital problems, and drug addiction put children at risk for unhealthy developmental outcomes. The research group, using ideas from child psychiatry and attachment theory, were specifically interested in why such infants tended to experience later developmental problems and in developing effective interventions to help these children. The report based on this study made no mention of brain research, however.

In 1977, as a result of the Clinical Infant Development Project, the scientists and advisors involved in the project started an informal "interest group" on early childhood. This interest group eventually became Zero to Three: The National Center for Infants, Toddlers, and Families. It was the first group to specifically declare a research and clinical interest in the first three years of life. Zero to Three, as they say on their Web site (www.Zero-ToThree.org), continues to "concentrate exclusively on these miraculous first years of life—the critical period when a child undergoes the greatest human growth and development . . . a period when you—the parent or professional—have the opportunity to make a great impact and positively influence a child's future."

The influences of this history are evident in *Rethinking the Brain*. In *Rethinking*'s discussion of brain development, synapse formation, and critical periods, there is a section entitled "The Importance of Attachment." It tells parents and caregivers that the stimulation children need is not reciting the multiplication tables and memorizing facts. What children need is "warm consistent care so that they can form secure attachments to those who care for them." As we saw in the last chapter, the lifelong importance of early, secure attachment is a fundamental message in I Am Your Child.

Infant determinism—the lifelong impact of enriching early childhood experience—has a long history in our cultural beliefs about childhood and parenting. Likewise, the determinist thesis has also been incorporated into our scientific theories about early personality development and mental health. From this very condensed historical sketch, we see that two strands of the Myth—critical periods and early enrichment—have been with us for centuries and were well entrenched in our scientific theories about child development by the mid-1950s. However, the brain had not yet made an appearance in the story. That came next.

The Brain and Child Development

Both neuroscience—the scientific study of the *brain*—and psychology—the scientific study of the *mind*—emerged as scientific disciplines in the late nineteenth century. As odd as it may seem now, given our contemporary interest in what brain development means for children's mental development, for most of their history these two disciplines evolved separately and independently. Neuroscientists were biologists who studied brain anatomy and physiology. Psychologists were behavioral scientists who studied patterns of behavior, mental processes, or the mind. Psychologists granted that the brain was important, but nonetheless claimed that they could study the mind without worrying about how the brain makes mental processing and thought possible. One might think, then, of psychologists as being interested in our mental software, happy to leave the task of figuring out how neural hardware ran the mental software to the neuroscientists. It is only in the last fifteen years that psychologists and neuroscientists have started serious collaborative research to study how the biological brain might implement mental processes, how the machine might actually run the software. For this reason, our theories of child development, including attachment theory, developed independently of what neuroscientists knew about brain development.

Attempts to think about the implications of neuroscience for child development began in the 1970s, when educators began to look at what brain science might tell them about how to help children with learning problems. Educators and psychologists initiated dialogues with neuroscientists.

In 1978, one of the first products of this dialogue was *Education and the Brain*, the seventy-seventh yearbook of the National Society for the Study of Education. All of the themes and neuroscientific ideas that characterize the Myth appear in that volume.

The volume's introductory chapter on brain science makes essentially the same argument that reappeared nearly twenty years later in *Rethinking the Brain*. The mature brain is the product of genetic blueprints plus environmental influences. Basic features of the brain are present at birth, but the brain undergoes tremendous growth and development in the early months and years. Citing neuroscientific research on critical periods and the effects of enriched environments on rats' brains, the author argues that the child's environment can profoundly influence this growth process. Genetics provides the neural framework and then the child's environment sculpts and fine-tunes the framework. Thus, by the mid-to-late 1970s, the third strand of the Myth—rapid early brain growth and synaptic exuberance—had also appeared, linked with the two prior strands of critical periods and early enrichment. The introductory chapter concluded,

"The social and political implications of this fact of brain functioning are obvious and far-reaching."

In a later chapter Herman Epstein, a developmental scientist then at Brandeis University, presented his theory of brain development. Epstein argued that there are predictable periods of brain growth, which he identified by measuring the circumference of children's heads. As a working hypothesis, Epstein suggested that educators should provide the most intensive intellectual input to children during the spurts in brain growth. He also used his theory to provide a biological explanation for why the Head Start program failed to have a permanent impact on disadvantaged children's intelligence. At the time, Head Start served children between the ages of 3 and 5. One should expect that gains from Head Start would be minimal and transitory, Epstein argued, because the 4-to-6-year age range is one of minimal brain growth. Based on his theory, Head Start should either serve 2-to-4-year-olds, the years during which there is a spurt of brain growth, or wait until children are 6 years old, the age at which the next spurt begins.

The editors of *Education and the Brain* developed three neuroscientific themes they thought were relevant to education. First, appropriate experience and stimulation could help overcome inherited or acquired brain deficits and assure healthy, optimal brain development. Second, the existence of critical periods implied that earlier stimulation was better than later, but that nonetheless, later stimulation could still be helpful. Third, the neuroscience of the day suggested that cerebral lateralization—right brain versus left brain—was important for human cognition and for understanding differences in children's learning styles. Just as today disadvantaged children are said to have too few synapses, they were then described as disproportionately right-brained. Right brain versus left brain, or hemisphericity, became a popular and influential theme in brain-and-education circles through the mid-1980s. It persists in the popular mythology and in educational circles, despite neuroscientists' criticisms that educational applications of hemisphericity are based on a highly oversimplified understanding of the underlying research.

Even in the 1970s, ideas about the brain, development, and infant determinism were not confined to academic journals. The first popular and fully fledged presentation of the Myth I have been able to find appeared in the 1977 book *Kindergarten Is Too Late*, written by Masaru Ibuka, one of the founders of the Sony Corporation. The one-line summary on the book's cover succeeds in telling the whole story: "From birth to three are the key years for developing your baby's intelligence—don't wait until Kindergarten." Ibuka wrote his book because he thought that student unrest in Japan during the 1970s might have had its origins in that generation's early childhood experiences and because he was deeply impressed by Dr. Shinichi Suzuki's method—the Suzuki method—for teaching violin to very young children.

To my knowledge, Ibuka's book had little impact in the United States, but it is interesting in that he formulates the same argument, using the same neuroscientific ideas, that the Myth used twenty years later. Neuroscience plus infant psychology show, he claims, that the key to lifelong intelligence is children's experiences during the first three years, because this is the time during which brain cells develop most rapidly. According to Ibuka, the brain's neurons are separate at birth and are formed into functioning circuits by the infant's sensory experiences. Seventy to 80 percent of the brain's neural connections, Ibuka tells us, are formed by age 3.

To assure that the circuits form properly, Ibuka recommends that parents touch and speak to their babies, teach children a second language, play and listen to (Western) classical music, teach them to walk correctly, and teach them to use the left as well as right hand (good advice today for parents looking to raise the next Michael Jordan). Reading to babies did not appear on Ibuka's recommended list.

In the mid-1980s, two other scholarly publications attempted to build interdisciplinary bridges among brain science, psychology, child development, and education. *The Brain, Cognition, and Education* included a pivotal chapter by the neurobiologist Patricia Goldman-Rakic, in which she described what was known about brain development in primates before, and in the months following, birth. Goldman-Rakic summarized research on synapse formation and synapse elimination in the brain—the Myth's first strand—dating back to the mid-1970s.

This volume is notable for two critical, skeptical chapters on the relation of neuroscience to child development and education. Mark Rosenzweig from the University of California at Berkeley, one of the pioneers in studying effects of enriched environments on rats, observed that educators often oversimplify what neuroscience does know about the effects of experience on brain development and tend to apply brain-based theories, like right-brain–left-brain, prematurely. He also warned that educators should be wary of overgeneralizing from single examples or cases. Most of the neuroscientific research on critical periods studied the development of the visual system. As it happens, critical periods in the visual system occur early in development, but from this single example educators should not infer that critical periods and brain plasticity in general are restricted to the early months and years of development. He related one aspect of his own work (work he reported in 1966) that raised the most interest, surprise, and skepticism among his professional colleagues. He had found that the brains of *adult* rats changed anatomically and chemically in response to the environment and that these changes were associated with better learning and problem-solving abilities.

Susan Chipman's chapter in *The Brain, Cognition, and Education* still offers one of the most thoughtful critiques of how neuroscience was (and is) being misinterpreted and misapplied in education and childcare policy. Most neuroscientists believe that their science may one day provide solutions for real-world educational problems, but they also tend to believe that it is premature to look for such applications now. Yet, the prestige of neuroscience remains seductive for practitioners and advocates of the educational and behavioral sciences. Chipman, a psychologist with the Office of Naval Research, argues that there are few, if any, tight links between the findings of basic neuroscientific research and sound educational practices or policies. She urged neuroscientists to take a more active role in formulating accurate descriptions of their work and its implications. "At a time when educators have become fascinated with research on the brain, it would be appropriate to develop a text for educators in training that reflects informed judgment and equips educators to defend themselves against irresponsible appeals to the authority of neuroscience." Today, if to "educators" we add "politicians, early childcare providers, and the public," Chipman's advice remains sound.

A 1987 issue of the journal *Child Development*, the flagship publication of the Society for Research in Child Development, devoted a special section to developmental psychology and neuroscience. Two articles from that issue still often appear in the birth-to-3 literature. William Greenough, James Black, and Christopher Wallace's "Experience and Brain Development" reviews research on the three strands of the Myth: synapse growth, critical periods, and enriched environments. Patricia Goldman-Rakic's "Development of Cortical Circuitry and Cognitive Function" discusses how the development of mental functions, like short-term memory, might be related to synaptic maturation during brain development.

Parents and Policymakers Take Notice

During the 1980s, popular articles and books appeared that presented the "new" brain science to parents and the general public. A 1985 *Children Today* article explained the process of synapse growth following birth and stressed the importance of early sensory stimulation for babies. The article mentioned the brain's unique period of rapid growth in the months following birth and cited research on the effects of enriched environments on brain development in rats as providing proof for parents that babies' brains grow with use. The article told parents that stimulation increases synaptic connectivity and that increased synaptic connectivity means increased brainpower. Parents should stimulate all the senses—place bright, intriguing objects around the nursery, play music, and show babies things, because "every time a baby responds to a stimulus, the brain stores the experience." All these ideas continue to appear today in the brain and early development literature. Unlike the recent brain and infancy literature, this 1985 article is not alarmist. If a child's early experiences are less than ideal, it tells parents not to worry. Children and their brains are remarkably resilient.

In a 1986 article for *Parents' Magazine*, "Brainpower: You Can Make Smarter Babies," the educational psychologist Dr. Jane M. Healy told parents about new, convincing neuroscientific evidence that the presence or absence of certain types of stimulation can influence infants' brain growth and their lifelong ability to learn. Healy discussed Marian Diamond's research on baby rats raised in enriched environments, rats which, according to Healy, developed "better brains" than their littermates raised in more spartan environments. Diamond also found, Healy emphasized, that stimulation could create new synapses throughout the rat's life span. Healy, sounding a note of reason, quotes Diamond on the dangers of extrapolating from rats playing with toys in cages to preschoolers responding to academic enrichment. She describes research on critical periods and visually deprived kittens, but cautions that there was no consensus on whether children could learn certain skills better at some ages than at others or whether lost ground could be regained. Healy cautioned parents against trying to use brain science to raise "superbabies"— babies who are unusually advanced in skills normally not acquired until school age—an idea that had some currency at the time. She elaborated on these ideas and the three strands of the Myth in her 1987 book *Your Child's Growing Mind*. In a 1990 book, *Endangered Minds*, she rehashes the same neuroscience to argue that television (including *Sesame Street*), video games, and other gewgaws of contemporary American culture, are changing children's brains, turning us into a nation of *aliterates* with short attention spans. Although this second book is more shrill and alarmist—"the future of society is at stake"—Healy still soft-peddles claims about critical periods, never specifically mentioning the unique importance of the first three years of life.

Also in the mid-1980s, brain science began creeping out of

parents' magazines into policy debates, at least on editorial pages. A May 31, 1985, editorial in the *Chicago Tribune* stated that "accumulating knowledge about how the brain develops in the first years of life indicates that appropriate mental stimuli can permanently raise a child's level of intelligence." Among other things, the editorial recommended that half- or full-day preschools, "preferably on a Montessori model, should supply non-pressuring mental stimuli." The 1985 *Tribune* recommendation anticipates a similar one it made on its editorial page over ten years later, when in an October 1996 editorial Joan Beck argued that applying neuroscience to education is the first step in improving America's schools. By age 2½ or 3, children should start in Montessori school, where, according to Beck, "the educational program comes closer to matching neurological findings than any I know."

In 1992, also in the policy realm, Zero to Three: The National Center for Infants, Toddlers, and Families published *Heart Start: The Emotional Foundations of School Readiness.* In two brief, early sections, "The Most Damaging Possibilities" and "The Consequences of Neglect," the report links Harry Harlow's work on social-maternal deprivation in monkeys and Bill Greenough's work on rats in enriched environments with ideas from child psychiatry and attachment theory. The report emphasizes the importance of early social and emotional development to help the child make a smooth transition into formal education. According to the report, ". . . we know that the infant's brain reaches two-thirds of its full size by the age of 3, that in size and complexity it evolves, in those years, more rapidly that it ever will again, and that certain kinds of learning occur far more readily in infancy than afterward." *Heart Start* concludes with a list of recommendations to improve early childcare policy and education.

Between April and December 1993, pursuing its interest in the brain and public policy, the *Chicago Tribune* ran two series of articles on the new brain science. In one series Ron Kotulak, a science writer at the *Tribune,* described how research was unraveling the mysteries of the brain. In 1996, Kotulak's Pulitzer Prize–winning series appeared as a book, *Inside the Brain: Revo-*

lutionary Discoveries of How the Mind Works, a book that has since assumed a central role in the Myth.

In his book, Kotulak presents the three strands of the Myth: synapse growth, critical periods, and enriched environments. When the critical learning windows are open, information flows into the brain easily, but, he tells us, these windows open only for short time periods. When they close, and many of them close by age 3, the fundamental architecture of the brain is complete. Learning is possible later, but it becomes much more difficult.

It is in Kotulak's articles and book that we first glimpse what is to become the neuroscientific theory of everything—viewing the world through the prism of the first three years, as Reiner put it. Unlike the articles of the 1970s and 1980s that gave advice to parents on how to raise their children or attempted to encourage interdisciplinary research in child development and education, Kotulak's articles suggested how the new brain science might serve as the scientific basis for broad policy recommendations and reform efforts.

As Kotulak relates, a question and a suggestion from his editor provided the starting point for his investigation. Kotulak's editor was disturbed by increasing levels of violence among Chicago's and the nation's young people. "Why do some children turn out bad?" the editor wanted to know. "Was there anything going on in brain research that could provide some answers?" On the basis of his journalistic research, Kotulak answered, "Yes." Modern molecular biology, genetics, and neuroscience allow us to understand how the brain works. The research tells us, according to Kotulak, that the first three years of a child's life are critically important to brain development. Children exposed to inner-city environments during the critical period are having their brains permanently wired in ways that predispose them to violence and crime. As he says, "Society needs to focus on this period if it is do something about increasing rates of violence and criminal acts."

Kotulak claims that research on the biology of violence allows us to pose the age-old question "Why do some kids turn out bad?" as "What happens inside a developing brain that turns a child into a killer?" (NOTE: The second question is not exactly the same one as the first!) Brain research explains the epidemic of violence. Kotulak's explanation appeals to the three strands of the Myth: "For millions of American children, the world they encounter is relentlessly menacing and hostile. So, with astounding speed and efficiency, their brains adapt and prepare for battle. Cells form trillions of new connections that create the chemical pathways of aggression; some chemicals are produced in overabundance, some are repressed." He continues, "What research can now tell us with increasing certainty is just how the brain adapts physically to this threatening environment—how abuse, poverty, neglect, or sensory deprivation can reset the brain's chemistry in ways that make some genetically vulnerable children more prone to violence."

Many children are raised in deprived rather than enriched environments. Kotulak cites the drop in the number of two-parent families, increased poverty, increased teenage pregnancy, and violence on television as factors that expose children to enormous stress. The problem, as he sees it, is particularly severe in America's inner cities. He quotes the psychologist Susan Clarke, who studies stressed monkeys at the University of Wisconsin: "'If you think about the fact that the inner-city population is chronically stressed, and there's a lot of that population that is chronically pregnant, then we can begin to see some of the biology that may be responsible for high rates of aggression in children.'"

Finally, "The rising tide of abuse and neglect of children occurs during the critical period when children are developing what Harvard's Felton Earls calls 'moral emotions.' These are emotions rooted in brain chemistry and are established in the first three years of life."

Thus, during the 1970s, a second starting point for the Myth emerged: neuroscience and our fascination with that mysterious organ inside our skull. Then a marriage occurred. There was marriage of our folk and scientific theories of child development to neuroscience—a marriage of infant determinism to brain science. As Susan Chipman pointed out, neuroscience, like infant determinism, exerts a seductive influence on parents, educators, and policymakers. Our tendency to accept neuroscientific research uncritically and often prematurely allows us, in this case, to look for biological justification for our abiding faith in the importance of early, enriched childhood experience. What we have is a new, neuroscientific version of infant determinism, the Myth of the First Three Years. A myth based both upon our beliefs about childhood and our fascination with the brain is particularly intriguing—doubly seductive. Such a myth can be surprisingly easy to propagate.

Starting Points

By the 1990s, the Myth had already been simmering in the background of education journals, parenting magazines, and the occasional newspaper article. In April 1994, only four months after Kotulak's *Tribune* series ended, the Carnegie Corporation of New York released *Starting Points*, the report of its Task Force on Meeting the Needs of Young Children. This report, along with the subsequent media campaign and coverage it engendered, brought the issue of the brain and early childhood into national prominence. It initiated a campaign to spread the beguiling Myth to a highly receptive audience.

The Carnegie Corporation, a private foundation that has been extremely active in addressing the needs of children and youth, established the Task Force on Meeting the Needs of Young Children in 1991. Its charge was to develop a report that would provide the scientific framework for an action agenda to ensure the healthy development of children from birth to age 3. The Task Force focused on this age group because, in the view of the Corporation, it was the most neglected. Dr. David Hamburg, then president of Carnegie, described the plight of underprivileged infants and toddlers as a "quiet crisis." There are no institutions, like school or preschool systems, dedicated to the needs of this age group. Head Start did not begin until children were 3 years old. Health, welfare, and education agencies that serve our youngest citizens work independently of one another and sometimes at cross-purposes. Thus, the Task Force began with a conviction that the needs of this age group had to be addressed and with the conviction that the first three years are particularly important in establishing the foundation for subsequent development and learning. They did not review the neuroscientific literature and come to this conclusion; rather, it was their starting point.

According to *Starting Points*, the scientific framework is at hand on which to build an action agenda to attack the "quiet crisis." Such an agenda would close the gap between what research has shown about the importance of the prenatal months and the first three years of life and the social polices that address the needs of young children. According to the report, the gap is particularly wide in two areas: "Our policies reflect neither our growing knowledge of early brain development nor our understanding of factors that tend to protect young children or place them at risk."

What is odd about *Starting Points*, as we noted in Chapter 1, is that despite pointing to the gap between our understanding early brain development and policy, it says very little about early brain development. According to Rima Shore, the writer who drafted the final report, *Starting Points* was never intended as a systematic review of the literature. An earlier draft contained very general references to brain development, a discussion like one might find in a high school or college text, but not one that was suitable for a document intended to provide a scientific basis for an early childhood action agenda. After reviewing scientific and medical journals, as well as newspaper and magazine accounts, and interviewing scientists, Shore drafted the few paragraphs appearing early in the report to at least partially answer the question: What do we know about brain development in the early years (0 to 3) that might inform policy and practice?

When *Starting Points* was officially released, it received extensive media coverage. The major dailies—*New York Times*, *Washington Post*, *Boston Globe*, and *Chicago Tribune*—ran stories, features, and editorials. All these articles emphasized how the report, relying on the latest scientific knowledge about brain development, provided a compelling argument that as a nation and as individuals we should pay more attention to children's earliest years. Most of the articles emphasized the *new* neuroscientific evidence. However, a *New York Times* article pointed out that when it comes to synapses, neuroscientists had long known that the principle of "use them or lose them" governs synaptic development.

The media coverage also picked up on the "first years last forever" theme, although this too was relatively poorly supported in the document. As a review of *Starting Points* published in the *Journal of the American Medical Association* pointed out, "The description of the critical importance of early environmental influences on child development is generally accurate, although the report's assertion of the permanence of early effects on later brain function is not well supported."

It is unusual for any foundation-supported policy report, no matter how excellent, to generate the initial, let alone the sustained, interest accorded *Starting Points.* The response surprised even the Carnegie Corporation and Task Force members, who entertained relatively modest expectations for the report. When *Starting Points* was first released, Hamburg commented that it would not have a far-reaching, immediate impact; rather, the Task Force members hoped it would provide momentum to various pieces of child welfare legislation that were then languishing on Capitol Hill. Hamburg hoped that the report would become a "pebble in the shoe of the national consciousness" to prompt action on behalf of the nation's youngest citizens.

Three years later, in an address given at the plenary session of the 1997 Winter Meeting of the National Governors' Association, Hamburg accurately observed: "Evidently the *Starting Points* report touched a nerve because when it came out in 1994 it had extraordinary news coverage. Never has anybody in the field of children, youth and families been able to recall a report that had such extensive, such constructive and largely accurate coverage. In an age of cynicism there was no cynicism to speak of in response to this report."

In subsequent policy reports and articles, *Starting Points* is justifiably cited as the seminal document in the brain and early childhood literature. Initially, however, it seemed as if even its authors were not aware of the power and appeal of its message that married infant determinism with brain science. *Starting Points* created a critical mass of interest in the Myth that initiated its move from obscure education journals and the odd parenting magazine into the public spotlight. *Starting Points* provided a seed that grew into a national campaign to increase public interest in the needs of children, a campaign in which brain science played a prominent role.

Starting Points contributed to Rob Reiner and the Reiner Foundation's active involvement in issues of the brain and early child development. The story of how Reiner and Hollywood become involved has been told numerous times.

Reiner had been thinking about brain development for thirty years, but he began working actively on the issue only in 1994. He and his wife, Michele Singer Reiner, as new parents and self-described "veterans of psychotherapy," had become acutely aware of how their own childhood experiences affected their adult lives. They were concerned about how their behaviors would affect their children, but could find little scientific research on the subject. His own psychoanalysis, said Reiner, had led him to the realization that how he functioned as an adult—as he once characterized it, like Harry in *When Harry Met Sally*—was the result of what had happened to him during his first three years. As he said, maybe "what happened to me in my first two or three years is not so far afield from what happens to everybody on this planet."

But, Reiner wondered, as a private citizen, what could he do with this insight? He called Tipper Gore, a person who he knew was deeply interested both in education and mental health. After a meeting in Washington with Mrs. Gore and representatives from the United States Department of Education, Reiner became convinced that the most important thing one could do would be to help all children arrive at school ready to learn. When children entered school, their minds should be unencumbered by emotional disorders caused by physical abuse or neglect.

Reiner met Ellen Gilbert, an agent at International Creative

Management, whom Reiner describes as having connections in the foundation world. He discovered *Starting Points,* a document that according to Reiner "validated everything I was thinking and . . . gave me the impetus to go forward." With a vision and the impetus, the Reiners convened a meeting at their Brentwood home. The meeting included representatives from the vice president's office and the Vermont governor's office, Los Angeles Mayor Richard Riordan, and "a number of educators, scientists, and media and foundation representatives." They decided to mount an effort to educate the public on the critical importance of children's first three years. This was the genesis of the I Am Your Child campaign. The centerpiece of the campaign would be a television special, supported by a CD-ROM, and a Web site. Reiner credits Teresa Heinz, president of the Heinz Foundation, as offering early support for the campaign from her foundation, a foundation that focuses on children and education. Heinz was no doubt familiar with issues and developments in early childhood from her work as a member of the board of the Carnegie Corporation.

While the campaign was being organized, *Newsweek* ran Sharon Begley's cover story, "Your Child's Brain," in its February 19, 1996, edition. Begley's article brought the new brain science and its potential implications for early childhood to mainstream America and the world.

Like most first-class science writers, Begley monitors scientific journals and conferences to keep abreast of new developments. She had been keeping a file on brain development and how experience affects the brain since 1992. Begley had noted the 1992 *Scientific American* issue on the brain and stories on the effects of early deprivation on Romanian orphans, as reported by Sandra Blakeslee in the August 29, 1995, *New York Times.* During late 1995, Begley noticed several articles on the brain that appeared in scientific journals. A common theme in these articles was that neural activity and stimulation contributed to brain organization and to the wiring and rewiring of neural circuits. She pitched the idea of a cover story on the brain to her editors and they approved.

At the time she began her research, Begley was unaware of both *Starting Points* and Kotulak's series of articles. She discovered these in a literature search early in 1996. In her research, she found that the neuroscientists she spoke to were reluctant about relating their work to anything practical, but that several were vociferous about the importance of early second-language learning. One behavioral scientist was passionate about the importance of early interventions to help disadvantaged children. Begley's article describes neuroscientific research on early synapse formation, critical periods, and enriched environments, using the classic examples. The article formulates the implications of this research as usually interpreted by early childhood advocates: Head Start begins too late; start music and second-language lessons early; read, sing, and play counting games with baby to develop its linguistic, musical, and logical brains.

On the critical significance of birth to 3, the article is somewhat ambivalent, as, Begley told me, she intended it to be. On the one hand, early experiences are exceedingly powerful and important. Her article states, "Children who are not stimulated before kindergarten are never going to be what they could have been." Yet, as the article concludes, there is new evidence suggesting that even after age 3 the appropriate kinds of intervention and stimulation can "rewire broken circuits." The example Begley discusses is the work of Rutgers University's Paula Tallal and UC-San Francisco's Michael Merzenich. Merzenich thinks that chronic middle-ear infections during infancy can result in abnormal brain circuitry that later cause reading problems and other language-based learning difficulties. Therapeutic interventions developed by Tallal and Merzenich given to 5-to-10-year-old children suffering with these language-processing disabilities alleviates their learning problems. From this example, Begley concludes that it is not necessarily the case, even when it comes to fundamentally and permanently rewiring the brain, that there is a magic learning window that closes forever at the age of 3.

Public reaction to Begley's article was overwhelming. *Newsweek* received more reprint requests for "Your Child's Brain" than it had for any articles it had previously published. The issue was the second-biggest seller of 1996, edged out of first place by the Easter edition. As Begley notes, "Religion still trumps science, at least on newsstands."

Summer 1996 saw two events that contributed to the development of the I Am Your Child campaign.

On June 13–14, 1996, the Harris Foundation, the Charles A. Dana Foundation, the Robert R. McCormick Tribune Foundation, and the Carnegie Corporation sponsored a conference at the University of Chicago, Brain Development in Young Children: New Frontiers for Research, Policy, and Practice. The conference was designed to extend and amplify the neuroscientific information and arguments to which *Starting Points* had only alluded and to develop the scientific research base for I Am Your Child. It resulted in the publication *Rethinking the Brain: New Insights into Early Development.*

After the Chicago meeting, the Carnegie Corporation sponsored a second meeting. Public relations experts, experienced in designing national campaigns to reduce drug abuse, child abuse, and smoking, met with Ellen Galinsky and Nina Sazer O'Donnell, both with New York's Families and Work Institute, the organization that was to manage I Am Your Child. These experts offered Galinsky and O'Donnell advice on how to mount a campaign to promote national interest in the needs of young children. The experts advised Galinsky and O'Donnell to avoid crisis-oriented messages that might evoke despair in favor of optimistic, positive messages "that build on what parents already know and are concerned about children's development." They were also advised to broadcast their message through a variety of media, both print and electronic, and to build a "business case" for their issue that would attract corporate and professional support.

The strategy adopted was to stage a media campaign drawing attention to early childhood issues built around the public's apparent interest (based on the response to *Starting Points* and Begley's *Newsweek* article) in early brain development. They recognized that brain development was of interest to both men and women. Talking about the brain's "hard-wiring" and soldering synapses presented a mechanistic image that appealed to men, an image they could use to frame issues in early child development that previously had been of overwhelming concern only to women. A message that appealed to both genders, they recognized, would be very useful in advancing policy initiatives. The organizers chose I Am Your Child as the name of the campaign to personalize its message and to establish the relevance of the campaign to families.

Also in 1996, Hillary Clinton's *It Takes A Village* appeared. Mrs. Clinton acknowledged the importance of *Starting Points* and often quoted Kotulak's book in her chapter "The Bell Curve Is a Curve Ball," in which she summarized what the new brain science tells us about early childhood development and its importance for both cognitive and emotional growth.

Just prior to the 1996 presidential election, the Reiners requested a meeting with President Clinton to discuss their ideas about I Am Your Child. According to Reiner, they met with the president for fifteen minutes. At the end of the meeting the president asked, "What do you want me to do?" The Reiners asked that Clinton declare early childhood a priority for his second term, mention it in his State of the Union address, and sponsor a White House conference on the topic. According to the White House, the Clinton's had already been planning a conference on children, but the Reiners' involvement gave the conference a higher priority.

On February 4, 1997, Reiner, along with Drs. David Hamburg and Bruce Perry, addressed the National Governors' Association at its winter meeting in Denver, Colorado. Reiner alerted his audience to the announcement that the president would be making in his State of the Union address that very evening. As promised, early childhood was one of the principles in the president's call to educational action and there would be a White House conference on the brain. Reiner told the governors, "We now know through science that the first three years of life is the most critical time period. It is the time period when the brain develops at a greater rate than at any time during the course of a person's life. . . . But by age 10 your brain is cooked and there's nothing much you can do."

The same week, *Time* magazine ran the cover story "How a Child's Brain Develops and What It Means for Childcare and Welfare Reform." Included in the special report on brain science, early childhood, and the day care dilemma was a piece titled "Hollywood Goes Gaga: The Stars' Newest Cause," describing an upcoming television special, Reiner's leadership, and the participation of other entertainers in the campaign.

The White House Conference, Early Childhood Development and Learning: What New Research on the Brain Tells Us About Our Youngest Children, took place on April 17, 1997. *Rethinking the Brain* was released in conjunction with the White House Conference. The I Am Your Child campaign, coordinated by the Families and Work Institute, was also formally launched and its Web site went on-line as a source of information on brain development, parenting, and early childcare. ABC aired the I Am Your Child special on April 28, 1997, and the network's *Good Morning America* actively promoted the special in the wake of the extensive media coverage of the White House Conference.

The public information blitz also included a special Spring/Summer 1997 edition of *Newsweek*. Following on the success of the February 1996 issue, Richard M. Smith, *Newsweek's* editor-in-chief felt that it would be useful to devote an entire special issue to an in-depth look at the "absolutely critical first three years of life." He notes in his letter to readers how in this effort they shared the company of the White House, Reiner, and corporate America. (Johnson & Johnson was the exclusive advertiser in the special issue.) The issue was a massive success, selling around 1 million copies, with huge overseas sales. The special issue went through several printings and news vendors could not keep it in stock.

The crusade that *Starting Points* initiated and I Am Your Child spearheaded has been exceedingly successful in increasing public interest in the brain and early childhood. Since the White House Conference, there has been a steady stream of articles in the media, parenting magazines, and teacher-educator publications on the significant, revolutionary implications of the new brain science for childcare, parenting, and teaching. Five years ago, it was difficult to find information about brain science and child development on the Internet. By late 1997, a simple search found forty-three "hits" on this topic, many being entire Web sites devoted to informing surfers about the implications of the new brain research for parenting, schooling, and childcare policy. In 1996, I received a single phone call from a journalist writing about the brain and early childhood. I now get calls several times per week and e-mail inquiries almost daily about brain science and early childhood from teachers, graduate students, journalists, and concerned parents.

Parents, especially, have taken keen interest in brain science and the I Am Your Child message. It was parents, not county libraries, who bought all those *Newsweek* copies off the newsstands. Recently, I had lunch with a professional colleague. He showed me pictures of his six-month-old grandchild. Without knowing what I was writing about, he told me that his daughter and son-in-law were following the developments in brain science and were deeply committed to providing the infant with experiences that would assure his optimal brain development.

Parental interest in the brain has reached the level where childcare experts have become concerned about possible public overresponse. Matthew Melmed is the executive director of Zero to Three, which is dedicated to providing information to parents and professionals on the critical importance of life's initial years. From his informed perspective as an information gatekeeper, there is "almost a sense of frenzy" among parents for information about early brain development. We have reached a point, as Stephen Hall wrote in the *New York Times Magazine*, where we now have "a neurotic national pastime: raising a scientifically correct child."

In a nationwide survey of parents with children under 3 years old, published in conjunction with the White House Conference, Zero to Three found that 92 percent of the parents believed that their children's experiences before age 3 would influence their children's ability to do well in school. Eighty-five percent of the parents believed that without appropriate stimulation their babies' brains would not develop well and 60 percent of these parents said that they would be extremely or very interested in learning more about research on brain development. According to the survey, parents "want more information about exactly *how* to influence their children in positive ways."

The Myth has found a large and receptive audience.

Marital Problems

Although a union of our most cherished beliefs and theories about early childhood with brain science might appear to be a marriage made in heaven from a public awareness and policy perspective, from a scientific viewpoint the partners may not be as compatible as we have been led to believe.

There are two problems with the marriage. These problems are particularly troublesome for the message that I Am Your Child is promulgating. First, although "the first years last forever" is a major I Am Your Child campaign theme, the scientific evidence we have does not support a strong, infant determinist interpretation of that claim. Second, whatever evidence we do have for this claim, as that claim is stated in I Am Your Child, comes from research in attachment theory, but currently there is no research linking early childhood attachment with brain development.

The cultural history of infant determinism as well as the scientific basis and contributions of attachment theory merit books of their own. In the present context, however, we should at least be aware that in the brain and early childhood literature we are getting only one side of the story about the lifelong, permanent impact of early experience. There is also a substantial body of research that supports the claim that experiences throughout one's life have a profound effect on personality, character, and mental health and that these effects swamp the impact of early childhood experience.

To help us see and appreciate this alternative point of view, here are two colorful counterexamples to the popular, deterministic adage that "as the twig is bent, so grows the tree."

A famous study of Jerome Kagan's (it was even cited in a 1985 article on early brain development!) found that in some Guatemalan villages parents raised their infants in isolation to protect them from the dangers of the evil eye. These infants were kept in dark huts for their first year of life, where they were not only malnourished but also rarely spoken to or played with. Yet, by adolescence, Kagan reported, the intellectual and social capacities of these children were comparable to those of middle-class American teenagers.

Deborah Blum in *Sex on the Brain* relates how some families in a few villages of the Dominican Republic carry a defective gene for an enzyme that aids in building the fetal penis and scrotum. Boys born with this defect have undescended testicles and a stunted penis resembling a clitoris. These boys are raised as girls until puberty, at which time the flood of male hormones transforms the girlish bodies into mannish ones. The villagers call this syndrome *guevedoces*, ("eggs at 12"). Immediately, the children switch genders. They wear male clothing, begin courting, and turn into normal males without a problem. One would think, given how the twig was bent, that individuals raised, cared for, and socialized as girls for the first twelve years of life would have had their brains fundamentally and permanently wired into patterns that conformed to female gender roles. You would think that such individuals would be rather confused about what their post-12 gender roles should be. Yet, despite their early experiences from birth through puberty, these children have no problem making the transition from girl to man. Early experience had not permanently wired female gender roles into the brains of these "males at 12."

One might say that these are rather bizarre counterexamples to the general claim that "the first years last forever." Nonetheless, they are counterexamples. If we are serious in wanting to know what *science* says about early childhood development as a guide for policy and parenting, we should be aware that, given counterexamples like these, it might be misleading, if not dangerous, to take the "first years last forever" claim simply at face value. If we look more carefully at this claim, as it is popularly understood and presented in I Am Your Child, we can see that that the evidence for it is far from overwhelming and that the claim is subject to considerable debate among developmental scientists.

As mentioned in the previous chapter, "the first years last forever" is a popular motto that has its research basis within attachment theory. Attachment, most simply stated, is the enduring emotional bond between two persons. Attachment theory maintains that the early interactions between infant and mother determine the quality of the attachment between them and that the quality of the infant-mother attachment has lifelong consequences. It bends the twig.

John Bowlby, who first formulated this theory, postulated that there are four stages of growth in the attachment relationship. Early in infancy there is an initial phase, ending at about 8 to 12 weeks of age, during which the child develops social orientation skills but does not discriminate between caregivers. During the second stage, ending between 6 and 8 months of age, there is a period when the child begins to make social discriminations among possible caregivers. This is followed by a stage in which the attachment relationship forms. This stage ends around age 3 or 4 years, when attachment gives way to a more goal-directed partnership between parent and child. Thus, part of the interest in the birth-to-3 age group arises because, according to attachment theory, this is the time during which the twig is bent. Some attachment theorists claim that there is a sensitive or critical period for the development of attachment during the first year of life.

How do scientists study the causes, results, and consequences of attachment between mother or caregiver and infant? In the late 1960s, Mary Ainsworth, a major figure in the study of early childhood, developed the Strange Situation procedure for assessing the character of the attachment relationship between infants and mothers. It is designed for use with children who are around 1 year old. The Strange Situation lasts approximately twenty minutes and consists of eight episodes involving different combinations of the infant being with the mother, with a stranger, and left alone. Observers record and score infants' behaviors during these episodes.

What is of greatest interest to the scorer-observers is how the infant reacts when he or she is reunited with the mother following separation during the Strange Situation. Among American middle-class babies, around 65 percent respond positively when the mother or caregiver returns. These are type B, or *securely attached*, babies. Around 20 percent of babies either fail to greet or delay greeting the caregiver when they are reunited. These are type A, or *insecure-avoidant*, babies. The remaining 15 percent of infants show resistance, anger, or distress toward the caregiver on being reunited. These are type C, or *insecure-resistant*, babies.

There is considerable variation across cultures, between countries, and within countries on the percentages of babies that fall into each of these categories. Among northern German babies, 50 percent were insecure-avoidant, 37 percent were secure, and 7 percent insecure-resistant (6 percent were unclassifiable). Among Japanese infants, one study reported no insecure-avoidant infants, 68 percent securely attached, and 32 percent insecure-resistant. Among low-income, high-risk U.S. infants, 22 percent were found to be insecure-avoidant, 56 percent securely attached, and 22 percent insecure-resistant.

Attachment theory research focuses on three questions: What kinds of maternal or caregiver behavior *causes* these different kinds of attachment relations? How *stable* is the attachment relationship once it is formed? What are the long-term *consequences* of these different kinds of attachment relationships? That is, what does early attachment *predict* about the infants' future behavior and development? Of course, it is the answer to this last question that is most relevant to the claim that the first years last forever.

At least two major research reviews have looked critically at the answers to these questions over the past fifteen years. The popular understanding of attachment is that securely attached infants (B infants) have more sensitive and responsive caretakers than insecurely attached infants (A and C infants). The evidence for this, however, is very weak. It does seem to be true that mothers who behave with their infants in a socially acceptable, American middle-class manner are more likely to have securely attached infants than mothers who do not behave in this way. The major difficulty is that the research has not shown any consistent pattern of what *specific* aspects of the mother's behavior result in secure, as opposed to insecure, attachment. The inability of the research to identify these specific behaviors is, no doubt, one reason why parenting advice based on the Myth, as found for example on the I Am Your Child Web site, is so vague. The research cannot tell mothers specifically what it is they should do to best promote secure attachment. Thus, the advice is no more specific than telling parents to "be attentive and talk, read, and sing to your baby."

Careful review of the evidence also suggests that the attachment classifications infants receive in the Strange Situation are not highly stable over time. One would think that when, or shortly after, the twig is bent into a type B baby, the infant would tend to remain a type B baby. Recent studies of even middle-class infants, however, do not show high stability in infants' attachment classification over time. What the evidence seems to suggest is that the classification remains stable as long as the life circumstances for mother and infant and the caring relationship between mother and infant remain stable. If the circumstances and relationship change sufficiently for better or worse, so can the infant's attachment classification. According to the research, as far as the stability of attachment goes, it seems to be more a case of "as the wind blows" than "as the twig is bent."

Finally, if early childhood experiences determine an infant's attachment classification during some early critical or sensitive period, then that early experience and the resulting classification should allow us to make long-term predictions about that child's behavior and personality years later. But this presents another problem for attachment theory and claims about the long-term consequences of the early years.

Attachment research has been able to make reliable predications about behavior at later ages based on infant attachment at age 1 year *only* in situations where the child-rearing conditions have remained stable between age 1 year and the later ages. When parenting, childcare, or family conditions change dramatically, for better or for worse, early experiences do not predict later behavior. Of course, this means that it is not only early experience that matters. What matters is early experience plus whatever happens afterward. If later experiences do matter and if later experiences do moderate early experiences, then the first years do not last forever, in any simple sense of that expression.

A 1984 review concluded that the research "suggests that early experiences per se may not be the crucial determinants and that future attempts to study the effects of early experiences must also consider the occurrence of intervening events which may ameliorate, accentuate, or maintain the 'effects' of early experiences."

After fifteen years of additional research, the conclusion remains pretty much the same. In a 1998 review of research on early sociopersonality development, Ross Thompson, a developmental psychologist at the University of Nebraska, concluded that the evidence "indicates that, except in extreme circumstances, early influences are not deterministic but rather predispositional, with the strength of their effects on later behavior moderated by a variety of factors that may subsequently enhance, undermine, or alter their relation to hypothesized consequences." As Jake recognized, a lot can happen between high chair and electric chair.

If so, this raises some problems for I Am Your Child's fundamental message that "the first years last forever." Although we might believe it, we might want to believe it, and some of our theories of child development assume it, we do not have compelling, unequivocal scientific evidence that supports it. The bottom line for worried parents and caregivers, as well as for policymakers, is that we should be wary of any strong, unqualified claims that the first years last forever.

A second problem for I Am Your Child is that the campaign suggests not only that the first years last forever, but also that brain science somehow supports the claim that early attachment has lifelong consequences. This message is most evident in the video clip on the Web site in which Bruce Perry gives expert advice to parents. Perry tells parents that the brain is organized by experiences the child has during his or her first three years. His example, however, is not how the visual system develops—it's not the blind kittens. Rather he tells parents that during this time, "if a child is held and touched and cuddled and loved then that child's brain and the part of the brain that will allow that child to love later on, gets healthy, patterned, neuronal activity and causes that part of the brain to grow.... Every time you hold that baby and coo and look in its eyes, as you feed and you love it, there are parts of that baby's brain that are being stimulated and that are being exercised, that are being grown so that when that child gets older, it will be very capable of loving other people." Of course, the implication is that children who are not so treated during their first three years will remain forever incapable of loving other people.

The message to parents is that there is research linking brain development and early attachment. As you can also read on the I Am Your Child Web site, "The new brain research informs us of the vital importance of the relationship between caregiver and child in the first years of life, and affords us a wonderful opportunity to enrich the lives of our children and help them realize their full potential."

There is no such new brain research.

In September 1998, I attended a meeting of the MacArthur and McDonnell Foundations' Research Network on Early Experience and Brain Development. The network, headed by Professor Charles Nelson of the University of Minnesota, has as its core members neuroscientists, developmental biologists, cognitive and developmental psychologists, and physicians committed to finding out what we do and do not know about early brain development as a basis for future research and sound policy. The topic for the September meeting was attachment theory and its relation to brain development. I Am Your Child and the related literature suggest, as indicated by the statements quoted above, that there is an intricate body of well-established research linking early brain development with attachment. The research network came to a different conclusion. Based on their discussions, in Nelson's words, "Nothing could be farther from the truth."

In a letter to Reiner, Nelson explained this conclusion and expressed his concern that I Am Your Child misrepresents and overstates what neuroscientists know about the link between brain science and attachment. As Nelson wrote, ". . . there is no such link. By this I do not mean to imply that scientists have unequivocally found that there is no such link; rather, it is that this link has not yet been established, certainly not in the human (there is some support for this in the monkey). The reason for this is that the investigators working on attachment have not incorporated into their theories work on the brain sciences, and similarly, those working in the brain sciences have paid scant attention to work on attachment." Nelson concluded, "The jury is still out about the importance of the first few years of life." While the early years are no doubt important, it remains unclear just how important.

I Am Your Child, to its credit, has succeeded in raising our awareness about the needs of children, but in doing so it has misrepresented what science does know about early brain and child development. If the scientific jury is still out, we should be reluctant to base parenting and policy too narrowly on what we see when we look through the prism of birth to 3. Looking through that prism tends to distort our vision. In this regard, I Am Your Child is a single but highly prominent example of what can happen if we uncritically embrace the Myth of the First Three Years. There are problems with the marriage of our beliefs about early childhood to brain science. The Myth creates misunderstandings in the minds of parents, caregivers, and policymakers. These misunderstandings can cause parents and caregivers undue anxiety and can contribute to poorly informed policy and legislation.

The Myth Grows

Despite neuroscientists' skepticism and problems with the Myth's fundamental message, as presented by I Am Your Child, the Myth continues to spread. Whereas in 1996 early childhood advocates had to advance the three-standard argument I outlined above to promulgate the Myth, in 1998 they no longer need to do so. Now their simple argument is accepted and asserted as scientific fact. In the November 15, 1998, *Boston Sunday Globe*, Thomas Oliphant wrote, "As things stand now—in the state and in the country—the undeniable fact that the human brain is almost entirely formed in the first three years is mocked by the fact that hardly any social resources are aimed at this critical period."

The Myth has not only had a profound impact on parents; it also is having a significant impact on legislation—legislation that some would see as ending the mockery. At the federal level, Senators John Kerry of Massachusetts and Kit Bond of Missouri introduced the Early Childhood Development Act of 1997 (S.756) to Congress.

As published in the *Congressional Record,* Section 2 of the bill states Congress's findings on the subject that are pertinent to the legislation. One of the findings states: "New scientific research shows that the electrical activity of brain cells actually changes the physical structure of the brain itself and that without a stimulating environment, a baby's brain will suffer. At birth, a baby's brain contains 100,000,000,000 neurons, roughly as many nerve cells as there are stars in the Milky Way. But the wiring pattern between these neurons develops over time."

Similarly, claims about research on early brain development are having an influence within state legislatures. The findings and implications of the new brain science have become accepted facts, no longer in need of explanation or justification, to support childcare initiatives at the state level. As stated in the June 1998 *State Legislative Report*, using language straight out of *Starting Points*, "New insights on how and when the human brain develops are affecting public policy relating to young children and their families at the federal, state, and local levels. The discovery that babies' brains develop more rapidly and earlier than previously understood has far reaching implications for education, health care, child care, and parenting."

According to the *Report*, "twelve governors mentioned the brain research in appeals to state lawmakers to support early childhood development programs during the 1998 sessions." Activities underway in twenty-five states in areas of childcare, school readiness, family support and home visits, maternal and child health, and early childhood infrastructure and coordination were based, at least in part, on policymakers and legislators understanding of early brain development.

In Iowa, "The General Assembly recognizes the significant findings of brain research indicating that early stimulation of the brain increases the learning ability of a child."

California legislation stated, "Neuroscience researchers now know that brain neuron connections occur rapidly after birth and are dependent on the experiences and stimuli of infants and children." After increasing childcare funding by $400 million in 1997, Governor Pete Wilson proposed a $742 million increase in the state budget for child assistance and, according to the legislative report, "The governor's fact sheet cites recent studies, including those that cover early childhood brain research and Carnegie's *Starting Points* report."

In Rhode Island, legislation to improve childcare and expand health care coverage for low-income families asserted, "Recent research in neuroscience and early brain development supports the critical importance of the early childhood years and their lifelong effects on a child's development."

In one of the most widely publicized state initiatives to put the new brain research into action, Georgia Governor Zell Miller, based on his understanding of the new brain research, asked state legislators for funding to buy and distribute classical music tapes and CDs for the state's newborns. He said, "No one doubts that listening to music, especially at a very early age, affects the spatial-temporal reasoning that underlies math, engineering and chess." Missouri's Governor Mel Carnahan initiated a similar policy.

Although the authors of the state legislative report are proud of this development, it is one that is hardly science-based. The January 30, 1998, issue of *Science*, the official publication of the American Association for the Advancement of Science, ran a short note on Governor Miller's announcement. Contrary to the governor's assertion that "no one doubts" that listening to music at an early age improves spatial-temporal reasoning, Frances Rauscher, one of the scientists who had done the studies on how music affected spatial reasoning, quickly and responsibly distanced herself from this recommendation. Rauscher pointed out that no one had looked at the effect of playing Mozart on infants' development. The governor, along with other brain and childhood advocates, had confused the results of a study on how listening to classical music affects college students' reasoning skills (for periods up to ten minutes) with the results of a study on the affects of musical keyboard lessons given to preschoolers (where spatial reasoning skills appeared to improve for several hours after the lesson). Far from no one doubting it, there is no evidence at all for the claim that listening to classical CDs improves children's spatial reasoning skills.

Advocates of the Myth, ever looking through the prism of the first three years, continue to find new social problems that they think they can solve using their understanding of brain science, if we would only give them the resources. The pediatrician T. Berry Brazelton offered one of the most astonishing new applications in a May 21, 1998, op-ed piece for the *Boston Globe* entitled "To Curb Teenage Smoking, Nurture Children in Their Earliest Years."

According to Brazelton, public discussion and congressional debate about restricting tobacco advertising and increasing the price of cigarettes miss the underlying reality. Children are vulnerable to the lures of tobacco, he argues, because of the experiences they have had during the first three crucial years of life. "If we wait until adolescence to help our children develop the sense of self that is needed to resist the draw of smoking, we will be sorry." Sound research, he goes on, shows that the brain wiring established in the early years creates a solid foundation for life, including a smoke-free future. Not only will the neglected brain be stupid, violent, unemployed, and breed more stupid children, as Kotulak claimed, in addition, according to Brazelton, it is also likely to smoke. "The research is conclusive," Brazelton tell us. "Early investments have a lifelong impact." Based on what we know about the brain, he concludes, we should invest the then-envisioned $500 million tobacco tax in better day care. If we did so, we could solve the teenage smoking problem, and apparently any other social ill one could possibly think of.

A myth grows and attracts adherents when it appears to provide emotionally evocative insights into a complex human problem. This is why many people—the childcare and early education research community, scientists, policy advocates, and parents—want to believe the Myth of the First Three Years. It is a myth that weaves together three strands taken from developmental neurobiology—early synapse formation, critical periods, and enriched environments—in an attempt to provide scientific, biological reassurance for our beliefs about childhood, parenting, and early childhood policy.

The weaving involves some fascinating and complex, but oversimplified and misinterpreted, science.

It is now time to look in detail at the science and the weaving.

CHAPTER 3

NEURAL
CONNECTIONS

Some You Use, Some You Lose

O ver twenty years ago, neuroscientists discovered that humans and other animals experience a rapid increase in
brain connectivity—an exuberant burst of synapse formation—
early in development. They have studied this process most carefully in the brain's outer layer, or cortex, which is essentially our
gray matter. In these studies, neuroscientists have documented
that over our life spans the number of synapses per unit area
or unit volume of cortical tissue changes, as does the number
of synapses per neuron. Neuroscientists refer to the number of
synapses per unit of cortical tissue as the brain's synaptic density. Over our lifetimes, our brain's synaptic density changes,
as we shall see, in an interesting, patterned way. This pattern of
synaptic change and what it might mean is the Myth's first neurobiological strand.

Popular discussions of the new brain science trade heavily on
what happens to synapses during infancy and childhood. Magazine articles often begin with colorful metaphors suggesting

that what parents do with their infant has a powerful, lifelong impact on their baby's brain that determines the child's adult intelligence, temperament, and personality.

The *Newsweek* Special Edition tells us, "Every lullaby, every giggle and peek-a-boo, triggers a crackling along his neural pathways, laying the groundwork for what could someday be a love of art or a talent for soccer or a gift for making and keeping friends." Also according to *Newsweek*, "You hold your newborn so his sky-blue eyes are just inches from the brightly patterned wallpaper. *Zzzt:* a neuron from his retina makes an electrical connection with one in his brain's visual cortex. You gently touch his hand with a clothespin: he grasps it, drops it, and you return it to him with soft words and a smile. *Crackle:* neurons from his hand strengthen their connection to those in his sensory-motor cortex."

Notice that these metaphors associate the neural crackling and zapping with rather mundane, commonplace activities—giggling, peek-a-boo, playing with clothespins. This is appropriate. Brain science has not pointed to new ways of raising or teaching children that will *really* stimulate those synapses above and beyond what normal experiences provide. Thus, the metaphors do properly convey that brain-based parenting amounts to doing no more than what most parents do normally. This is in keeping with the vague and commonplace brain-based parenting advice we reviewed in the previous chapter.

In popular articles, the crackling, zapping metaphors are often followed by similes that provide accessible, colorful analogies of what goes on early in brain development. They tell us that although some of the neurons in the newborn's brain are genetically hard-wired at birth to control vital functions, like breathing and controlling body temperature, trillions and trillions of others "are just waiting to be hooked up and played like orchestra instruments in a complex musical composition. Parents, educators, the babies' early experiences—all these factors will determine which neurons connect and which connections will eventually wither and die from lack of use." Or to use a more technological image, infants' neurons "are like the Pentium chips in a computer before the factory pre-loads the software. They are pure and of almost infinite potential, unprogrammed circuits that might one day compose rap songs and do calculus, erupt in fury and melt in ecstasy. . . . It is the experiences of childhood, determined by which neurons are used, that wire the brain as surely as a programmer at a keyboard reconfigures the circuits in a computer. Which keys are typed—which experiences a child has—determines whether the child grows up to be intelligent or dull, fearful or self-assured, articulate or tongue-tied."

These metaphors and similes convey the image of infinitely modifiable infant brains. Neurons are in place awaiting the appropriate experiences and stimulation that will build synaptic connections among them. This figurative language and the picture it paints captures the popular understanding of early brain development and the understanding conveyed in the Myth literature. We are left with the idea that infant brains are exuberantly growing and connecting in direct response to the actions of watchful singing, reading, and talking parents and caregivers.

But, does this idea accurately capture what neuroscientists know about synapse formation early in brain development? How well does the neuroscientific evidence that the Mythmakers cite support this popular understanding?

Neurons, Synapses, and Brain Development

What happens to synapses during development, and why, are fundamental questions for modern neuroscience. As one prominent textbook, Eric Kandel and James Schwartz's *Principles of Neural Science*, says, "Behavior depends on the formation of appropriate interconnections among neurons in the brain." Or as Patricia Goldman-Rakic, another neuroscientist who has conducted extensive research on primate brain development, puts it, "The synaptic architecture of the cerebral cortex defines the limits of intellectual capacity, and the formation of appropriate synapses is the ultimate step in establishing these functional limits."

Neuroscientists do know that rapid synapse formation occurs early in the development of complex nervous systems, like those of cats, primates, and humans. Before we proceed to look at what neuroscience has learned about early, rapid synapse formation, we should first have a better idea of what developmental events precede it.

Figure 3-1 shows the main features of a mature neuron. Neurons come in a variety of shapes and forms, but they all have a cell body that contains the cell nucleus. Most neurons have branches extending from the cell body. Axons, the long branches in the cells shown, carry nerve impulses away from the cell body to other neurons. Dendrites, the shorter branches, generally receive nerve impulses from the axons of other neurons and transmit those impulses toward the cell body.

Usually, nerve cells are not in direct physical contact. There are microscopic gaps between the axons of one neuron and the dendrites of its neighbors. Communication between neurons takes place across these microscopic gaps, or synapses. Chemical neurotransmitters move across the gaps from the presynaptic ending of the axon to the postsynaptic membrane of the adjoining dendrite. These chemical messengers then either excite or inhibit electrical activity in the postsynaptic cell. Via their synaptic connections, brain cells form the neural circuits that somehow support our sensory, motor, and cognitive skills, and that ultimately regulate all of our behavior.

Neurons do not begin life in the mature state shown in the figure. They take time to develop. Neurons begin to form very early in fetal development. All our neurons derive from a single, thin layer of tissue in an embryonic structure called the neural tube. In humans, the first neurons that will eventually become part of the brain's cortical "gray matter" begin to appear at around 42 days after conception. All our cortical neurons form during the next 120 days, 280 days before birth. The formation of our cortical neurons is complete four months before we are born. We humans, along with our primate cousins, acquire all the cortical neurons we will ever have during the middle third of gestation. When one considers that a fully developed human

FIGURE 3-1 A MATURE NEURON

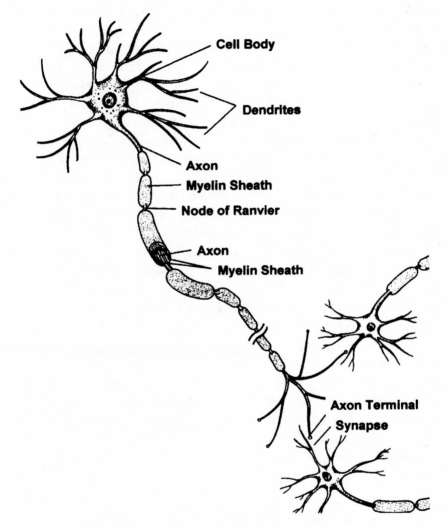

A typical mature neuron has a cell body, an axon (usually enclosed in a myelin sheath), and dendrites. The terminal axon branches form synapses with other neurons. Nerve impulses travel away from the cell body on the axon and are transmitted neurochemically across the synapses, where the dendrites pick up the impulse and carry it toward the body of the next cell.

Reproduced with permission of the publisher from Gudrun Arnodottir, *The Brain and Behavior* (St. Louis: Mosby Publishing Company, 1990), p. 30.

brain contains on the order of 100 billion neurons, this means that during those 120 days, neurons form at a rate of around 580,000 per minute.

As cortical neurons form and the fetal brain grows, the neurons migrate from where they are first formed to their final position in the cortex. During this migration, neurons begin to grow axons and dendrites, the structures that will eventually allow them to form synapses and to build neural circuits.

The process by which axons reach their dendritic targets is not an arbitrary, random one. The brain has to form the correct contacts and circuits between axons and dendrites. Sometimes, the axons must traverse relatively vast distances—on an axonal scale, distances equivalent to our making a coast-to-coast U.S. trip—to find their appropriate target cells. Genetic mechanisms guide this neural mass migration. Following a trail blazed by physical, mechanical, and chemical markers, axons reach and identify their appropriate target cells. They even find the appropriate sites on the target cells' dendrites. In humans, the migration begins about four months before birth and ends shortly after birth. Once the axons and target cells recognize each other, synapses begin to form almost immediately. In humans, synapse formation starts at around two months before birth and continues at least through the first year of life. The popular and policy interest in brain development begins at this point. It begins with considering what happens to synapses following birth, during infants' first three years of life.

Synaptic Density:
Counting Needles in the Neurological Haystack

Neuroscientists discovered the period of rapid, postnatal synapse formation nearly twenty-five years ago. In these studies, scientists take samples of brain tissue from the same brain area of animals or humans that differ in age. In animal studies, the animals are sacrificed at different ages to obtain the tissue samples. In human studies, scientists must rely on samples of brain tissue taken at autopsy. This makes human studies a bit more difficult, because scientists are limited in the number of brains they can study and have little control over how many brains at each developmental age they can include in a study. In the animal and human samples, the scientists then count synapses, or structures associated with synapses, to see how synaptic densities—the number of synapses per unit area or unit volume of cortical tissue—vary over the life span in a species.

Counting synapses in studies like these is the scientific equivalent of estimating the number of needles in a haystack, when both the number of needles and the size of the haystack are changing at constantly differing rates. This is not work for the timid, impulsive, or impatient. For a series of studies on rhesus monkeys done during the 1980s, Pasko Rakic and his colleagues at Yale University first used electron micrographs to enlarge the tissue specimens 14,000 times. They then counted the synapses in each of at least four specimens from dozens of animals. They counted over 500,000 synapses in 25,000 electron micrographs. From these counts, they calculated average synaptic densities.

Calculating reliable densities also presents a series of needle-in-the-haystack methodological problems. Brains grow and undergo age-related changes, with different kinds of brain tissue growing at different rates—neurons, nonneuronal brain cells, the space around cells, myelin sheaths on axons, and the number and size of blood vessels. Synapse counters must take account of and adjust for all these factors. They have to make reasoned assumptions to compensate for possible sampling errors, because there is no way they can count all the synapses in even one brain area. Scientists differ in how they choose to address these problems. These technological and methodological differences can complicate direct comparisons across studies and certainly across species.

This work is sufficiently demanding that relatively few scientists do it and even fewer do it well. The result is that we have a relatively limited database—much more limited than policymakers and the public are aware—on synapse formation and synapse change over species' life spans. As Goldman-Rakic reminded me, despite its importance for developmental neurobiology, "this is a sparsely populated field. In fact one might say that the study of postnatal brain development is so sparsely populated that it does not really exist as a *field* of scientific inquiry at all."

In 1975, Brian Cragg first documented a phase of rapid increase in synapses, followed by a phase of synapse elimination in the visual area of the cat brain. In the cat, some synapse formation occurs before birth, but Cragg saw that there was a period of rapid synapse formation from 8 to 37 days following birth. He observed peak synaptic densities at around the age of 7 weeks in kittens. There followed a protracted "pruning" phase, during which synaptic densities and related neural measures decreased to adult levels. From the peak values, Cragg saw a 40 percent decrease in average synaptic density and a 29 percent decrease in the average number of synapses per neuron.

Two years later, Jennifer Lund and her colleagues reported a similar pattern in the development of monkey visual cortex. They reported that synapses peaked at around 8 weeks of age in the monkey. From 8 weeks, but continuing through at least 9 months of age, there was a gradual reduction until synapses stabilized at adult levels. From these early studies, neuroscientists concluded that, at least for the brain's visual area, there is an early developmental phase, during which the rate of synapse formation exceeds the rate of synapse elimination. This is followed by a second phase, during which the rate of synapse elimination exceeds the rate of synapse formation.

Although Cragg, Lund, and others documented this phenomenon, they were cautious in interpreting their discovery. Like archeologists who had just stumbled upon Stonehenge, they could describe their find in some detail but knew it would take more time and study to figure out what their discovery meant. Their studies assessed neither how changes in synaptic densities affected the animal's ability to see nor how synaptic change contributes to the functional maturation of the visual system.

They did raise an interesting idea that has remained part of neuroscientific theorizing but that has been largely lost in the popular discussion of brain development. They suggested that the *loss* of synaptic contacts might be an important and positive aspect of brain development. "It is perhaps important to realize," Lund concluded, "that the elimination of contacts may be as selective and as constructive towards the final function of the visually altered neuron as the formation of specific synaptic contacts."

By the 1980s, other researchers began to study the pattern and timing of synapse formation in monkeys and humans. Unlike Cragg's and Lund's initial studies, these later studies looked at various areas of the brain's cortex, not just the visual area. Some of the best work of this kind has been that of Pasko Rakic, Patricia Goldman-Rakic, and their colleagues on brain development in rhesus monkeys.

The gestation period for rhesus monkeys is around 165 days, and the first cortical neurons form 40 days after conception. All the monkeys' neurons are formed over the next 60 days, and the process is complete 65 days before the monkeys are born. Rhesus monkeys (unlike humans) reach sexual maturity at age 3. In their studies, Rakic and his colleagues used animals that ranged in age from a few days postconception to mature 20-year-old adults.

In these animals, Rakic with his colleagues, Jean-Pierre Bourgeois and Nada Zecevic, examined developmental changes in synaptic densities in the visual area and three other brain areas: the somatosensory area involved in the sense of touch, the motor area involved in movement, and the prefrontal cortex involved in some memory tasks, planning, and other higher brain functions.

In all four areas of the monkey brain, they found the same general developmental pattern. First, there was a period of extraordinarily rapid increase in synaptic density. This period of rapid increase began 2 months prior to birth. At birth, infant monkeys' synaptic densities were approximately the same as the densities found in adult monkey brains. Synaptic densities continued to increase rapidly, peaking at age 2 months in all areas except the visual area, which peaked at 3 months. The peak densities were twice those seen in adult monkeys. Densities remained at this high plateau level until around age 3 years, the age of sexual maturity. At age 3, synaptic densities began to rapidly decrease, finally stabilizing at adult levels at age 4 to 5 years. The single exception to this pattern was the prefrontal area. There, rather than a rapid decline following the onset of puberty, there was a slight but significant decline in synaptic density starting at age 3 that continued throughout the monkeys' lives.

Further analysis of their data led Rakic and his colleagues to the conclusion that decreases in synaptic density were due to genuine synapse elimination in the brain, not to the number of synapses remaining constant while the brain grew in volume. The rate of synaptic loss is staggering. In the monkey, over a period of 2 to 3 1/2 years, 2,500 synapses disappear every second from the primary visual area in each brain hemisphere.

This research confirmed that a rapid increase followed by a decrease in synaptic density occurs throughout the rhesus monkey brain and is not confined to the visual area, as had been known since Lund's study.

The work of Peter Huttenlocher and his colleagues at the University of Chicago has revealed that a similar pattern occurs during human development, but on a different time scale. Of course this is no surprise, because monkeys and humans have very different life spans. Monkeys mature sexually at 3 years and are old at 20. Humans mature sexually early in their second decade and live another 60 to 70 years.

Over the past two decades, Huttenlocher's research group has been one of the very few that has studied changes in synaptic density over the human life span. They have counted synapses in around fifty human brains, looking at three brain areas. These brains were obtained at autopsy from patients ranging in age from 28-week-old fetuses to 90-year-old adults. Although twenty-four of the brains were from children in the prenatal-to-3-year age range, unfortunately only three of the brains were from children between 4 and 11 years old, an important period in brain development for which we would like to have more data. Huttenlocher has reported results from three such studies in four research papers.

In a 1979 paper, Huttenlocher reported results on changes in synaptic density over the life span in the frontal area of the human brain. He found that at birth infants have synaptic densities that are nearly the same as those found in adults. There was a rapid increase in synaptic densities between birth and age 1 year. Synaptic density peaked in the frontal cortex at around 1 to 2 years of age, when it was 50 percent higher than average adult values. Between the ages of 2 and 16 years, densities declined to mature levels and remained there throughout adulthood. Using data on changes in brain volume with age, Huttenlocher, like Rakic, argued that the decline in synaptic density could not be accounted for by a stable number of synapses confined within a growing brain. At age 7 years, the human brain has nearly reached adult volume, but synaptic density is still 36 percent higher than in adults. Decreases in density must be due to a relative loss of synapses during development. He concluded: "This finding confirms the fact that synaptic density in mammalian cerebral cortex declines late in development, after brain growth is nearly complete."

In 1982 and 1987 publications, Huttenlocher reported changes in synaptic densities over the life span in the human visual cortex. Again, at birth, synaptic densities in this brain area were near adult levels. Densities increased most rapidly between 2 and 4 months of age and peaked between 8 and 12 months of age at levels 60 percent higher than those seen in adults. In the visual area, there was then a longer period of decrease in density extending beyond 3 years of age, stabilizing at adult levels at around age 11.

In his most recent published study, Huttenlocher looked at two brain areas—frontal cortex (the same area studied in the 1979 paper) and auditory cortex—in the same human brains. He found that synaptic density peaked in auditory cortex at around 3 months of age, but that it did not peak in the frontal area until around 3 1/2 years, a later peak than he had found in his 1979 study. This suggested to him that synaptic development in the frontal area lags behind that in the auditory area. Synapse elimination also appeared to be on different timetables in the two areas. Synapse elimination appeared to be complete by age 12 years in auditory cortex, but continued in the frontal area until mid-adolescence. Huttenlocher did point out, however, that his conclusions on rate of elimination were only tentative because he had only four adolescent brains in the study and these showed considerable variability.

The Rakic and Huttenlocher data figure prominently in developmental neuroscience and in the early childhood literature because they present the best direct evidence we have in humans and nonhuman primates on how synaptic densities change over the life span. As we noted, methodological and technical problems can make precise comparisons between studies and across species problematic, yet the research points to striking similarities between rhesus monkeys and humans. First, in both species, synaptic densities peak at around the same absolute level in all brain areas and final, mature synaptic densities are around 60 percent of the peak values in all brain areas that have been studied. This suggests, as Rakic and Huttenlocher have pointed out, that there might be a normal range for synaptic density throughout the primate brain. Having either too few or too many synapses, as we will see below, might be detrimental to brain function.

The studies also show that in both species there is a three-stage pattern of change in synaptic densities over the life span. In both species, there is a stage of relatively rapid synapse formation early in life. In monkeys, this initial stage begins 2 months before a monkey is born and continues until the monkey is 2 to 3 months old. In human infants, the stage of rapid synapse formation begins in the first few months following birth, with synaptic densities reaching peak levels between 3 months of age (auditory cortex) and 2 to 3 1/2 years of age (frontal cortex).

Next, in both species, there is a plateau stage during which synaptic densities exceed adult densities. In monkeys, this stage begins at around 2 to 3 months of age and ends with the onset of puberty at age 3 years. In humans, because Huttenlocher examined so few brains from subjects between 4 and 11 years of age, the plateau period is not as well characterized. Huttenlocher believes, however, that this stage is present in humans and lasts from approximately 1 year of age to between 2 and 16 years of age, again depending on the brain area.

Finally, in both species there is a third stage, beginning at puberty, during which synaptic densities decrease to adult levels. In monkeys, this final stage begins at approximately 3 years of age and ends at around 4 to 5. In humans, based on the three brain areas Huttenlocher studied, this stage begins in late childhood and is complete by age 11 in the visual cortex and by age 12 in the auditory cortex, but continues until at least age 16 in the frontal cortex.

These three stages of synaptic development constitute the "interesting pattern" that I mentioned in the chapter's opening paragraph. What we see from the research is that synaptic densities follow an inverted-U pattern over our lifetimes, as it does over the life span of rhesus monkeys. At birth, we have approximately the same synaptic densities in our cortex that we do as adults. Rapid synapse formation following birth leads to a plateau period. Synapse elimination beginning at puberty reduces densities to adult levels. It will be helpful to have this inverted-U image in mind when we begin to consider how neuroscientists and Myth advocates interpret what this pattern might mean for behavior, intelligence, and learning.

PET Scans and Synaptic Development

In humans, we also have some indirect evidence that brain development and changes in synaptic density change over the life span. A 1987 positron emission tomography (PET) study by Harry Chugani, J. C. Mazziotta, and M. E. Phelps provides this indirect evidence that corroborates Huttenlocher's more direct evidence.

Brain imaging technologies, like PET, allow neuroscientists to monitor brain activity in living human subjects. PET studies use radioactively labeled oxygen and glucose to measure rates of brain energy metabolism. In human studies, scientists inject these substances into experimental subjects. The blood supply delivers the substances to the brain. The scientists assume that the more active brain areas would require more energy and would use more of the radioactively labeled, energy-providing substances. After a period of time, the labeled substances undergo radioactive decay and emit positrons. Positrons are subatomic particles that have the same mass as an electron but that, unlike electrons, carry a positive rather than a negative electrical charge. Positron detectors arranged in a ring around the subject's head detect these emissions and, using some geometry, some physics, and some high-powered computing, scientists can calculate the paths that the positrons traveled. The path data allow scientists to construct images showing which areas of the brain are burning more or less of the oxygen or glucose in response to energy demands.

In their oft-cited work, Chugani and his colleagues report results of PET scans on twenty-nine epileptic children, ranging in age from 5 days to 15 years. These children needed PET scans for diagnostic purposes, so in one sense the children were not totally normal neurologically. We have no PET data (at least none that I have been able to find) from normal children, because PET scans require the injection of radioactive substances that researchers cannot administer to normal, healthy children. Chugani and his colleagues do address this issue, arguing that apart from their epilepsy, the children were otherwise neurologically sound. The researchers compared the epileptic children's scans to those taken on seven young, normal adults, ranging in age from 19 to 30.

In this study, the scientists gave the children radioactively labeled glucose and measured the rate at which specific brain areas took up the glucose. While the scans were being acquired, the scientists made every effort to eliminate, or at least minimize, all sensory stimulation for the subjects. Thus, they measured the rate of glucose uptake when the brain was (presumably) not engaged in any sensory or cognitive processing. That is, they measured resting-brain glucose metabolism.

Despite this study's popularity and importance, it is a single study of only twenty-nine epileptic children, many of whom had been medicated since infancy and eighteen of whom had received medication on the day they were scanned. However, it provides almost the only imaging data we have on which to make guarded inferences about what might happen during "normal" human brain development.

With these cautions in mind, what did Chugani and his colleagues find? They saw that, during the first year of life, glucose uptake in the infant cortex was between 65 and 85 percent (depending on the specific brain area) of that found in adult brains. In newborns, the area with the highest metabolic activity was the primary sensorimotor area, the area that supports the infants' sense of touch and bodily sensation. During the second and third months of development, there was a gradual increase in resting metabolic activity in other brains areas, for example, those areas associated with hearing and vision. By age 8 months, metabolic activity began to increase in some frontal areas of the brain. At age 1 year, the anatomical distribution of glucose uptake in infants' brains had the same qualitative pattern as that found in adult brains. However, the infant rates were still quantitatively lower than the adult rates.

After year 1, the maturational curves for all brain areas followed a similar pattern. In all the areas examined, metabolic levels reached adult values when children were approximately 2 years old and continued to increase, reaching rates twice the adult level by the age of 3 or 4. Metabolic levels remained at this high-plateau level until children were around 9 years old. At age 9, rates of brain glucose metabolism started to decline, and stabilized at adult values by the end of the teenage years. Like the synaptic densities Rakic and Huttenlocher calculated, rates of brain glucose metabolism follow an inverted-U pattern from birth to early adulthood.

Huttenlocher counted synapses, whereas Chugani and his colleagues measured glucose metabolism. To connect what they measured—glucose metabolism—to what Huttenlocher counted—synapses—Chugani and his colleagues reasoned as follows. First, they referred to Rakic and Huttenlocher's work. In rhesus monkeys and humans, there is initially a vast overproduction of synapses, followed by synaptic loss that continues until early adolescence. What Chugani and his colleagues see in the PET scans, they argue, is consistent with the process of synaptic overproduction and elimination. They cite other evidence to show that synapses and dendrites account for most of the glucose the brain consumes. So, they reason, as the density and number of synapses and their associated neural processes wax and wane, so too does the rate of brain glucose metabolism. Thus, what Chugani and his colleagues measured provides an *indirect* measure of what Huttenlocher counted. Changes in measures of glucose metabolism over time are correlated with changes in synaptic density and numbers over time. Chugani and his colleagues also note that there might be other explanations for the pattern they observed.

Chugani's 1987 PET study is one of the all-time favorites in the Myth literature. It is one of those "all things to all people" studies and possibly one of the most overinterpreted scientific papers of the last twenty-five years. Part of the reason for this is our fascination with brain images. Imaging studies have assumed a central but problematic role in how the public understands the brain.

We are fascinated and mystified by how the brain functions. But until recently we have not been able to "see" a living, functioning human brain "in action." Vividly colored pictures that purportedly show the brain actually perking or bubbling along give us concrete images of what before we had thought of as hidden and mysterious processes. Before brain imaging, the brain was indeed a "black box" for most of us.

We should not forget, however, that PET images of a brain are not Polaroids. They are images that represent complex data after considerable statistical processing and enhancement. Our brains are not red when we look at an intense black-and-white checkerboard and blue when we close our eyes. The colors represent increases and decreases in brain metabolism or cerebral blood flow over some baseline level. Far from being Polaroids, brain images are difficult to acquire and even more difficult to interpret, even for the experts.

Nonetheless, Chugani's PET study is taken as the paradigmatic example of how neuroscience is now providing "hard data" about the importance of the first three years of life.

According to *Starting Points*, new neuroscientific research, showing that "the brain development that takes place before age one is more rapid and extensive than we previously realized," underscores the importance of the first three years of life. The report cites Chugani's study as evidence for this claim.

Rethinking the Brain further elaborates on the significance of this imaging study, emphasizing the changes in the brain's metabolic activity during the first year of life: "Cortical activity rises sharply between the second and third months of life—a prime time for providing visual and auditory stimulation. By about eight months, the frontal cortex shows increased metabolic activity. This part of the brain is associated with the ability to regulate and express emotion, as well as to think and to plan, and it becomes the site of frenetic activity just at the moment that babies make dramatic leaps in self-regulation and strengthen their attachment to their primary care givers." This is the period, according to *Rethinking*, when parents and caregivers can most help infants develop self-regulatory skills.

The interpretations of Chugani's PET study these policy documents offers are, to be kind, highly convoluted and go well beyond the evidence presented in the original scientific paper.

Let's just consider the passage quoted above from *Rethinking the Brain*. If you look at the published data, it is not the case that cortical activity rises sharply between the second and third months of life. It is more accurate to say, as Chugani does, that one can observe increases in glucose metabolism in various cortical areas at that time. Where there was at 2 months of age very low metabolic activity in the cortex, at 3 months, there is more metabolic activity—nothing so dramatic as a sharp rise. Similarly, the frontal cortex is not "frenetic" at 8 months; rather, its rate of metabolic activity increases to levels comparable to other brain areas. One might say it begins to come "on-line" at 8 months. It is not clear what the rationale is for thinking that the PET results give reasons for providing visual and auditory stimuli at age 2 months and self-regulatory training at 8 months. Although the frontal cortex might come on-line at 8 months, it will not mature, at the synaptic level, until puberty, no matter what kind of stimulation a parent might provide.

A PET study showing when brain areas come on-line metabolically, or a neuroanatomical study that shows when synaptic densities increase, does not speak to when, or even to whether, parents might be able to train brain areas. The simple fact is that although we know these events occur, we do not know what they mean for child development or to what extent, if at all, environmental and parental stimulation affects these events.

More interesting, however, is that Chugani and his colleagues do not interpret their PET study as indicating that birth to 3 is the most important period for parents and caretakers to have an impact on brain development. In their original paper, they conclude that "our findings support the commonly accepted view that brain maturation in humans proceeds at least into the second decade of life." For Chugani, however, it is the plateau period of high metabolic activity and high synaptic connectivity—the years from 3 to 8 or 9—that is most significant developmentally. It is during this developmental period, Chugani consistently claims, that experience fine-tunes neuronal circuits and makes each individual's neuronal architecture unique. Of course, this too is an interpretation that goes beyond the data he presents in the PET study.

What we must always keep in mind is that this PET study *is* important because it corroborates, using indirect evidence, the existence of the inverted-U pattern that Huttenlocher documented with more direct evidence based on counting synapses. What that pattern might mean for child development and parenting is a substantial, difficult question that is not adequately addressed in either Chugani's original article or in the discussions of early synapse formation in documents like *Starting Points* and *Rethinking the Brain.* In the remainder of this chapter, we will explore what current neuroscience might contribute to answering this question.

Digging Beneath the Metaphors:
Neuroscience, the Myth, and Synapse Formation

The neuroscience we have just reviewed plays a fundamental role in the Myth literature. Policy and popular descriptions convey this neuroscience via the neural crackling, zapping metaphors that link early brain development, particularly rapid synapse formation, with the amount and quality of stimulation infants receive during their first years of life. Now that we have a better understanding of what the relevant neuroscience says, we can better assess the extent to which the science supports the ideas and images the Myth conveys about early brain development.

Three Myth claims in particular are based on the phenomenon of early, rapid synapse formation, which is on the Myth's first strand.

First, the Myth literature maintains that this period in development is crucial because it is the time during which most synapses form and that the more synapses we have the more intelligent we are. One often sees claims in the popular birth-to-3 articles that more synapses mean more brainpower. The Myth suggests that the reason why we should talk, sing, and read to infants is to stimulate the baby's brain, thereby facilitating synaptic growth. This increases the infant's brainpower, thus building a better brain than baby would have otherwise. More synapses are better than fewer. "The evidence indicates," we read, "that the more connections you have, the smarter you are."

Second, there is a claim that early environmental stimulation *causes* synapses to form. According to the Education Commission of the States, the early years are developmentally crucial because "brain connections develop especially fast in the first three years of life in response to stimuli, such as someone talking to, singing to, reading to or playing with the infant or toddler." In *It Takes a Village*, we are told that "with proper stimulation brain synapses will form at a rapid pace, reaching adult levels by the age of two and far surpassing them in the next several years." According to *Inside the Brain*, "Growing evidence indicates that early mental stimulation promotes the growth of synaptic connections between brain cells." Another article tells us that the "more experience or stimulation that an infant undergoes, the more brain connections are made."

Third, there is a claim that the period of rapid synapse formation is the time during which basic learning skills are "hard-wired" and that somehow this process ends when the period of rapid synapse formation ends. Joan Beck, the *Chicago Tribune* columnist, provides an example of this claim. During the first three years of life, she tells us, "the brain grows most rapidly and then becomes hard-wired into an organ of thinking." What happens, she concludes, during the first three years—the time of rapid synapse formation, the only time we have to build a better brain—affects the child for the rest of its life.

Let's now look at each of these claims individually.

Neural Accounting: Brain Power and Synaptic Density

The Myth propagates a profound misconception about the relation between synapses and "brainpower" and what neuroscientists know about it. The misconception is that there is a linear relation between the number of synapses in the brain and brainpower or intelligence. More simply, the Myth literature suggests that more synapses equal more brainpower. This misconception contributes to both the popular and policy appeal of the Myth. It allows us to think about brain development and intelligence in a concrete, quantifiable way. We can measure our success as parents, caregivers, or teachers by doing a little neural reckoning. Seductive as this view might be, the neuroscientific evidence we have does not support it. Whatever the relation is between synapses and brainpower, it is not a simple one.

The neuroscientific findings on humans and animals show, as we have seen, that synaptic density follows the inverted-U pattern—roughly, low, high, and low—from birth through childhood to adulthood. However, none of the studies looked at whether monkeys or humans with more synapses or with higher resting rates of brain metabolism were smarter. Data like Rakic's,

Huttenlocher's, and Chugani's do not speak to this issue at all, and there are no reliable data that do.

However, there have been a few cases where researchers have studied defective brains. People suffering from the genetic disorders that cause Down syndrome or Patau's syndrome do have brains with abnormally low synaptic densities. As early as 1975, however, neuroscientists also had found cases of human mental deficiency, where the patients' brains had abnormally high synaptic densities. Huttenlocher reported a case of a mentally defective child whose brain had synaptic densities higher than those found in normal patients. He speculated that patients whose brains had undergone developmental arrest at an early age would likely have abnormally high synaptic densities as adults and not be the better off for it. Again, following the theme first enunciated by Lund in the mid-1970s, synaptic loss is fundamental to normal brain development. At the synaptic level, normal brain development may be a regressive, rather than a progressive, process. Creating more synapses or preserving as many of them as we can into adulthood may be neither possible nor desirable. Although the phrase "use them or lose them" is a popular one in discussing synapses and the brain, it gives a misleading overall description of what goes on during normal brain development. It tends to conceal that losing synapses is also part of the maturation process for our brain circuitry and that such loss is normal, inevitable, and beneficial.

Recent research on fragile-X syndrome also suggests that too many synapses are detrimental rather than beneficial to efficient mental function. Fragile-X syndrome is the second-most-common form of mental retardation in humans after Down syndrome. It affects approximately 1 in 2,000 males and causes severe mental and behavioral impairments. Mature brain tissue removed from fragile-X patients at autopsy contains long, thin, twisted postsynaptic spines that resemble the spines seen during early brain development. Synaptic densities are also higher than normal in these tissue samples. Scientists have constructed an animal model of fragile-X in a strain of genetically altered mice. Brain tissue removed from these mice shows the same twisted dendrite structures and higher than normal synaptic densities that are found in the human samples. In adulthood, fragile-X mice have more synapses than do normal mice. Fragile-X syndrome may result from a developmental failure that prevents synaptic maturation and proper synapse elimination during development. With fragile-X, more is indeed less.

One final, commonsense reflection on the inverted-U pattern should convince us all that more synapses do not necessarily mean more brainpower. Synaptic densities follow an inverted-U pattern, but our intellectual capacities and ability to learn do not. At birth and in early adulthood, synaptic densities are approximately the same. However, by any measure one cares to use, adults are more intelligent, have more highly flexible behaviors, and show capacities to learn subject matter and reasoning skills that we do not see in infants, toddlers, and 3-year-olds. Furthermore, the late adolescent and early adult periods of rapid synaptic loss do not result in a drop in brainpower. Despite what many parents might express about the difficulties of having teenagers in the house, the problem that parents confront is not that their teenagers become rapidly less intelligent as they leave junior high school and enter high school. They may be emotionally and temperamentally difficult, but as massive synapse elimination begins at puberty, adolescents are just beginning a stage in their lives during which they have the ability to learn and master diverse, complex, and abstract bodies of knowledge. Based on observed behavior, measures of intelligence, and our ability to learn, there is no clear connection between synaptic densities or synaptic numbers and brainpower.

Goldman-Rakic summarized what she and many brain scientists believe, given the evidence they currently possess, about the relation between early synapse formation, learning, and intelligence. As she told the participants at the Denver meeting sponsored by the Education Commission of the States: "While children's brains acquire a tremendous amount of information during the early years, most learning takes place after synaptic formation stabilizes. From the time a child enters 1st grade, through high school, college, and beyond, there is little change in the number of synapses." It is during the time when no, or little, synapse formation occurs that most learning takes place.

While neuroscientists believe that there is some relation between brain connections and intellect, they are still trying to discover what that relation might be. Based on their studies of synapse formation and elimination in nonhuman primates and humans, neuroscientists like Huttenlocher and the Rakics draw a cautionary conclusion. In a 1986 article, Goldman-Rakic wrote, "Although neuroscientists believe that the ultimate explanations of behavioral phenomena will come from an understanding of cell-to-cell communication at the synaptic level, at the same time, no one believes that there will be a simple and linear relationship between any given dimension of neural development and functional competence." That is, despite what we read in the papers, the neuroscientific evidence does not support the claim that "the more connections you have, the smarter you are."

Making Synapses Grow: Stimulation and Early Brain Development

The Myth literature also conveys a misconception that early environmental stimulation or experience *causes* synapses to form. This, too, runs counter to the existing neuroscientific evidence. Rather, the research suggests that genetic and developmental programs, not environmental input, control early synapse formation.

Data from several species, including humans, shows that environmental input does not *initiate* rapid synapse formation. Rapid synapse formation begins in the rat visual cortex about two days after birth and increases rapidly until the rat is around 3 weeks old. However, rats do not open their eyes until they are around 2 weeks old, long after the rapid growth is well under way. Rapid synapse formation begins before the animals have any sensory stimulation from their environments. In the monkey visual cortex, as we have seen, rapid synapse formation begins two months prior to birth. According to Huttenlocher's data, synapse formation also begins in some areas of the human brain before birth. If in these species rapid synapse formation begins before the animals have any sensory input from the environment, then sensory input does not initiate rapid synapse formation.

Furthermore, following birth, environmental input does not appear to drive the process of rapid synapse formation, to cause more synapses to form. Of necessity, evidence for this claim comes from studies done on monkeys.

Somatosensory, or tactile, skills in rhesus monkeys appear very early in their development. At around 2 months, rhesus infants can make tactile discriminations of size and texture with the same precision as adults. This is also the age, based on the Rakic data, at which synaptic densities peak in the monkey somatosensory cortex. Neuroscientists take this correlation as suggesting that when synaptic densities peak, a critical mass of synapses forms. This critical mass of connections allows brain circuits to come "on-line," thus allowing the monkey to make the tactile discriminations.

In one experiment, Mary Carlson raised an infant monkey with its right hand restrained in a soft leather mitten. The mitten kept the monkey's hand in a tightly fisted position from birth until the animal was over 4 months of age. During that time, the animal received no sensory stimulation to its right hand. Carlson expected that this extended sensory deprivation would retard the animal's ability to make size and texture discriminations. When the mitten was removed, the animal showed some initial, transient impairment, but, to Carlson's surprise, the monkey quickly began to perform at the same levels as normal animals. If a critical mass of synapses is necessary to perform this task, then the monkey possessed that critical mass. It had tactile skills comparable to normally reared animals. Yet, the animal's right hand had not received any sensory stimulation for the first four months of its life, nor had the part of the brain that would process those stimuli. Therefore, for the tactile system at least, it is not true that stimulation causes synapses to form. The synapses formed in the absence of any simulation.

A few studies have examined both the effects of sensory deprivation and increased sensory input on the rate of synapse formation and on synaptic density in rhesus monkeys. In the deprivation experiment, researchers removed the retinas from fetal rhesus monkeys during the first half of gestation, around eighty days before the monkeys would normally be born. After the monkeys were born, they compared the visual areas of these totally deprived animals' brains with the visual areas of normal, age-matched monkeys. There were some differences. The blind animals had fewer neurons going into their brains' visual areas than the sighted animals and, for that reason, blind animals had smaller visual areas than the sighted animals. However, despite the fact that the experimental animals had been totally deprived of any visual stimulation, there were no significant differences in synaptic densities between the blind and the sighted monkeys. The rate and extent of synapse formation was the same in blind and sighted animals of the same age.

In the increased sensory stimulation experiment, three-week-premature rhesus monkeys received intensive visual simulation from birth to see if such stimulation could accelerate synapse growth in their visual areas. This experiment directly tested the claim that "the more experience or stimulation that an infant undergoes, the more brain connections are made." Contrary to the experimenters' expectations, despite all the extra stimulation, the synaptic densities of the preterm, highly simulated monkeys were no different than those of the full-term, normally stimulated control monkeys.

Together, experiments like these show that the rate of synapse formation and synaptic density are impervious to the quantity of stimulation, either to deprivation or to overstimulation. Contrary to what the Myth suggests, early rapid synapse formation appears to be under genetic, not environmental, control. This was clearly stated in one of the most recent scientific reviews on the relation between synaptic change and mental development: ". . . the *developmental* accumulation of synapses [i.e., the phase of early rapid increases in synaptic density] is altered much less by environmental stimulation than has been appreciated or would be expected by conventional wisdom."

Rapid Synapse Formation and
Hard-Wiring the Brain

Finally, let's consider the Myth's claim that it is only during the early years of life that we have the opportunity to "build better brains." The Myth suggests that after the period of rapid synapse formation ends, a period which, based on Huttenlocher's data, ends in the human brain at around 3 to $3^1/2$ years of age, the mechanisms for learning are established and brain circuits become hard-wired. To adequately assess this claim, we will have to look at how behaviors and abilities change during and after the period of rapid increase in synaptic densities.

One of the best examples to consider in assessing this claim is a series of studies done by Goldman-Rakic and Adele Diamond, a developmental psychologist. These studies examined how short-term, or working-memory, skills develop over the early months of life in both infant monkeys and human infants. Specifically, they studied how monkeys and infants improved on what psychologists call delayed-response tasks.

In delayed-response tasks, the experimental subject observes the experimenter hide an object or morsel of food in one of two wells on a tray. The experimenter then obscures the tray from the subject's view for a delay period. After the delay, the subject selects one of the two locations. The task requires that the monkeys or infants remember information about where the object was hidden for a period of time (the delay) and then to "find" the object when the only information available to guide the choice is their memory of where the experimenter had hidden the object. To do this, the infant monkey or human must have a mental representation, or a memory trace, of the original "hiding" and the ability to hold that memory "on-line" during the delay. Such simple tasks tap into a highly significant mental skill. Delayed-response tasks measure the emergence of representational memory—the ability to create and maintain a mental representation of an event that is no longer present to the senses. Representational memory is "a building block, if not cornerstone, of cognitive development in man," according to Goldman-Rakic. Furthermore, there is an abundance of neuroscientific studies, using a variety of techniques and measures, that provide strong converging evidence that this building block of cognitive development is dependent upon a specific part of the monkey brain, the dorsolateral prefrontal cortex. The association between this brain area and the ability to do delayed-response memory tasks is one of the best-established brain-behavior relations in neuroscience. This allows us to compare improvement on delayed-response tasks with changes in frontal brain areas. It allows us to understand how improved representational memory corresponds with changes in synaptic density.

In their studies, Goldman-Rakic and Diamond tested monkeys and infants on delayed-response tasks on a regular basis, starting when the monkeys or babies could first make reaching movements. When the monkeys were 1½ months old (the age at which the monkeys could first make reaching motions at the tray), the experimenters began testing them on delayed response tasks five days per week. Testing continued until the monkeys were around 4 months old. The mark of success on delayed-response memory tasks is the length of delay the animal or infant can tolerate before they start making incorrect choices. The longer the delay tolerated, the better the ability to hold information "on-line" in memory to guide the choice.

Infant monkeys first showed an ability to succeed at delayed-response tasks when they were a little less than 2 months of age, tolerating delays of around 2 seconds. By age 2½ months, they could tolerate delays of 5 seconds and by age 4 months delays of up to 10 seconds. The young monkeys showed a gradual, constant developmental improvement on these tasks, improving at a rate of around 1 second per week in the delays they could withstand.

Although Diamond and Goldman-Rakic did not count synapses in these monkeys, one can relate the improvement on the memory tasks to the developmental changes that Rakic and his colleagues found in their studies of frontal areas in the monkey brain. They found, remember, that synaptic density peaks in all areas of the monkey brain at around 2 months. This is precisely the time at which the monkeys began to show their first successes on delayed-response tasks. This suggests to Goldman-Rakic that the first appearance of basic skills and abilities associated with a brain area occurs when synaptic densities, as measured by Rakic, peak in that brain area. Here the ability to form representational memories in monkeys is correlated with the peaking of synaptic densities in the frontal areas of the monkey brains. The pattern seems to be that synaptic densities increase under genetic control and when they peak, the associated skills and behaviors first appear in elementary form.

We can tell the same, although a bit more complicated story, about the emergence of representational memory in human infants. Diamond tested infants on delayed-response tasks every two weeks starting at around 6 months (the age at which babies could first make reaching movements toward the tray). She tested the infants once every two weeks until they were 12 months old. Infants first started to succeed at delayed-response tasks at delays of up to 2 seconds when they were around 7 months of age. The infants improved on the tasks at a rate of about 2 seconds per month, until at age 1 year, they could tolerate delays of up to 10 seconds. What happens to the monkey's representational memory abilities between 2 and 4 months of age occurs in the human infant over the period of 7 to 12 months.

Using Huttenlocher's data, we can also relate improvements in the infants' representational memory abilities to development of the frontal areas in the human brain during the second half-year of life. However, to compare accurately the monkey and human data, we must first deal with one complication. Earlier, I mentioned that neuroscientists differ in the assumptions and methods they use to calculate synaptic densities and that this can complicate direct comparisons across studies. This is true for the Rakic and Huttenlocher studies.

In his human studies, Huttenlocher computed number of synapses per unit of whole cortical tissue, including the neural tissue as well as blood vessels, glial cells, and nonneuronal cells and spaces. In the monkey studies, Rakic computed synapses per unit of neuropil—that is, whole cortical tissue, less blood vessels, glial cells, and nonneuronal cells and spaces. Thus, Rakic and Huttenlocher used different denominators in computing densities. Different denominators matter because the different kinds of brain tissue included in the denominator grow at different rates during development.

Using his original whole brain tissue denominator, Huttenlocher found that synaptic densities peaked in the frontal areas of the human brain at around 3 years of age. However, when he recomputed his data for the frontal area using neuropil as the denominator, thus making his data more readily comparable to Rakic's, he found that synaptic density peaked in the frontal area of the human brain at around 7 months of age. Goldman-Rakic and Diamond found that seven months is the age at which human infants can first reliably succeed at delayed-response tasks. Thus, in both infant monkeys and human infants, representational memory abilities first appear when the number of synapses per unit of neuropil in the associated brain area reaches peak value.

The Diamond and Goldman-Rakic studies also provide some additional insight into how experience contributes to improved representational memory skills. In their study, in addition to the group of infants tested biweekly, they had another group of infants, ranging in age from 2 months to 12 months. They tested each of these infants only once on a delayed-response memory task. This allowed them to determine if improvement on the memory task might be due to practice. It allows us to consider whether experience or increased stimulation affects the development of basic representational memory.

In their first study, Diamond and Goldman-Rakic found that there was no difference in performance on delayed-response tasks between 9-month-old infants tested once at that age and 9-month-old infants who had been tested every two weeks. That is, infants who had already been tested at least ten times by age 9 months did no better than 9-month-old infants doing the task for the first time. They also found that the same rate of improvement, of about 2 seconds per month in delays tolerated, occurred in infants from all social classes.

In a later study, Diamond did find that over a variety of ages, infants who were repeatedly tested could tolerate delays 1½ to 2 seconds longer than infants of the same age that had been tested only once. However, she also found that the advantage for the repeatedly tested infants disappeared by the time the infants were 12 months old. Together these findings suggest that representational memory develops at approximately the same rate independent of practice or exposure to the task and independent of any class-related differences in early childhood experience.

When neuroscientists attempt to interpret their findings on rapid synaptic development in behavioral terms, they tend to list examples that exactly parallel the case of representational memory. In monkeys, synaptic density peaks in all cortical areas between 2 and 3 months of age. At around 2 months of age, infant monkeys can make precise tactile discriminations of size and texture (a sensorimotor function). They begin to visually track small objects, reach for objects guided by vision, and visually discriminate objects (visual functions). They show some ability to use individual fingers independently (a motor function). So, the argument goes, in the monkey, all these behaviors emerge between 2 and 3 months of age, at exactly the time when synaptic densities peak throughout monkeys' brains. In interpreting the human data, neuroscientists like Huttenlocher and Chugani allude to the correlations between synapse change and behavior found in monkeys, then argue by analogy that the same is probably true for infant humans, citing a few additional examples of language development that are unique to humans.

Neuroscientists also generally agree that this relationship between first appearance of a skill and peak synaptic density is only a part of the story. Skills continue to improve and behaviors continue to become more sophisticated long after rapid synapse formation ceases and well into the synaptic plateau period. Sensory, motor, visual, and memory skills continue to develop in the monkey, some reaching mature levels only at sexual maturity, when synaptic densities start to decline. The same is true for humans. Among primates, both humans and monkeys, childhood and adolescence—the plateau period for synaptic densities—is a time of massive learning and rapid behavioral change, when adult-level skills emerge in language, mathematics, and logic. On delayed-response tasks, adult monkeys can tolerate delays of two minutes or more. Adolescent children and adults are able to tolerate delays of hours if not days, in addition to developing other sophisticated representational memory skills. The circuitry we need to do these things is not complete, hard-wired, or permanently fixed during early development. It is not limited to the time when synapses form most rapidly.

The Synaptic Preservation Strategy

There is one other subtle wrinkle about early synapse development we should address. According to Huttenlocher's data, the period of rapid synapse formation in the young human brain appears to end at around 3 years of age. The neuroscientific data suggests that environmental stimulation neither initiates this process nor causes more synapses to form. However, this leaves open the possibility that early experience might strengthen existing synapses and that these strengthened synapses would be more likely to survive through the high-plateau period and into adulthood. In this view, building better brains is best accomplished via an aggressive synaptic preservation strategy. We talk, sing, and read to babies to save synapses from elimination, not to cause synapses to form in the first place. In some of the early childhood discussions we read that the brain "ruthlessly prunes" synapses that have received inadequate stimulation prior to puberty. This line of reasoning suggests that building optimal brains requires that we use as many synapses as possible before puberty or lose them for sure afterward. The more you use, the fewer you will lose.

Chugani has both offered and encouraged this interpretation of his PET study. According to a Wayne State University article on his work, "The trick . . . is to keep desired connections alive and permanent to allow for efficient processing of a variety of functions." In an academic review of his own work, Chugani wrote, "The individual is given the opportunity to retain and increase the efficiency of connections that, through repeated use during a critical period, are deemed to be important, whereas connections that are used to a lesser extent are more susceptible to being eliminated."

Rethinking the Brain makes the same argument: "As pruning accelerates in the second decade of life, those synapses that have been reinforced by virtue of repeated experience tend to become permanent; the synapses that were not used often enough in the early years tend to be eliminated. In this way, experiences—positive or negative—that young children have in the first years of life influence how their brains will be wired as adults."

The strategy for optimal brain development is to stimulate as many synapses and circuits as much as possible during the period of high connectivity in order to mitigate the effects of the imminent, ruthless pruning at puberty. We should engage in an aggressive program of synaptic conservation with our children. We should provide experiences and environments that promote, as the Bee Gees might describe it, neural staying alive.

Superficially, this strategy makes sense, but there is no neuroscientific evidence to support it. First, neuroscientists have little idea how experience before puberty affects either the timing or the extent of synaptic pruning. Scientists—Rakic, Goldman-Rakic, and Huttenlocher among them—have documented that pruning does occur at puberty. None of these studies we have, however, compared differences in final adult synaptic densities with differences in the individual's experiences before puberty. Neuroscientists do not know, for monkeys or humans, whether early experience increases or decreases synaptic densities or synaptic numbers after puberty. They do not know if prior training and education affect either loss or retention of synapses at puberty. They do not know what kinds of synapses—excitatory versus inhibitory—are selectively pruned. Nor do they know whether the animals with greater densities in adulthood (pathological conditions like fragile-X syndrome aside) are necessarily more intelligent and developed.

Some neuroscientists are frankly puzzled about this synaptic preservation strategy. When I asked Bill Greenough about the soundness of such a strategy, he replied, "The evidence strongly suggests that excess connections need to be removed to establish normal function."

David A. Lewis, a neuroscientist at the University of Pittsburgh, studies the development of the prefrontal cortex in monkeys, a brain area that undergoes considerable reorganization at puberty. The prefrontal cortex contains discrete stripelike clusters of axon terminals. During puberty, the stripes shrink dramatically in size and some disappear entirely. Lewis believes that these changes occur because axon terminals containing excitatory synapses are eliminated during puberty. This change, Lewis hypothesizes, produces modifications in how the prefrontal cortex processes information. Fewer and smaller stripes after puberty may give the adult animal a more focused, restricted, and sustained neuronal response to the stimulus that the animal must remember during the delay period. Our improved performance on delayed-response tasks that occurs throughout puberty might depend on eliminating axons and their associated excitatory synapses, rather than preserving more of them. Pruning is normal. Less is more.

Reflecting on his studies, Lewis thought that the synaptic preservation argument presented an "interesting interpretation" of the little we do know about the pruning that occurs at puberty. He would argue, however, that pruning or eliminating synapses is critical to achieve mature levels of cognitive ability. As he points out, working memory capacity in the monkey progressively improves as pruning in the prefrontal cortex proceeds and reaches mature levels only when pruning ends.

This synaptic preservation strategy, despite its initial, intuitive plausibility, does not make much neuroscientific sense. Any plausibility it has derives from our desire to understand the mind and intelligence in terms of synaptic numbers and densities. A neural accounting approach gives us a concrete, quantitative measure for something that we otherwise find abstract and mysterious. Once we buy into the quantitative neural accounting image, it is natural to think that more is always better. Unfortunately, the brain—at any age—is more complicated than that.

The First Strand Unraveled

Neuroscientists have made astounding progress over the past hundred years in their quest to understand how, as Kandel and Schwartz said, "behavior depends on the formation of appropriate interconnections among neurons in the brain." They also realize that despite a century of research, they remain closer to the beginning than to the end of this quest. Making the connection between behavior and synapses remains more of a neuroscientific Holy Grail than commandments engraved on stone tablets. Neuroscientists engaged in this work are more like Lancelot than like Moses. This is not to demean the neuroscientific enterprise, but rather to emphasize the difficulty of the task.

Neuroscientists who study how the brain's fine structure—neural circuits and synapses—govern human behavior and cognitive capacity take justifiable pride in their progress and are rightly optimistic about the future of their science. Yet, they are appropriately cautious in interpreting their work, emphasizing that much remains to be done before we can use the research to support specific policy-relevant claims about parenting, childcare, and education. As Huttenlocher acknowledges, "The persistence of exuberant synaptic connections during early childhood raises the question whether these connections may be of functional importance for the emergence of cognitive functions in the young child, and for compensation of the child's brain focal injuries. Answers to these questions are not available at the present time." And as Pasko Rakic states, ". . . the connections between neuroanatomy, neurochemistry, and neurodevelopment on the one hand and behavioral research in cognition on the other are rather tenuous."

The hundreds of thousands of measurements that neuroscientists have made that document a pattern of change in synaptic density in our brains over our lifetimes allow them to generate and support general hypotheses about how synapses support behavior. However, there is still much work to be done before we can move from general hypotheses to formulating and establishing specific relationships between particular changes in the brain and the appearance, acquisition, or learning of specific skills and behaviors. We have every reason to believe that behavior and intellect do ultimately depend, *somehow*, on how brain cells are connected. We are far from knowing *exactly* how behaviors, like negotiating a busy street, recognizing a familiar face, understanding a voice-mail message, reading *TV Guide*, or even the development of representational memory depend on specific neural connections.

Goldman-Rakic cautions that every time policymakers, educators, childcare providers, and parents look to brain science for answers to pressing questions, there is a danger and tendency to take what little is known about neural development, accept it uncritically, and interpret it as *the* neural basis of behavior. This is what has happened with the little that we know about early synapse formation and modification early in development. This time around, uncritical acceptance and misinterpretation of what neuroscientists do know about these processes—taking it as *the* neural basis of behavior—has given us the first strand in the Myth of the First Three Years.

The neuroscience and its interpretations that we have reviewed in this chapter are the basis for Carla Shatz's cautionary statement that I cited in Chapter 1: "Much research remains to be done before anyone can conclusively determine the types of sensory input that encourage the formation of particular neural connections in newborns."

Parents and caretakers should take some solace from this. Brainpower does not depend on the number of synapses formed before age 3. Environmental input, including stimulation provided by parents, neither initiates early synapse formation nor influences when or at what level synaptic densities peak. If the development of representational memory is a suitable example, the brain develops, synaptic densities peak, and elementary behaviors first appear. Rather than this marking the end of the time we have to "build better brains," it more likely marks only the beginning of a long developmental and maturational period during which environmental stimulation and experience do matter.

Although the synaptic preservation strategy does not make

much neuroscientific sense, we do know that for some brain systems normal development does require that certain kinds of experiences occur at certain times during development. This time-dependent experience seems to be essential for the selective elimination of synapses and neural structures in these systems. This brings us to the Myth's second neurobiological strand, the strand of critical periods, blind kittens, and the research program that David Hubel and Torsten Wiesel initiated forty years ago.

Is birth to 3 *the*, or even *a*, critical period in brain development?

CHAPTER 4

BE ALL THAT YOU CAN BE

Critical Periods

D onald Bailey, Director of the National Center for Early Development and Learning at the University of North Carolina, Chapel Hill, told me about an experience he had when he appeared on a radio talk show to answer questions from the listening audience on issues in child development. One mother called and said that what she was hearing about brain research made her anxious because it sounded as if the early years were a critical period in her child's life and she was worried that she would not know all of the right things to do. Bailey and the other panelists reassured the mother by giving her some general principles to follow, such as responding to the child's needs and holding and reading to the baby. There was not, the panelists told her, a precise curriculum that she should follow; rather she should use responsive caregiving practices.

Claims about critical periods constitute the Myth's second neurobiological strand, a strand that has a considerable impact on how parents and the general public think about early brain development. The North Carolina mother is just one example of a concerned parent who was made overly anxious by a superficial understanding of what neuroscientists know about the brain and critical periods in its development. And, of course, among the general public and on the policy front, emphasizing the critical nature of the early years lends urgency to claims that we must reform early childhood policies and practices.

Are critical periods "windows of opportunity" that nature flings open, starting before birth, and then slams shut, one by one, with every additional candle on the child's birthday cake? According to the popular understanding, critical periods have both an upside and a downside for child development. On the upside, they imply that "with the right input at the right time, almost anything is possible," because the young human brain is almost infinitely modifiable. On the down side, critical periods imply that if a child misses one or several, that child will go through the game of life with a permanent handicap: "children whose neural circuits are not stimulated before kindergarten are never going to be what they could have been."

The most dramatic, compelling, and oft-cited example in the Myth literature accentuates the downside. In the mid-1960s, David Hubel and Torsten Wiesel reported that kittens deprived of visual input in one eye during the first three months of life remained permanently blind in that eye. Hubel and Wiesel's blind kittens have acquired an iconlike status within the brain and early development myth. They generate a powerful mental image—blind little kittens pathetically groping for a ball of yarn.

This image can have a profound impact on parents, conjuring up their worst fears about severely disabled, developmentally impaired children. If birth to 3 is *the* critical period in brain development, when not only vision, but hearing, motor skills, intelligence, temperament, and circuits that support learning are developing, then these years, the average parent would think, must be critical indeed. And, if it is true that with the right experiences anything is possible, but with insufficient stimulation our children will never be what they could have been—or worse, they could end up like the kittens—parents, it would seem, have a lot to worry about.

We shouldn't be surprised, then, if writers for parenting magazines want to tell parents what neuroscience says about choosing childcare or a nursery school. And we shouldn't be surprised that parents' initial reaction to the Myth argument, particularly the critical-periods strand, is one of guilt. One parent was quoted in *Working Mother* magazine: "I have to admit when I first read the research, I felt as though I'd already failed my three kids." And, as Hillary Clinton suggested, the new brain science does "ratchet up the guilt."

Before any of us become too guilty, anxious, or concerned, however, we should ask whether what we know about critical periods has such far-reaching implications, for good or bad. Critical periods do exist. Hubel and Wiesel's kitten experiment is but one, albeit the most famous, example from a decades-long research program that includes both their Nobel Prize–winning work and the work of many scientists. From this research, we have learned an enormous amount about brain development in kittens, as well as in monkeys and humans. However, the implications of this research for our children's development, behavior, and learning potential is decidedly different, more limited, and less certain than we have been led to believe.

When we look carefully at the research on critical periods, four points emerge that should reduce the level of guilt and anxiety among parents, care providers, and teachers. First, there are critical-period constraints only for specific and limited kinds of learning and development. Most learning is not subject to critical-period constraints, not confined to windows of opportunity that slam shut.

Second, neuroscientists do not think that the quantity of experience or simulation during the critical period is the key variable in brain development.

Third, critical periods are complex. There are distinct phases within critical periods; there are distinct critical periods for specific functions within a system like vision or language; and the periods and phases within them extend over considerable periods of time—years—and well into children's second decade of life.

Finally, critical periods do not at all fit neatly into the first three years of life.

However, to be reassured and to see what critical periods can tell us about parenting and childcare does require that we understand what the research says. At first glance, understanding the research seems to involve obscure and complicated details about brains, neurons, and axons, where the details are based primarily on animal research. Bear with me on this one. It should be worth your while.

Critical Periods: What Are They? Why Do We Have Them?

Critical periods are time spans in development during which, and only during which, animals, including humans, can acquire specific traits, behaviors, or skills. Sometimes you also see the term "sensitive" period. At one time, sensitive periods were thought to be critical periods that ended gradually rather than abruptly. More recently, neuroscientists have learned that *most* critical periods end gradually rather than abruptly, rendering the original distinction between critical and sensitive periods less useful. Readers should be aware that there is no consistent usage of these terms in the scientific literature, let alone in popular articles. I will use the term "critical period" here, however, because that is the term that is most often used in the early childhood literature.

Critical periods are always defined against a background of what scientists assume to be normal development. If during the critical period for a trait an animal has experiences that are normal for its species, the animal will develop the trait normally. If during the critical period for a trait the animal has abnormal, species-atypical experiences, it will develop the trait abnormally. If the environment is sufficiently abnormal, the animal may not acquire the trait at all.

There are some classic, textbook examples of critical periods in animal development. Nearly a hundred years ago, the ethologist Konrad Lorenz found that newly hatched graylag goslings fix, or *imprint*, on the first large, moving object that they see after hatching. The goslings will follow that object around wherever it goes and do not easily transfer their "affection" to a different object. After a day or two, the goslings' tendency to imprint disappears. Lorenz concluded that there was a critical period for imprinting in the goslings. Normally, the first thing a gosling sees is its mother and it imprints on her. Thus, imprinting would appear to have some evolutionary survival value.

Scientists have also studied critical periods in the development of male songbirds. The young male must hear its species' song, as sung by a mature male, to learn the song completely and correctly. For the zebra finch, this critical period begins no earlier than twenty-five days after hatching and ends no later than eighty days after hatching. If the male is unable to sing the proper song, it will fail to attract females and will not reproduce.

Clinical observations suggested that critical periods also exist in human development. By the mid-1950s, doctors who treated visual problems were well aware that a congenital cataract in an infant's eye presented a much more serious problem than a cataract that developed later in life. The abnormal visual experience caused by a cataract damaged the visual system in young children but not in adults. Hubel and Wiesel's work, as Carla Shatz mentioned at the White House Conference, provided an animal model for this well-known clinical problem.

Clinical observation has also suggested there are critical periods in human development for acquiring a first, or native, language. There have been a few famous cases of feral or wolf children, like the character in Truffaut's film *L'enfant sauvage*. Feral children are raised in the wild—for a mythical example, think of Romulus and Remus raised by the she-wolf—without normal human social and linguistic contact. The general observation was such that children, if their first exposure to linguistic experience occurs much after puberty, fail to acquire language. In our own day, there is the case of Genie, an abused child raised in social and linguistic isolation to the age of 13. Genie eventually managed to learn a few words but was never able to master English grammar. In contrast, Isabelle, a child first exposed to language at age 6½, acquired a vocabulary of several thousand words and had mastered complex grammatical constructions in English by age 8. Cases like these suggest that something changes in a child's ability to learn a first language between 6 and 13.

The critical period for learning a first language may extend into middle childhood or late adolescence.

Infants raised in conditions of extreme isolation or social deprivation can have serious, irremediable behavioral problems. In the late 1940s, R. A. Spitz published studies on infants raised in orphanages under conditions of extreme neglect. These children developed persistent behavioral problems, including depression. These observations have led many scientists to conclude that there is an early critical period for the development of social and emotional traits and behaviors. Harry Harlow's research on the effects of isolation on infant monkeys provides a well-known animal model for this critical period. More recently, there have been numerous reports about Romanian orphans, who were (and are being) raised in conditions of intolerable institutional neglect. Some of these children suffer long-term and apparently irreversible linguistic, social, emotional, and intellectual impairments. Such long-term problems are reported to persist in around 25 percent of Romanian children adopted into American families.

These classic examples of critical periods share at least one characteristic. They all deal with very basic traits, traits necessary for survival and reproductive success—recognizing the mother, mating, seeing, language, and social-emotional development in a highly social species like humans. For traits and behaviors like these, abnormal experiences during a critical period can result in permanent, abnormal, and nonadaptive outcomes that no subsequent amount of normal experience can correct.

This might prompt you to ask, "Why do critical periods occur at all? Isn't it a risky business to rely on a time-limited game of environmental roulette for the development of extremely sensitive systems, like vision, that are basic for our survival? Brain development that requires certain kinds of experiences to occur at particular times hardly seems to be a fail-safe system. What evolutionary advantage could it possibly confer?"

To answer this question, we have to take a longer perspective than merely thinking about what might or might not happen to our own children during their early years. We have to look at what critical periods might mean for a species over evolutionary time. In this longer view, critical periods are adaptive, clever, and efficient feats of biological engineering that facilitate the construction of highly complex nervous systems.

Carla Shatz alluded to this engineering feat in her White House Conference remarks. The human brain has a Saganesque number of synapses—billions and billions. What is the most efficient way to hook them up, especially those most needed to assure the species' survival? Nature could hard-wire brains completely at birth or it could rely totally on experience to connect the synapses. Neuroscientists now know that nature does neither; rather, nature relies on an in-between solution. Carla Shatz, with her phone-line metaphor, explained how nature implements this solution. Genes play a role and experience plays a role. According to her metaphor, our genes lay down the neural trunk lines, and stimulation or experience completes the fine-wiring, through the competitive strengthening and weakening of synapses.

Early in development, as we saw in Chapter 3, the genetic program results in an oversupply, or redundancy, of synaptic connections. Stimulation and experience drive a competitive process among these synapses for a limited supply of neural growth factors. More active synapses attract more of the sustaining growth factors than inactive ones. Active synapses flourish— become stabilized—and inactive synapses perish. Under normal circumstances, as synapse-bearing axon terminals survive or wither in response to stimulation, this competition completes the brain's fine-wiring and increases the sensitivity and specificity of our neural circuits.

Based on animal studies, this competitive process appears to be a general feature in the development of complex nervous systems. Once we reflect on how common this scheme appears to be in the development of neural systems across many species, we can infer that it must work pretty well.

Viewed from an evolutionary distance, nature's solution has some interesting consequences. One is that the brain is "plastic," or modifiable by experience, and that it relies on this plasticity to fine-tune its neural circuits. Bill Greenough and his colleagues have provided a useful way to think about this developmental phenomenon: it is as if evolution has resulted in there being neural systems that *expect* to find certain kinds of stimuli in the environment in order to fine-tune their performance. Greenough calls this kind of brain plasticity that underlies critical periods *experience-expectant* brain plasticity. Some species, humans among them, have evolved neural mechanisms designed to take advantage of experiences and stimuli that normally occur during development in the species' typical environmental niche. These expected experiences shape, refine, and fine-wire our basic neural systems, like those for seeing, hearing, and movement. The overabundance of synapses early in development is the raw material upon which these experiences work. Deprivation is the absence of experiences that would normally occur during development. Deprivation experiments in the laboratory, like those to which Hubel and Wiesel subjected the kittens, take this to an extreme, involving levels of abnormality that are the equivalent of smashing normal development with a sledgehammer.

If critical periods and the mechanism of experience-expectant brain plasticity has its origins in our evolutionary history, we can begin to delineate what kinds of traits, behaviors, and learning are most likely subject to critical-period constraints. For instance, under normal circumstances, the first large, moving object a gosling sees is the mother goose, and it is almost a guarantee that a young male zebra finch will hear the song of a mature male within eighty days of hatching. With vision, in the normal course of things, it is overwhelmingly likely that an infant will be in an environment that includes moving edges, differences in dark-light intensity, and formed patterns. For speech, it is just as likely that an infant will hear speech sounds and receive maternal attention in the context of a social group.

Experiences like these are so overwhelmingly likely to occur that nature has bet successfully on them for eons. The odds that our children will end up with appropriately fine-tuned brains are incredibly favorable, because the stimuli the brain *expects* during critical periods are the kinds of stimuli that occur everywhere and all the time within the normal developmental environment for our species. It is only when there are severe genetic or environmental aberrations from the normal that nature's expectations are frustrated and neural development goes awry.

All this helps us to conclude that critical periods are most likely to exist for acquiring species-typical traits—sensory skills, motor skills, some primate-typical social behaviors, and, in humans, language. Conversely, this suggests that critical periods are less likely to exist for traits and behaviors that are not species-typical, that is for traits and behaviors that are unique to the experiences of individuals, social groups, or cultures. There is a critical period for vision, but it is unlikely that there is a critical period for sushi making, to borrow an example from the developmental psychologist Rochel Gelman.

Sushi making is an example of a culturally specific skill, not a species-wide one. Even within Japanese culture, some individuals acquire this skill and others do not. Learning to make sushi *depends* upon a person having the appropriate specific experiences. Somehow brain plasticity must also underlie this kind of individual learning. In contrast to *experience-expectant* brain plasticity, Greenough calls the neural mechanism underlying an individual's ability to learn from its own unique, personal experiences *experience-dependent* brain plasticity. Greenough believes that this kind of plastic change in the brain depends on growing new synapses and/or increasing the efficiency of existing synapses, unlike experience-expectant plasticity that relies on synaptic pruning.

Experience-dependent plasticity allows an animal to acquire knowledge that is specific to its own environment and to learn about specific features of the particular environment it inhabits, environmental features that are not ubiquitous for the entire species. For example, an animal must learn where to find water, food, and shelter in its environment and must learn to recognize significant conspecifics—its mother, its siblings, and, for social animals, members of its group. Humans also have to learn these kinds of things, as well as how to play chess and make sushi. We must also learn the particular, specific features of our native languages, most notably vocabulary, a feature of our language that varies widely depending on the sociocultural and personal niches we inhabit. The brain's *experience-dependent* plasticity allows us to acquire new knowledge of these specifics throughout our lives, as our personal, social, and cultural environments change.

Understanding critical periods from the perspective of experience-expectant brain plasticity should already make parents, like the mother in North Carolina, less anxious. Critical periods make evolutionary sense because they rely on stimuli that are ubiquitous within normal human environments—patterned visual input, the ability to move and manipulate objects, the presence of speech sounds. These kinds of stimuli are available in any child's environment, unless that child is abused to the point of being raised in a sensory deprivation chamber, as Genie was raised in social and linguistic isolation. The stimulation children need during critical periods to fine-tune their neural circuitry are everywhere around them—at home with mother or in a Montessori preschool, in the inner city, the suburbs, rural areas, in the hills of New Guinea, or on Manhattan's Upper West Side.

Understanding critical periods in this way should help ratchet down parental guilt and anxiety to more appropriate levels. For example, for most children in most environments, vision, although subject to critical period constraints, develops normally. There is little parents need do other than to make sure the infant's eyes are working normally. You can buy the black-and-white, Calder-like mobile to hang over the crib if you want. It may amuse you and may even amuse the baby. But it won't make the infant see either better or earlier than it would otherwise. You can play Mozart softly in the nursery, but it won't make your baby hear better or earlier than it would normally.

This longer, evolutionary perspective on critical periods can also alleviate parents' anxiety along a different dimension. It has implications for when and how children learn culturally transmitted skills, like reading, math, music, and chess. These are not species-wide skills with long evolutionary histories. Literacy is a very recent cultural phenomenon among humans. It is only in the last century that universal literacy has become the norm in the industrialized world. As with sushi making, it is unlikely that there are critical-period constraints on learning how to read. Acquiring literacy skills most likely depends on experience-dependent, not experience-expectant, brain plasticiticy.

The Myth literature tends to paint a different picture, by suggesting that critical periods pervade all areas of learning, extending to specific cultural skills and to an individual's ability to learn from experience that is unique to his or her personal history. This is a monumental misconception derived from the Mythmakers' overlooking the difference between experience-expectant and experience-dependent brain plasticity, between acquiring species-wide traits and learning from personal experience.

For example, *Rethinking the Brain* and Kotulak's *Inside the Brain* claim that experience-expectant plasticity allows young children to adapt to many different kinds of conditions. Overproduction of synapses ensures that infants and young children have enough "extra wiring" to process and organize input from any environment, Borneo to Boston, as Kotulak puts it. Children in the rain forest acquire the perceptual and motor skills needed to hunt and survive. Children in the cities develop street smarts, the skills they need to survive, including "the capacity to filter out certain kinds of experience." The implication is that the time of synaptic excess during childhood is a "critical period" for acquiring all these socially and culturally distinct skills and behaviors. If so, critical periods would be extensive indeed—critical periods for adapting to monkey meat rather than McDonalds, to become expert with a blowgun rather than Flight Simulator. However, it is more likely that critical periods and experience-expectant plasticity function to help children acquire species-wide skills, characteristic of children both in Borneo and Boston. If, however, learning those things that make Borneo and Boston different depends on experience-dependent neural mechanisms, then critical periods are not as pervasive as the Myth suggests. Much of our learning depends on experiences that are unique to our personal, social, and cultural environments, not on experiences that all humans, everywhere, have.

The popular belief that critical periods constrain learning in many subject matters and skill domains has also raised needless concerns among educators. Schools are the cultural institutions that we have designed for the intergenerational transfer of culturally valued skills, like reading, math, and music. For the past fifteen years, at least, there have been debates about whether lost academic ground could be made up after a critical period ends or whether skills usually learned by young children early in their formal schooling could be learned as easily, if at all, in adulthood. Educators on the negative side of this debate tend to assume that there are critical-period constraints on learning school subjects. This assumption, however, is not warranted.

Reading is an example of a highly valued, culturally transmitted skill. As Isabel Beck, a noted reading educator and researcher, told me, critical periods have never been associated with learning to read. Typically, in our culture, children learn to read in the early primary grades, acquiring both word recognition skills and high-level comprehension skills at a relatively early age. Most children fully master these skills around age 10 or 11, in the late elementary grades of American schools. However, children who do not follow this normal trajectory are not necessarily condemned to a life of illiteracy. With proper instruction, junior high and high school students, and even adults, can acquire these skills, and with the appropriate instruction they can do so in a relatively short period of time.

Reciprocal teaching, a method to teach high-level comprehension skills, developed by Ann Brown and Annemarie Palincsar, provides an excellent example. After less than a month of reciprocal-teaching instruction, junior high school and high school students in remedial reading classes were able to read at grade level. Among these students was a seventh-grader with an IQ of 70 who had entered the program reading at the third-grade level.

Adult literacy programs provide additional evidence that acquiring and improving literacy skills is not time-limited or subject to critical-period limitations. The U.S. Department of Defense has devoted considerable time and resources to improving the literacy skills of recruits. For example, the Army's Functional

Literacy Program provided recruits a six-week literacy program associated with their job training. In one evaluation of this program, after six weeks, the trainees showed a twenty-four-month increase in job-related reading skill and a seven-month improvement in general reading skill. Eight weeks after the course had ended the trainees retained 80 percent of the gain on job-related reading skills. Tom Sticht, a psychologist who has worked extensively in military and adult education, concludes from his experience that even short-term workplace literacy programs can improve job-related literacy. With continuing opportunities for education and learning, adults can and do develop high levels of literacy. Raising literacy skills, and verbal intelligence that is closely associated with literacy skills, depends on ongoing experiences and opportunities to read and learn. These experiences and opportunities benefit adults as well as children. Reading educators have good reason to reject the significance of critical periods for acquiring literacy skills.

We can tell a similar story about number skills and mental arithmetic. Although most children in our culture learn basic number skills at an early age, not all children do. Yet, those individuals who do not, if given the appropriate instruction and experiences, can acquire number skills even as adults.

For example, until recently, developmental psychologists thought that all children learned to compare numbers for size—which is bigger, five or seven?—at around 4 years of age. Most children do. However, as the developmental psychologists Robbie Case and Sharon Griffin discovered, disproportionate numbers of children from lower socioeconomic-status homes do not. Lacking this middle-class skill that comes from playing board games and counting invitations to birthday parties, these children are missing a number skill that is implicitly assumed in most elementary arithmetic curricula. Children who lack this skill—who did not learn it at the "normal" time—readily learn it, if the curriculum teaches it. Case and Griffen developed a curriculum that explicitly taught numerical comparison and related elementary number skills. After one year in this curriculum, these "deprived" children acquire this simple, but missing, skill

THE MYTH OF THE FIRST THREE YEARS

and other concepts based on it, and when they acquire it their arithmetic and number abilities become comparable to those of middle-class American and Asian children.

Children use their counting and comparing skills to invent strategies to solve simple addition and subtraction problems. To solve 4 + 2, a child would reason that 4 is bigger than 2 and then "count on" two numbers beyond 4. The child would mentally count like this: "4 . . . and two more . . . 5, 6." Children find these strategies most useful when they have to do "mental arithmetic"—that is, compute sums and differences when they do not have visible physical objects that they can actually count to solve the problem.

Cognitive psychologist Geoffrey Saxe documented a more exotic case of inventing these same counting strategies among the Oksapmin, an isolated, agrarian people in the hills of New Guinea. Traditionally, the Oksapmin had a subsistence economy based on barter. They did not use currency. The Oksapmin did use numbers to count or order things ("third pig on the left"). Typically, however, the kinds of problems they had to solve involved visible physical objects that they could see and count. They had no need to do mental arithmetic.

Oksapmin males who left their villages to work on plantations in Australia used their savings to establish trade stores when they returned to their home villages. With stores, currency entered everyday life. The Oksapmin had to learn to tally accounts, make payments, and give and receive change. All of a sudden, they had a need for mental arithmetic. To solve these new problems that now arose in their environment, the Oksapmin adults spontaneously and without instruction invented the same counting strategies that young Western schoolchildren invent. Although in our culture, children usually invent these strategies when they are 4 to 5 years old, the Oksapmin invented them as adults when experience so dictated and the need arose. Inventing these strategies and learning arithmetic skills does not appear to be constrained to a critical period early in development.

Music, especially classical music, is another highly valued

cultural activity. In the literature surrounding the Myth, we often see claims and suggestions that there is an early critical period for learning to play a musical instrument.

One important neuroscientific study is commonly cited in the Myth literature as providing evidence that there is a critical period for music. Scientists at the University of Konstanz used brain-recording technology to examine how playing a string instrument reorganizes the brain. The average age of the subjects in the experiment was 24 years. Half of the subjects played string instruments and had been doing so on average for about 11½ years. The remaining subjects had never played a string instrument.

Using a technology called magnetoencephalography (MEG), the scientists measured the magnetic fields that emerged from the subjects' scalps when the subjects moved the fingers on their left hands. These magnetic fields were generated by the electrical activity of tens of thousands of neurons involved in finger movement. The left hand is the hand a string player uses on the instrument's fingerboard.

The published report of this study presented two results. First, the researchers found that the magnetic response from brain areas controlling the left-hand fingers of string players (their fingerboard fingers) was greater than the response from the same areas in the nonplayers' brains. Second, the researchers found that among the string players, the magnitude of the magnetic signal seemed to depend on how old the person was when he or she began playing the instrument. The younger the age at which the person began playing, the larger the magnetic response from the brain area that controlled the left hand.

Popular articles about this study reported that early music training is particularly effective in reorganizing the brain and concluded that parents should provide music lessons before age 12, before the critical period ends. But this brain-recording study does not support that conclusion.

First, anxious parents should realize that this experiment is only incidentally about music or musical training. The experiment measures brain responses to a highly overlearned motor skill, fingering a violin keyboard. Scientists would likely have found the same differences in right-hand responses, if they compared compulsive computer-game joy stick users with nonusers. (I suppose this would have been interpreted as neuroscientific evidence that computer games are *bad* for brain development.)

Second, the experimental design the scientists used in this study prevented them from drawing any conclusions about the existence of a critical period. Although among the string players, those who began playing earlier did have a larger brain response, it is also likely that those who began playing at a younger age had been playing longer. The larger brain response could be the result of time on task—how long they had been playing—rather than the result of a critical period for violin playing—when they first started instruction.

Third, the study design does not address critical periods, because that was not the point the scientists were trying to make. The authors believe that their results are important because they tell us something new and significant about more mature brains, not about critical periods in young brains.

I asked Edward Taub, one of the study's authors, about the media coverage the article received. He told me, "I am definitely not happy with the interpretation and treatment of this article. In fact, I am quite unhappy about it. The interpretation and coverage missed the main point of the work entirely, which was not that you have a greater plasticity in the immature brain than in the mature nervous system, but rather that this plasticity persists, at least in reduced form, into maturity. It is the latter that is contrary to the previously established view in neuroscience and that gives the paper whatever importance it has."

Emphasizing the larger response in earlier beginners appeals to parents anxious about how their children will ever get to Carnegie Hall (or Opryland). What is of neuroscientific interest, what is new here, is that string players who started late, after age 12, also showed significant brain reorganization compared to people who had never played. The scientists' conclusion is that the neural circuitry of the mature brain reorganizes itself in response to what people do and the experiences they have throughout life. Even after the great synaptic pruning, changes in brain structure "conform to the current needs and experience of the individual." (We will trace additional implications of this new understanding of the brain for the Myth in Chapter 5.)

We have seen that critical-period learning is limited to acquiring species-wide behaviors—the ability to see and the ability to use language in humans, for example. The experiences children need, that is, the experiences brain expects, to acquire these skills are so widely available and hard to miss that parents need not worry about having to provide them or about their children missing critical periods in development.

But equally important, it is highly unlikely that there are windows of opportunity that slam shut for learning culturally transmitted skills, like the skills children learn in school. It is true that children in our cultural normally learn these skills—reading, arithmetic, or playing the piano—at certain ages, but we should not confuse this kind of learning with the existence of critical periods for those skills. What is culturally normal is not biologically determined.

As you read articles on parenting and childhood that talk about windows of opportunity, always ask yourself this question: is the article talking about a genuine critical period for some species-typical trait, or is the article concerned only with some culturally specific skill that children normally acquire at a certain age?

Don't worry about cramming all those music, dance, and sports lessons into a child's early years. As far as we know, the windows of opportunity stay open much, much longer than that.

"Looking Inside": Synaptic Competition and Critical Periods

Konrad Lorenz discovered the critical period for imprinting in the goslings by carefully observing the goslings' behavior. However, for a critical period to exist, something besides an animal's observed behavior has to change. Why? Because what makes critical periods interesting is that at time 1 in an animal's life certain kinds of experience, or the lack of it, allow the animal to change its behavior, while at time 2 the same kinds of experience have no effect. Critical periods in a species' development imply that something changes inside the animal between time 1 and time 2. During maturation, some intrinsic, constitutional change must occur that affects how the animal can use experience to change its behavior. The significance of Hubel and Wiesel's work was that it launched a research program in which neuroscientists began to "look inside" the organism and to identify the cellular and molecular changes underlying critical periods.

To understand this part of the neuroscientific story, we will look in some detail at animal research that may seem a bit far removed from the concerns of parents and childcare providers. Animal research must suffice because we can't do deprivation experiments or examine slices of our children's brains under the microscope to gain insights into what does occur in a child's brain during a critical period.

Although the blind kittens are the most famous example of a missed critical period, Hubel, Wiesel, and their colleague Simon LeVay also studied critical periods in the development of the monkey visual system. Because we are more similar to our primate cousins than we are to cats, we will focus on the monkey research here.

Hubel, Wiesel, and LeVay found that abnormal visual experiences, typically different kinds of visual deprivation, affected neural structures in the primary visual area of young monkeys' brains. In a normal monkey brain, there are columns of neurons, approximately .5 millimeter wide in the visual cortex. Each such column responds preferentially, or predominately, to stimuli presented to one eye or the other. The columns are arranged so that columns preferring, or dominated by, input from the right eye alternate with columns preferring, or dominated by, input from the left eye. For this reason, neuroscientists call these neural structures *ocular dominance columns.* Neuroscientists believe that ocular dominance columns are the neural structures that first allow the brain to begin integrating and combining information that comes into the brain from each eye along separate visual pathways. Integrating and combining this information makes binocular vision possible.

We typically hear about the kittens that had *one eye* surgically closed at birth. Hubel, Wiesel, and LeVay did a similar experiment on monkeys. Six months of closure, starting at birth, rendered the monkeys permanently blind in the deprived eye. When the scientists examined the brains of these animals, they found that the ocular dominance columns for the normal eye had become wider than usual and that the ocular dominance columns for the deprived eye had become narrower than usual. In adult monkeys, closing one eye for six months had no effect on either the animal's vision or on the width of the ocular dominance columns.

But what would happen to animals that had both eyes, or alternating eyes, surgically closed early in life? Hubel, Wiesel, and LeVay did those experiments. And much to their surprise the monkeys that had both eyes closed for the first six months of life had normal vision in both eyes and normal ocular dominance columns at maturity.

In the alternating closure experiment, the scientists alternately sutured and opened the animals' eyes during the critical period. Both eyes received the same total amount of stimulation during the critical period, but never at the same time. At maturity, these monkeys had normal vision in each eye, but never developed normal binocular vision. They also had more sharply defined and highly separated ocular dominance columns than did normal monkeys.

Hubel, Wiesel, and LeVay also did a "reverse closure" experiment. In these experiments, they closed one eye at birth, then some time later opened the closed eye and closed the open one. If they did the reverse closure before the monkey was 3 weeks old, the monkey had normal vision and normal ocular dominance columns for both eyes. Reverse closure at 6 weeks resulted in a normal ocular dominance pattern, but incomplete recovery of visual function. Reverse closure at age 1 year had no effect on the damage caused by the early, initial deprivation.

Finally, they found that a monkey raised in total darkness had normal ocular dominance columns. This means, as more recent studies have confirmed, that monkeys have normal, adult-like ocular dominance columns at birth and that visual experience is not required for the ocular dominance columns to form. In monkeys, spontaneous neural activity that occurs in their visual systems prior to birth—Carla Shatz's neural autodialing—is sufficient to form ocular dominance columns.

Taken together, Hubel, Wiesel, and LeVay's experiments tell us how activity-dependent competition occurs in one model case—ocular dominance—of experience-expectant brain plasticity. Early in development (before birth in monkeys) the fine axon terminals from both the right and left eyes make synaptic contacts on all target cells in the structures that will become ocular dominance columns. Because of the genetic or developmental programs that control axon growth and early synapse formation, the number of axon terminals is slightly biased in favor of one eye or the other on alternate groups of target cells.

Under normal conditions—both eyes open—there is *balanced* and *simultaneous* activity along the visual pathway from both eyes to their target cells. Under these conditions, synapses on the axon terminals compete for neural growth factors subject to the synaptic bias nature bestowed. On those target cells where nature has awarded a slight numerical advantage to the right eye, axons from the right eye win the competition and axons from the left eye retract. Where nature favors the left eye, it wins. This results in the normal segregation and formation of ocular dominance columns. Under normal conditions, axon terminals, with their synapses, sprout or retract according to the rules of nature's game.

Closing both eyes decreases the level of activity along each visual pathway to the target cells, but alters neither the *balance* nor the *simultaneity* of activity. As a result, the competition still proceeds under the natural handicap and there is no change in the ocular dominance patterns.

Closing one eye during the critical period upsets both the *balance* and *simultaneity* of input from the two eyes to their target structures in the brain. The deprived eye's target cells receive no stimulation. This puts the axon terminals from the deprived eye at an extreme competitive disadvantage and upsets the odds in the axons' struggle to control target cells in the visual area. In this abnormal competition, axons from the closed eye retract from their target cells and axons from the open eye sprout and expand onto target cells formerly controlled by the closed eye. This unnatural competition makes the ocular dominance columns for the closed eye narrower than normal and those for the open eye wider than normal.

Alternate eye closure maintains the overall *balance* in activity from the two eyes but disrupts the *simultaneity* of activity along the two visual pathways. This kind of abnormal stimulation appears to increase the competition for target cells, reinforcing the initial advantage each eye had with regard to its groups of cells, resulting in more distinct and clearly separated columns than normal.

Reverse closure—reversing the imbalance and lack of simultaneity—if done early enough in the critical period, grants a competitive advantage to the closed eye over the normal eye. Axon terminals from the initially deprived eye recapture control of target cells they had previously lost, and axon terminals from the newly closed eye retreat from previously won territory, restoring the normal ocular dominance pattern.

These animal experiments have direct analogues and therapeutic implications in treating visual problems in children. Of the cases Hubel, Wiesel, and LeVay examined, closing one eye early in development had the most serious consequences for the monkey. This is also true for human infants. Congenital cataracts in one eye are a much more serious condition than congenital cataracts in both eyes. Children with cataracts in one eye will be permanently blind in the affected eye if the condition is not surgically treated early in life. Even if treated, these children seldom recover visual acuity better than 20/200 (compared to the normal 20/20) in the treated eye. Children with congenital cataracts in both eyes who are treated before the age of 2 show much better recovery. In some cases, these children have visual acuity in the 20/30-to-20/40 range.

Strabismus is another common childhood visual problem

that if left untreated can result in poor vision. With strabismus, the visual axes of the two eyes cannot be directed simultaneously to the same object. Being cross-eyed is a form of strabismus called internal strabismus, where the visual axes of the two eyes cross. Strabismus, however, is not as serious a condition as cataracts. In strabismus, visual input from the two eyes to the brain is balanced but is out of synchrony. Visual input that falls on the retina of one eye reaches the brain either slightly before or slightly after input that falls on the retina of the other eye. This is like the case of alternate closure in the monkeys. Here, once the strabismus is surgically corrected, the effects of the abnormal experience can be reversed using corrective lenses or by patching the child's good eye, thus forcing him to use the damaged eye. How best to use reverse deprivation and eye patching in children and what animal models can tell us about it is now a substantial research area.

However, if the critical period for ocular dominance columns is the paradigmatic example of experience-expectant brain plasticity, there is a larger message here for parents and caregivers. Hubel, Wiesel, and LeVay disrupted *normal visual input* from the eyes to the brain. Normal visual input is balanced and simultaneous along the neural pathways from each eye to the brain. As long as the visual input is normal in this way, so is brain development. Problems occur and the brain develops abnormally during the critical period, when either the balance or timing of input is disrupted. The crucial case to keep in mind is what happened when both of the monkey's eyes were closed at birth. This kind of deprivation caused no damage, because even though the overall amount of visual stimulation was far below normal, the stimulation that did occur was balanced and synchronous. This leads neuroscientists to an important, but not widely appreciated, conclusion: when it comes to critical periods, if the visual system is our best example, the *amount* of neural activity is less important than the *pattern* of neural activity in causing synapses and axons to reorganize.

Understanding this neuroscientific conclusion gives parents and caregivers another tool to use in evaluating some of the advice conveyed in the Myth literature. Some of the advice we have reviewed, like stimulating infants as much as possible or apply-ing a full-court developmental press during the critical years, is based on the assumption that the amount of stimulation a child receives during the critical period is what matters. However, the deprivation experiments show that the amount of stimulation during the critical period is not the key variable in normal synapse elimination and experience-expectant brain plasticity. The key is balance and overall timing of neural activity among the competing axons and synapses. These experiments provide no support for the popular belief that during a critical period more stimulation is necessarily better than less. As Jeff Lichtman, a neuroscientist at Washington University, told me, "We know from these experiments that deprivation is bad. We do not know from these experiments that more or earlier stimulation is good." What seems to matter during the critical period is the pattern, not the amount, of stimulation.

Critical-Period Complexity: Distinct Phases and Multiple Periods

Neuroscientists have also learned that critical periods, far from being windows that slam shut, are complex.

First, there can be distinct phases within a critical period. Again, the best example is the development of the monkey visual system. As we learned above, monkeys are born with nearly adultlike ocular dominance columns. So in monkeys, there is a phase of rapid early development in the visual system that re-quires neural activity along the visual pathways, but which re-quires no visual experience. We can think of this as phase one of the visual system's critical period, the phase during which the system rapidly approaches mature, adultlike form.

From deprivation experiments, we know that closing one eye early in the monkey's life alters the normal structure of the al-ready formed ocular dominance columns. This is the second phase of the critical period, during which the nearly adultlike oc-ular dominance columns are susceptible to damage by abnormal, unbalanced visual experience. Recent research done by Jonathan

Horton and Davina Hocking at the University of California-San Francisco varied the age at which monkeys had one eye closed. They found that the earlier in a monkey's life that the deprivation occurred, the greater the effect of the deprivation on its ocular dominance columns. Closing one eye during the first week of life caused the ocular dominance columns for the deprived eye to disappear. Closing one eye of a 12-week-old monkey, however, had no effect on the monkey's ocular dominance columns. This experiment tells us that the second phase of the critical period ends at around 12 weeks of age.

Finally, reverse closure experiments show that there is a third phase. In the late 1980s at the University of Texas-Houston, M. L. Crawford and R. S. Harweth did a series of reverse closure experiments on monkeys. One monkey had its eye closed when it was 1 month old, during the second phase of the critical period when abnormal experience causes damage. Three and half months later, when the monkey was 18 weeks old, the scientists did a reverse closure and kept the "normal" eye closed for three months. At maturity, this monkey had normal-to-near-normal performance in all the visual functions the scientists tested and had normal ocular dominance columns. Reverse closure restored normal visual function and rewired the brain into a normal pattern. During this third phase, damage caused by earlier abnormal experience can be reversed. That is to say, there is a final stage in the critical period, extending beyond the phase when the system is sensitive to deprivation, during which the system remains sufficiently plastic to benefit from therapy.

These same three phases also occur in children's development of visual acuity. We all know from our frequent visits to the eye specialist that normal visual acuity is 20/20. In children, visual acuity develops during the first three years of life. From birth to age 6 to 8 months, there is rapid improvement in visual acuity from 20/600 to near-normal, (young) adultlike 20/30 vision. Then there is slower improvement until age 3 years during which time acuity reaches 20/20. Thus, for visual acuity there is a phase early in development when this function develops rapidly to adultlike, mature levels.

Strabismus—for example, having crossed eyes—in children can damage visual acuity, if the condition develops before the child is 7 or 8 years old. Yet, strabismus and even cataracts do no permanent damage to children's vision, if they first occur after age 7 to 8. So, like the monkeys, abnormal visual experience—here caused by strabismus—can affect visual acuity well into childhood (age 7–8 years), long after visual acuity first reaches the normal, mature 20/20 level (age 3 years).

Doctors treat strabismus by using a variation of alternate closure. For several hours every day, the child wears a patch over the normal eye, forcing him or her to use the abnormal, misaligned eye. For many years, doctors assumed that poor vision caused by strabismus could not be corrected much after the child was 6 or 7 years old—that is, much after the stage of sensitivity to abnormal experience had ended. In treating these conditions, the criterion of success is having the patient achieve a visual acuity of 20/30 or better. Since the mid-1970s, several studies have reported that children over 8 years old respond to therapy as well and as fully as children under 8. Another study, which employed a more stringent criterion of successful recovery, showed that all patients under age 16 responded equally well to treatment. These studies show that in strabismic children there is an extended third phase to the critical period, during which damage caused by abnormal experience during the second phase can be partially, if not completely, reversed.

Neuroscientists also know it is inaccurate to speak simply of *a* critical period for vision. Each specific visual function—acuity, color vision, motion vision, depth perception, binocular vision—has its own critical period, some stretching as we have seen at least into the teenage years. Even for a well-studied system like vision, researchers and clinicians are still investigating how and when to use therapies like eye patching and corrective lenses to repair damage caused by abnormal early visual experience.

What is the significance of this complexity for parenting and childcare? To begin with, rather than thinking of critical periods as windows that slam shut, we might do better to think of them as reservoirs that gradually evaporate during normal development and that can be partly refilled if we know which valves to open and when to open them.

What is most important to remember is that for each specific function—in our example visual acuity, color vision, depth perception, etc.—critical periods and the phases within them are linked to the maturational timetable for very specific parts of the brain. Neuroscientists are only beginning to understand the neural mechanisms and timetables that governs these processes.

To make use of critical periods to understand how children develop and to help children develop requires detailed knowledge of specific functions and skills and highly specific knowledge of the maturational timetables for the brain areas that support those specific functions. We know more about critical periods for vision than we do for any other brain system, and even there we have barely scratched the surface. We have no idea of what the critical periods might be for the development of social and emotional skills or even if they exist. Because critical periods are complex, using what we know about critical periods to guide therapy, let alone parenting, is a complex task, where the wrong therapy used at the wrong time can cause more harm than benefit.

Critical Periods and the First Three Years

If it makes little sense, given the complexity of critical periods, to speak of *the* critical period in the development of the visual system, it makes even less sense to speak of *the* critical period in brain development.

If it is incorrect to speak of *the* critical period in brain development, it is highly misleading to identify *the* critical period with the first three years of life, as the Myth literature tends to do.

We have seen that critical periods in the development of the visual system extend well beyond the first three years of life. The phase during which that system is sensitive to abnormal visual experience lasts until children are 8 to 9 years old; the phase during which some of this damage can be reversed may last well into the teenage years. In the next section of this chapter, we will look at the language system and see that the critical periods for learning phonology and grammar, in first and second languages, also last into children's second decade of life.

We should pause to recall that so far in our discussion of the Myth's purported *neurobiological* basis, we have encountered only one research-based finding that mentions the first three years of life. In the previous chapter, we reviewed Peter Huttenlocher's work. He found that synaptic density (computed using whole cortical tissue as the denominator) peaks in the frontal areas of the brain at around 3 years of age. Of the brain areas studied so far, it appears that the brain's frontal areas are where synaptic densities reach their peak values latest in development. So, based on the brain science, we could make the general claim that synaptic densities peak in all parts of the brain by age 3; that is, by age 3 the period of exuberant synapse formation has ended in all parts of the brain's cortex that neursoscientists have so far studied.

We have seen in this chapter that critical periods in humans extend well into the synaptic plateau period, continuing at least until developmental programs prune back excess synapses starting in puberty. Although the period of rapid synapse formation ends at age 3, critical periods in development last far longer. Given what the research says, critical periods do not fit neatly into the first three years of life or into what we know is happening in the brain during those years.

Rob Reiner and the authors of I Am Your Child oversimplify and mislead both politicians and parents when they claim, "We know through science that the first three years of life is [*sic*] the most critical time period."

Thoughtful scientists who study child development are well aware of how misleading such a simplistic claim can be. Sam Meisels, a developmental psychologist and board member of the national organization Zero to Three, provided one such thoughtful formulation when I asked him why researchers focus on the birth-to-3 age range. He told me, "We chose the birth-to-3 period because there is very strong empirical and clinical evidence that this is a period of life when valuable pathways are laid down for cognitive and emotional growth. There is substantial research that shows that the first years of life—while not formally a "critical" period—are central to later social, emotional, and cognitive functioning."

The empirical and clinical evidence to which Meisels refers comes primarily from research in child psychiatry and the attachment theory tradition. As we saw in Chapter 2, despite the popular perception that there is a critical period for the development of attachment relations, the evidence for such a belief is weak to nonexistent. In addition, as Charles Nelson reminded Reiner, there is at present no link between brain science and theories of infant attachment. If, as according to careful scientists like Meisels, what happens in the early years is not a formal critical period at all, then citing research on what happens during formal critical periods—the blind kittens—is a red herring.

As Meisels told me, the brain science is interesting, but many early childhood researchers would continue doing exactly what they are doing independent of what neuroscience says now or what it might say in the future. Brain science and critical periods are sideshows to what is going on under the big top, where scientists are carefully studying how and why children's behavior changes. Parents, childcare providers, and policymakers should be encouraged to come to the same conclusion.

Critical (and Uncritical) Periods in Language Learning

Unlike other areas—reading, numbers, music—where there is little if any research, but an abundance of anecdote claiming that critical periods exist, language learning is different. Psychologists, psycholinguists, and linguists have devoted considerable attention to critical periods for language acquisition. In 1967, Eric Lenneberg reviewed the existing research on first, or native, language acquisition. He argued that a person could completely acquire his or her native language only within a critical period, extending from early infancy until puberty.

Brain-related claims about critical periods in language learning are not new either. Forty years ago, based on their pioneering studies of brain development, Wilder Penfield and Lamar Roberts, speculated that "the time to begin what might be called a general schooling in secondary languages, in accordance with the demands of brain physiology, is between the ages of 4 and 10." Recently, neuroscientists have joined in the research on critical periods in language learning and are starting to make some fascinating discoveries.

For all these reasons, language learning provides an opportunity to further explore what critical periods are, to appreciate their complexity, and to see what brain science might contribute to our understanding of how we acquire our first language and learn second languages. It will allow us to see some interesting parallels between what we know about critical periods in vision and what we know about critical periods for language.

First of all, language, like vision, is a species-typical behavior and as such might well involve critical periods and experience-expectant brain plasticity. Just as every neurologically normal child acquires the ability to see, every neurologically normal child also acquires the ability to use his or her native language, despite dramatically diverse beliefs about language learning across cultures. American middle-class mothers (and fathers) tend to constantly bathe their children in language. We like to think that we are teaching our children to speak. Parents in other cultures do not share our belief, as Steve Pinker described in *The Language Instinct*. In some cultures, parents do not speak directly to their children at all. Why should they? they reason. The child cannot say anything back. Nonetheless, these children master their native language as completely as the linguistically bathed American children. Children also acquire their native language much in the same way that they acquire the ability to see, hear, and walk—easily, automatically, and unconsciously, very unlike learning reading, arithmetic, and violin. All these factors suggest that first-language learning might well occur as it does because the human brain has evolved to expect that the necessary linguistic stimuli will be present in a child's environment to fine-tune its language circuits.

The language system, like the visual system, is also a complex of distinct skills. At the crudest level of analysis, mastering a language requires learning to hear and produce the speech sounds the language uses; that is, one must acquire the language's phonology. One must also learn the language's grammatical rules, its syntax and morphology. Finally, one must learn what specific words in the language mean—that is, the language's vocabulary and semantics. There are different critical periods associated with each of these three sets of language skills. In fact, for vocabulary and semantics, as we shall see, there is no critical period at all.

Researchers distinguish between learning a first, or native, language and learning a second language. Learning a first language presents a very different, and intuitively more difficult, learning problem than does learning a second language. Once we acquire a first language in childhood, we can use our understanding of that language plus our general intelligence to construct analogies between the two languages to help us learn the second one. When we acquire our first language, we do not have this same leg up on the problem—no language at all, no general learning strategies, and no ability to generate analogies. The very different learning problems first and second languages present create the possibility that there might be different critical periods involved in each case.

Let's first look at what we know about a critical period for phonology, or "accent," first. There is relatively little research on critical periods in first-language phonology learning, although the experts universally agree that such a critical period exists.

One well-known body of research that does have some bearing on this issue and that is highly prominent in the brain and early childhood literature is the work of Patricia Kuhl, who spoke at the White House Conference. Kuhl and her colleagues have studied how early language experience alters infants' ability to perceive speech sounds, the first step toward learning phonology.

She found that, at birth, infants could discriminate all possible human speech sounds, but by age 6 months they lost this ability. Children's early speech experience, just listening to adult speech around them, fine-tunes their ability to perceive speech sounds. But this fine-tuning comes at a price. It limits children's ability to discriminate speech sounds to the sounds that occur in the language that they hear. Also, as we saw for the critical period in the development of visual acuity, this perceptual ability develops to near adult levels very rapidly, by age 6 months. Kuhl suggests, consistent with the notion of experience-expectant brain plasticity, that this rapid perceptual tuning taps into an underlying species-wide cognitive capacity to notice and process certain kinds of stimuli that the neural system needs to fine-tune itself.

Tuning an infant's system for speech perception relies on the phonetic equivalents of objects, moving edges, and patterned forms that tune the visual system. As we might expect for experience-expectant brain plasticity, whatever language stimuli are available in a normal human environment seem to be enough to do the job. At the White House Conference, President Clinton asked Kuhl how much we should talk to our children every day. She responded that scientists do not really know, but that there seems to be a natural balance between parents' tendencies to talk to their babies and the babies' ability to benefit from that linguistic stimulation.

For learning second-language phonology, everyone's favorite example is Henry Kissinger. Kissinger, who arrived in the Unites States at around age 12, speaks excellent English, with a German accent. His brother, younger by two years, speaks unaccented English. Research generally supports the Kissinger brothers anecdote, although on the "accent" issue, different researchers have come up with varying claims about when the critical period ends. Some think there is a critical period for unaccented language learning that closes at around 5 or 6 years of age. Others argue that a critical period ending at about age 14 could account for most of the observed differences in accent. James Flege has recently published data showing a gradual, linear decline, far from a slamming window, in unaccented learning that begins at age 2.

We know almost nothing about the stages within the critical period for phonological learning, but Kuhl's infants and the Kissinger brothers point to some constraints. Rapid tuning appears to occur during the first six months of life. Both Henry and his brother were no doubt well tuned to German phonology at this tender age. However, the system remains plastic and able to tune itself to a second phonology, based on different linguistic experience, as Henry's brother shows, until early in the second decade of life. All we can say is that acquiring phonology is similar to acquiring visual acuity in that there is rapid early development followed by a longer period during which the system remains malleable by "abnormal" experience.

We know a little bit more about critical periods for learning a language's grammar. We cannot do deprivation, or linguistic isolation, experiments on children, but there are some "experiments of nature" that allow scientists to study humans in ways that are comparable to deprivation experiments. The subjects in these experiments are the congenitally deaf, who learn American Sign Language (ASL) as their first language.

ASL is a language that is expressed by hand gestures and comprehended through the visual system. It has a sophisticated grammar based on spatial relationships. Congenitally deaf children of deaf ASL-using parents acquire ASL as their first language, in the same way that hearing children of hearing parents acquire their first spoken language. These children are "native" ASL speakers.

Deaf children of hearing parents, because of their disability, often receive no linguistic input at all, until the parents discover the child is deaf. For some of these children, their first linguistic experience does not occur until 4 to 6 years of age, when they are first exposed to ASL. These children can be thought of as early, although not native learners. There are other children who receive their first exposure to language via ASL even later, at age 12, and sometimes past the age of puberty.

In what is considered to be one of the best studies of critical periods in first-language grammar acquisition, Elissa Newport compared how well these three groups of ASL users had mastered the grammar of their first language. She found that native learners had a better mastery of ASL grammar than did the early learners and that children in both these groups were superior to the late learners. She concluded that normal grammar acquisition occurs only when children are exposed to language early in life. With later exposure, the ability to master the grammar of a first language gradually declines. It is not a window slamming shut—the rate of decline in the ability to learn is slow but steady through the childhood years and flattens out in adulthood—but the window does seem to close. On the basis of her results, she concludes, and most investigators agree, that there are maturational, presumably biological, brain-based constraints that allow completely successful first-language grammar acquisition only early in life. There is a critical period for acquiring the grammar of one's native language that closes around puberty.

Newport, along with Jacqueline Johnson, also studied critical periods for second-language grammar learning. Newport and Johnson designed an experiment in which they could separate the effects of brain maturation from practice effects and time on task in second-language grammar learning. The subjects in the Newport and Johnson study were native-speaking Koreans and Chinese, ranging in age from age 3 to 39 years. These subjects, who had been exposed to English for between three and twenty-six years, were divided into two groups, those who arrived in the United States before puberty (age 15 years) and those who arrived after. On average, time of exposure to English—that is, the time on task, or practice time—was the same for both groups, around ten years. This allowed Newport and Johnson to compare the effects of ten years of exposure to English as a second language when that experience occurred either before or after puberty.

Newport and Johnson found that after ten years' experience with English as a second language the earliest arrivals—those who came to the United States before age 7—were indistinguishable from native English speakers in their mastery of English grammar. Those who arrived at later ages, but before their mid-teens, after ten years of exposure to English, had a grammatical facility with English that was related in a linear, predictable way to their age of arrival in the United States. The younger they were when they arrived, the better mastery they had of English grammar. However, for those subjects who were older than 17 when they arrived in the United States, even after ten years of practice, their grammatical skills remained poorer than those of the earlier arrivals and were not at all related to their age of arrival in the United States. Interpreted this way, the Johnson-Newport study is generally accepted as showing that there is a critical period for second-language grammar learning that ends at around puberty. However, this interpretation is not universally accepted. Recent research has caused some psycho-linguists to reconsider questions of how long the grammar-learning window stays open and how tightly it ever shuts.

Learning a language's semantics or vocabulary is a totally different story. There is *no* good evidence for a critical period effect in vocabulary learning. Children start learning words in their native language when they are around 12 months old and learn quickly. It is a good thing that they do, because there are a lot of words to learn. The average 6-year-old, just by listening and conversing, can recognize around 13,000 words. Generally, school-age children learn vocabulary faster than do preschool children. The average high school graduate probably has a "passive," or receptive listening, vocabulary of 60,000 words. A high school graduate who reads a lot might have a vocabulary twice that size.

From birth until the end of high school, we learn about ten new words a day. Vocabulary learning begins to plateau around high school; however, college students show an additional spurt in vocabulary learning, as again do graduate students, when they acquire the specialized vocabularies of law, medicine, or other advanced fields. As adults, we continue to learn new names, words, slang, and professional jargon throughout our entire lives.

Based on such observations, psychologists and psycholinguists do not believe that there is a critical period for learning vocabulary. Rather, they believe that the limiting factor in vocabulary acquisition is exposure to new words. Learning slows down when we enter into a comfortable, familiar semantic and communicative niche in which there are few new words to learn.

We continue to acquire new vocabulary as we develop new interests, take on new hobbies, and engage in literate activities. What matters for vocabulary learning, at any age, is experiencing and using new words.

The rate of exposure to new words varies from person to person and from social group to social group. This seems to be equally true for learning vocabulary in a second language. If you want to increase your vocabulary, even in middle age, learn some neuroscience or study Italian. Unlike experience-expectant plasticity and critical periods, exposure to and learning of words depends entirely on experiences that are unique to each individual, not on experiences that are ubiquitous in any normal human environment.

This general pattern is consistent with another oft-cited finding in the early childhood literature. Betty Hart and Todd Risley found significant differences across social classes in vocabulary learning. Professional mothers speak to their infants and children more than do working-class and welfare mothers. Because of this exposure, the children of the professional mothers have larger vocabularies and are, no doubt, better prepared for school than the other children. However, their finding is not an instance of a critical-period phenomenon. As far as we know, it is possible to increase our vocabulary at any age, and learning vocabulary is an area in which children who happened to have less talkative mothers can make up lost ground later on.

We are only beginning to understand how changes in the brain's structure and neural circuitry relate to the critical periods, and lack of them, for language learning. What we are learning about language and the brain is exceedingly interesting, however. This research suggests that there are very different kinds of brain organization and reorganization involved in critical-period grammar learning versus noncritical-period vocabulary learning.

Helen Neville with her colleagues first at the University of California-San Diego and now at the University of Oregon have studied both first- and second-language grammar and vocabulary acquisition. They use a brain-recording technology called evoked response potentials (ERP). ERP records electrical currents on the scalp's surface that are generated by the firing of tens of thousands of neurons as those neurons process information. By recording the timing and pattern of these scalp-current patterns, neuroscientists can begin to trace the neural circuitry involved in processing different kinds of information and to see how that circuitry changes during development.

In a series of ERP studies on first-language grammatical processing, Neville found that normal, English-speaking adults all registered a distinct pattern of brain activity when they were engaged in grammatical processing: a localized response in the front part of the brain's left hemisphere, near the temple. However, this pattern is not present in young English-speaking children. It begins to appear only at around 11 years of age and takes on the clear, mature adultlike pattern by age 15 or 16.

In her study of second-language grammar learning, Neville looked at native ASL users, who had learned English late in life as a second language. When these late second-language learners processed English grammatical information, they did not have the characteristic left-hemisphere response found in mature native English speakers. These studies suggest, first, that late exposure to a second language results in the brain processing grammatical information in the second language differently than it does for the native language. Second, they suggest that the critical period for acquiring grammar might come to an end when the brain finally shows the mature left-hemisphere pattern for grammatical processing early in adulthood.

Brain-imaging studies are also allowing us to make some tentative connections among what we know about critical periods, learning a language's grammar, and changes in synaptic densities over the life span.

Brain-imaging studies in normal humans have revealed that the gray matter in our brain cortex decreases markedly in volume between the ages of 8 and 30 years. These decreases might be associated with the synaptic pruning that we know begins around puberty, based on Rakic's and Huttenlocher's anatomical studies. Decreases in gray matter might further be associated with decreases in some kinds of brain plasticity, but with increases in functional capacity, as we saw with the development of representational memory abilities in humans and monkeys in the previous chapter.

Neville hypothesized that these anatomical changes in the brain might also be somehow related to increased grammatical knowledge and processing skill. In an ERP study of children between 8 and 13 years old, she found that the amount of left-sided asymmetry in the brain's electrical activity when processing grammatical information was correlated with the children's grammatical knowledge of English. Children with higher scores on a grammar test showed more pronounced left-sided asymmetries; those with lower scores showed less left-sided asymmetry. In a group of children between 8 and 14 years old, Neville also found that ERPs which were *larger* and more asymmetrical to the brain's left side were directly related to *lower* volumes of cortical gray matter. Together these two studies suggest that higher grammatical knowledge is related to greater left-hemisphere asymmetry and to lower gray matter volumes; that is, greater grammatical knowledge is associated with greater asymmetry in brain response and with fewer, rather than more, synaptic connections. If so, during the critical period for learning grammar, this learning seems to be associated with the loss, not the preservation, of cortical gray matter. Once again, this points to the idea we discussed in previous chapters: as far as synapses go, for some brain functions at least, fewer are better. Less is more.

We have also seen that psychologists and psycholinguists, based on their behavioral studies, have concluded that there is no critical period for vocabulary learning. Neville's studies of how the brain processes semantic information and how those processes developed in childhood and adolescence provide some neuroscientific insight into why there may be no critical period for vocabulary learning.

When normal adults processed semantic information, Neville found a characteristic electrical pattern of brain activation over the rear portions of both the left and right brain hemispheres. This normal adultlike pattern was already present in the youngest children Neville tested, a group of 4-year-olds, and it did not appear to change significantly from early childhood through adulthood. Native ASL users, who learned English relatively late, as a second language, showed exactly the same brain response when they were asked to process written English words. Native English speakers and speakers of English as a second language, thus, both seem to process semantic information in the same way throughout life. Based on Neville's brain recordings, how we process vocabulary does not change with brain maturation, as one would expect it would if it were a form of time-limited, experience-expectant learning. It seems instead that the neural circuitry we need to process semantic information and learn vocabulary comes on-line early in development and does not change as we mature.

There is one final, interesting twist to the story (as we understand it now) of critical periods in language learning. Neville gave English grammar tests to both hearing English-speaking children and to deaf children who were native ASL users. Deaf children, many of whom learn English relatively late, find it extremely difficult to master English grammar, as we might expect given what we know about how the critical period for grammar acquisition gradually closes. However, a few of the deaf children had nearly perfect scores on the English grammar test despite their late start with English and their highly abnormal early language experience. Furthermore, these grammatically skilled deaf children showed the same brain response found among the highly grammatically adept native English-speaking children. Despite their early handicap, these children seemed to have acquired "native" levels of grammatical skill and the native-language brain response for processing grammatical information.

This interesting result is also consistent with another phenomenon that psychologists, psycholinguists, and linguists have observed. Despite the existence of critical periods for learning phonology and grammar, there are exceptional learners. As with Neville's unusual deaf children who have perfect command of English grammar, about 5 percent of adult bilinguals can achieve native mastery of a second language, even if they begin learning the language in adulthood, after the critical period comes to a close.

Neuroscience is also pointing to other insights into how the brain reorganizes itself that may be relevant to the way we might best teach language skills.

Recall from Chapter 2 that Sharon Begley's cover story in *Newsweek* was ambivalent about the claim that the first years last forever. In support of her ambivalence, Begley mentioned the work of Paula Tallal and Michael Merzenich. Tallal and Merzenich have developed therapeutic interventions that help language-learning-impaired (LLI) children as old as 10 years of age overcome their learning impairments. From this example, Begley concludes that it is not necessarily the case, even when it comes to fundamentally and permanently rewiring the brain, that there is a magic learning window that closes forever at age 3 years.

We can now begin to see how this research relates to our understanding of critical periods for language learning. Kuhl's work shows that by age 6 months infants' phonetic perceptions become tuned to the specific language they hear around them. This normally occurs automatically and effortlessly for most children. Nonetheless, it appears that 3 percent to 6 percent of otherwise normal children fail to develop normal speech and language. These children suffer language-learning impairments that make learning to read exceptionally difficult. Tallal and Merzenich believe that some of these children suffer from phonological processing deficits that result from early, abnormal auditory experience. Even though they are developing in a normal human language environment, many of these children have a history of chronic middle-ear infections that muffle normal speech sounds. This abnormal auditory experience—we might think of it as auditory "strabismus"—seems to result in the LLI children's being unable to process rapidly changing auditory inputs, the kind of auditory inputs that carry information about consonants and vowels in a language. For example, LLI children find it difficult to distinguish the syllable "ba" from the syllable "da." These two simple syllables can be reliably discriminated only if the child can hear the rapid frequency changes that occur in the first few tens of milliseconds of each syllable.

Merzenich and Tallal ran experiments in which they trained LLI children using temporally modified speech sounds. They made the speech sounds 50 percent longer and made fast changes in the speech signal louder. The children listened to these altered speech sounds on CDs and played computer games in which they were rewarded for making correct discriminations among the altered speech sounds. As the children's ability to discriminate improved, the speech sounds used in the therapy were gradually speeded up and reduced in volume. The children in the Merzenich-Tallal studies were from one to three years delayed in language development. After one month of training, three to five hours per day, using altered, exaggerated, and abnormal linguistic input, the children's speech discrimination and language comprehension scores improved by around two years. All the children in the study reached or exceeded normal speech discrimination levels for their chronological ages.

As Merzenich and Tallal point out, these children, some already 10 years old, were at or quickly approaching the end of the critical period for phonological processing in their native language. Nonetheless, the training rapidly and permanently (as far as Merzenich and Tallal know at this time) improved the children's speech perception and comprehension by presumably rewiring and reorganizing the children's speech discrimination brain circuitry. Merzenich and Tallal believe that providing similar therapy earlier in the critical period for phonological processing would result in even larger improvements. What is most interesting and counterintuitive, however, is that the stimuli that helped children's brains reorganize were not normal speech sounds, clearly presented, but rather highly distorted speech sounds that would never occur in a child's normal linguistic environment.

Jay McClelland and his colleagues at Carnegie-Mellon University, following a similar line of thinking and research, did both modeling and experimental studies of how to cause changes in *adults'* perception of phonological distinctions that are not present in their native language. The case McClelland looked at was the inability of Japanese adults to distinguish between the

English phonemes /r/ and /l/, sounds that do not occur and are not discriminated in their native language. A native Japanese speaker's phonological perception is tuned, presumably very early in life, to the Japanese phoneme called the *aveolar liquid* /AL/ that combines the English /r/ and /l/. If the brain is tuned in this way at a very early age, McClelland argues, every time a native Japanese speaker hears either of the English phonemes, those phonemes simply reinforce the Japanese adults' perception of the Japanese /AL/. As he points out, "The result will be that the phonological categories the person brought with them from Japan will simply be reinforced rather than eliminated by experience in the new environment."

McClelland and his colleagues designed a study to teach Japanese adults to distinguish /r/ from /l/. They developed a list of eighty training items that ranged from exaggerated versions of /r/ to exaggerated versions of /l/. Japanese adults began by trying to discriminate the most exaggerated versions of each phoneme, and as their English phonological perception improved, they were tested with ever more difficult pairs. Although in this pilot study, McClelland and his colleagues studied only four subjects, the subjects improved from around 60 percent correct in their ability to discriminate /r/ from /l/ to between 80 and 100 percent correct rather rapidly. To reach this level of performance, the Japanese adults needed only three days of 480 training trials. Apparently, this rather limited training was sufficient to reorganize the phonological maps in these adult subjects. Like Merzenich and Tallal, McClelland's experiment used distorted, exaggerated speech sounds that never occur in a normal linguistic environment to drive this kind of brain reorganization.

Neville's deaf but proficient English grammarians, Merzenich and Tallal's LLI children, and McClelland's Japanese adults all point to the importance of the question "*How* can we best teach second languages or overcome language deficits acquired during a critical period?"

Why is it that some of Neville's deaf subjects have native command of English grammar? Why is it that 5 percent of adults can achieve native competency in a second language? What is different about these exceptional learners? Are their brains different initially? Is their experience of how they learned the second language different? Are both their brains and their experience different? Answers to these questions would contribute immensely to our understanding of how second languages might best be taught.

What do Tallal, Merzenich, and McClelland's studies tell us about how we might teach phonology to language learners even after the critical period might have closed? Are unnatural, artificially created speech sounds the key to "re-activating" dormant experience-expectant brain mechanisms? If so, how could we use this in language instruction? Can this idea by extended to teaching and learning grammar?

We should not overlook the importance of these *how* questions. The brain and early childhood literature is correct to emphasize that second-language learning is increasingly important and that often American schools provide too little language instruction too late. We also know, primarily from behavioral research, that there is a sensitive period for acquiring second-language phonology and that there may be some maturational constraints on second-language grammar learning. No doubt, as language experts have said for years, our children, most of whom are not among the lucky 5 percent, would be better off if they began second-language learning before these windows of opportunity close. One of Harry Chugani's oft-quoted sound bites is right on target: "Who's the idiot who decided that youngsters should learn foreign languages in high school?" Although it may be a no-brainer to decide *when* children should study foreign languages—earlier is probably better—there is still a lot we can learn about *how best* to teach second languages. One of the dangers of the Myth, with its emphasis on critical periods, is that it prompts us to pay too much attention to *when* learning occurs and too little attention to *how* learning might best occur. It is in this area, in generating answers to the *how* question, that research on brain plasticity and brain reorganization might eventually have the greatest impact.

Merzenich and Tallal's and McClelland's research also point

to a larger, emerging question in neuroscience. There is a strong assumption within the Myth, as we have seen, that across all kinds of learning, the brain is better able to reorganize in response to experience before puberty than it is later in life. In the domain of language, the degree to which adults experience difficulty in mastering second languages supports the assumption that some neural mechanisms responsible for experience-expectant brain plasticity might be shut down or be seriously compromised after puberty. However, if we can alter phonological perception as children approach puberty or, as in McClelland's experiments, even in adults, maybe loss of experience-expectant brain plasticity is not the issue. Based on these few experiments, it seems that there are cases where brain plasticity that disappears in the face of continued normal experience can be rejuvenated in response to abnormal stimuli, stimuli that do not occur in our linguistic normal environment.

This suggests that the brain might be much more plastic than the Myth literature acknowledges. We will explore this suggestion further in the next chapter.

CHAPTER 5

CLUB MED OR SOLITARY

The Importance of Enriched Environments

The Myth's third and final neurobiological strand builds on what is known about how enriched environments affect brain development. According to the Myth, although stimulating synapses at any time during our lives matters, stimulating them early in development matters most. Why? Because, as we read in *Starting Smart: How Early Experience Effects the Brain*, "Early experiences can have a dramatic impact on this brain-wiring process, causing the final number of synapses in the brain to increase or decrease by as much as 25 percent."

In statements like this one, we see how the Myth's three strands ultimately come together: the period of rapid synapse growth or high synaptic density is *the* critical period for brain development and the time during which enriched environments can have the most profound and long-lasting impact on brain circuitry.

Within the Myth literature, it has also become an accepted "fact" that early experiences can cause synapses in the brain to increase by 25 percent. This fact does have a basis in a substantial body of published brain research, but when we unpack what that research says, it does not have the implications for early childhood that the Mythmakers claim.

The 25 percent figure refers to one of Bill Greenough's findings on how complex environments affect brain structure and synapse formation in rats. Unfortunately, however, Greenough's research is consistently misinterpreted because the Mythmakers fail to take notice of three significant caveats about his important finding. First, there is disagreement among neuroscientists about what the oft-cited 25 percent figure derived from rodent research implies for human brain development. Second, Greenough found an increase of this magnitude in only one area of the rats' brains. Third, complex environments have similar effects on rats' brains throughout their lives.

Changing Brains, Young and Old

Scientists have been intrigued about the possible effects of experience and training on brain structure since at least the eighteenth century, when an Italian investigator, Vincenzo Malacarne (1744–1816), studied the effect of training on birds. Malacarne trained one bird extensively and the other not at all. When he examined their brains, he found that the trained bird had more folds in its cerebellum than did the untrained bird. In 1868, Charles Darwin noted that wild animals have brains 15 to 30 percent larger than their domesticated offspring. Fifty years ago, Donald Hebb, a Canadian psychologist at McGill University, initiated research on the effects of early experience on rats' abilities to solve problems, like learning to run mazes. Hebb brought several very young rats home as pets for his children and gave them the run of the house. When Hebb compared his "enriched rats" with their laboratory-reared littermates, he found that his former houseguests learned to run mazes more quickly and made fewer errors while learning than did their institutionalized peers. Starting in the 1960s, a research group at Berkeley that included Mark Rosenzweig and Marian Diamond began to publish their findings that rats raised in enriched environments had heavier brains and thicker cortices in certain brain regions than did rats raised alone in a cage. Also, in the 1960s, Rosenzweig reported that they had seen similar changes in the brains of adult rats. (See Chapter 2.)

In the early 1970s, Greenough and his colleagues began what is an ongoing research program on how rearing conditions affect brain structure in rats. His group's work, often cited in the early childhood literature, is the most representative, current, and rigorous of its kind.

Experiments that attempt to measure how different rearing environments affect behavior and the brain typically employ three different environmental conditions: isolated environments, social environments, and complex environments. A rat in an isolated environment inhabits a small laboratory cage by itself. It is the rat equivalent of solitary confinement. A rat in a social environment lives in a large cage with several other animals. It might be the rat equivalent of living in stripped-down, institutional barracks. Rats in complex environments live in larger enclosures with other animals. There are also obstacles and toys in the enclosures that are changed regularly to keep the rats interested and amused—a Club Med for rats.

Notice that neither I nor Greenough and his colleagues describe any of these environments as "enriched" or "deprived." Greenough prefers to make clear that the environments they are providing are enriched or deprived only in relation to how lab rats are usually housed. No matter how one does it, Club Med or solitary is still an unnatural condition for a rat. Calling the environments complex or isolated rather than enriched or deprived, as we will in this chapter, also prevents us from making unwarranted inferences about how the rat research relates to humans who inhabit diverse sociocultural environments. When it comes to humans, we should be careful not to read "Upper East Side/Palo Alto" for "complex/enriched" and "South Bronx/East Los Angeles" for "isolated/deprived."

In some studies, researchers consider the social environment to be the normal or baseline condition for lab rats. On this assumption, complex and isolated environments are departures from the "natural" baseline. Greenough, on the other hand, views complex environments as providing the best laboratory-based simulation of a natural or wild environment. In his view, both social and isolated rats live in relatively unnatural environments, in a barracks or in solitary. Although the complex environments are more like the rats' natural environment, they are still far different from the animals' feral state. What goes on in the rat Club Med is most likely quite different from real rat life in a New York subway tunnel or under an Iowa corncrib.

What is a rat's life like? Laboratory rats live around two years. They probably live longer than do rats in the wild. These rodents are born with their eyes shut. At birth, their nervous systems are not nearly as well developed as those of primates. A 5-day-old rat is developmentally equivalent to a human newborn. A weanling rat is 21 to 25 days old. Rats reach puberty at 30 days and full sexual maturity at 45 days. They are young adults at 105 days, middle-aged at 285 days, and elderly at 400 days.

In the early 1970s, Greenough and Fred Volkmar raised weanling rats for 30 days in complex, social, or isolated environments. When they examined the rats' brains at around the age of 55 days, the complex-environment rats had 20 percent more dendritic area in the visual area of the brain than did the isolated rats. The social rats showed a small increase in dendritic area, but were more similar to the isolated than to the complex rats. If one assumes, as these scientists did, that the number of synapses per unit length of dendrite is about the same for rats in each of the three living conditions, then the amount of dendrite per neuron provides an *indirect* measure of how many synapses were made on each neuron. Therefore, 20 percent more dendritic area translates into around 20 percent more synapses. Like Hebb's rats, the weanling rats raised in complex environments not only had more synapses, but they also learned to run mazes more quickly and made fewer errors as they learned.

In 1985, Greenough and Anita Turner repeated the earlier work using new, more precise electron microscopic techniques. In this study, they estimated both the *number of neurons* per unit volume of brain tissue and the *number of synapses* in the same unit volume of brain tissue. With these data, they computed the number of synapses-per-neuron. They found that the weanling rats raised in a complex environment had 20 to 25 percent higher synapse-per-neuron ratios than did the animals raised in isolated environments, thus confirming and refining the earlier finding.

These studies are the scientific source for the 25 percent figure that is universally cited in the Myth literature. So far so good, one might say. But here we should raise one cautionary note. Greenough's research on how complex environments affect brain structure in rats is research that attempts to discover the neural mechanisms responsible for *experience-dependent* brain plasticity. It is an attempt to figure out how the brain remembers and learns from environmental experiences that may be unique to an individual animal.

There are various views within neuroscience about what these mechanisms might be. Some believe—and I emphasize, nobody knows—that learning occurs as a result of *pruning* or *eliminating* synapses that are already formed. Others believe the primary way the brain learns from new experiences is through strengthening *existing* synapses. Others, Greenough and his colleagues among them, argue that learning occurs when *new* synapses are formed in response to the brain's need to store information. Greenough's research on what happens to rats in complex environments tends to support his view that new experience causes new synapses to form. Neuroscientists who study primates point out, however, that given the techniques they use to count synapses, they have not seen similar new synapse formation in primates. How the brain learns—how brains change in response to complex environments—is an exceedingly important and difficult question. This is one of those cases where studying different species with different techniques leads to different results and interpretations of those results. We should just be aware that when we see the 25 percent figure it is based on rodent research, and there are neuroscientists who question whether the finding generalizes to primates and humans at all.

However, having flagged this possible problem concerning deep theoretical issues within the field of neuroscience, let us proceed, as the Myth literature does, to assume that complex environments do cause new synapses to form in the brain. Even on this assumption, things get rapidly worse for the Myth.

In 1973, with Janice Juraska, Greenough and Volkmar reported that increases in synapses on the order of 20 to 25 percent are not seen in all brain areas of the rat nor for all kinds of neurons. For example, rats raised in complex environments also had more dendritic branches in the temporal cortex than the animals raised in isolated environments. However, the increases they saw in the temporal area were much smaller than what they had found in the visual area and were seen only on certain kinds of neurons, but not all neurons in the temporal area. In the frontal brain area, they did not find *any* changes in dendritic branching for rats reared in complex environments as compared to those reared in isolation. Therefore, neuroscientists have also known for nearly thirty years that rats raised in complex environments do not show a 25 percent increase in synapses throughout the brain. As far as we know, changes of this magnitude occur only in the visual areas of the rat brain. Greenough's research provides no reason to think, as the Myth suggests, that early enrichment will result in 25 percent more synapses throughout a young child's brain.

There is yet another problem with the Myth's interpretation of Greenough's research. Both developmentally and reproductively, rats are very different beasts from primates and humans. So, making meaningful, accurate age-based comparisons between rats and humans is not always straightforward. But consider this. The rodent research we have reviewed thus far was done with weanling rats, rats that were 21 to 24 days old at the beginning of the experiment. After 30 days of living in a complex environment, they are over 50 days old, past puberty, and sexually mature. So, in these experiments the differential rearing began when the rats were quite advanced into "childhood," not early in rat infancy. What the rats are getting at the Club Med might be more like a complex childhood experience, not an intensive infant program. Experiments on weanling rats might not be that relevant to brain development in infants and toddlers.

It gets worse yet for the Myth: what happens to weanling rats in complex environments is far from the whole story.

Although researchers, influenced by Hebb's findings on the impact of early experience, began their studies on weanling rats, it was not long before studies also included adult and elderly rats. As early as 1964, scientists knew that complex environments and extensive training on mazes increased brain weight in quite ancient, 400-day-old rats. In 1971, W. H. Riege found that 285-day-old rats that had spent between 30 and 90 days in complex environments had both heavier brains and heavier visual areas in their brains. One-year-old rats that spent 1 to 3 months in a complex environment also learned mazes more quickly than rats reared in isolation.

In the late 1970s, scientists found that rearing adult rats in complex environments caused certain areas of the cortex to thicken, increased dendritic branching in some kinds of brain cells, and increased the length of dendrites on neurons, again mostly in the visual area of the rat brain. Changes in rat brain structure were also correlated with changes in rat behavior. Running mazes increased the growth and branching of dendrites in adult rat brains. These studies, some done nearly twenty years ago, were among the first to show that the effects of experience on the brain are not limited to an early "critical period" in development. There is considerable neuronal plasticity even in adult animals.

In 1983, Greenough's group found that complex rearing of 450-day-old rats resulted in their having significantly more dendritic material than isolated rats, suggesting that experience affects brain structure over much of the animal's life. In 1986, Greenough and Hwa-Min Hwang reported that adult rats reared in social conditions (large cages, companions, but no toys) and then placed in a complex environment (a rodent Club Med) at age 120 days had synapse-per-neuron ratios comparable to those found earlier by Greenough and Turner in weanling rats. These changes occurred after as little as 10 days in the complex environment. Furthermore, the changes they saw in both weanlings and adult rats, after spending 30 days in a complex environment, also persisted through at least 30 days of subsequent isolation. In rats more than 2 years old, the rat equivalents to elderly humans, there were detectable effects (although smaller than those found in the weanling rats) of complex environments on their fine-brain structure.

Although the picture that emerges from this research is very different from the one presented in the early childhood literature, we should not jump to the conclusion that there are *no* differences between young and old brains. As new synapses form, they must be fed and maintained. So, if the new synapses are to survive, the brain must grow new "life-support" structures, including new blood vessels, for the synapses. For rats, Greenough's group has found that the brain's ability to grow these supporting structures diminishes with age and diminishes well before the brain's ability to make new connections declines. In rats, this inability to support new synapses occurs at the relatively advanced age of 1 year, late middle age for a rat. One-year-old rats are still capable of making new connections in response to a complex environment, but their brains' capacity to support these connections is already starting to wane. How rapidly rats' ability to support new brain connections decreases with age is a complex question that researchers are addressing.

The possibility that the brain has limited resources to support synapses has led some neuroscientists to rethink what they know about synaptic density. Some feel, as we saw in Chapters 3 and 4, that there may be an optimal synaptic density for efficient nerve transmission and information processing in the brain. The need to provide metabolic support for synapses might place a biological limit on this density. We should not expect, they reason, that ever-increasing environmental complexity will result in ever-increasing synaptic density. In support of this conjecture, Greenough and his colleagues have observed that "super-enriched environments" produce little additional change in the visual cortex of rats beyond what a "garden variety" complex environment produces. He and James Black conclude in a 1992 review, "We feel, however, that there will be limits to the degree that the brain can form new connections, in the aggregate, and that the solution that instead must be employed is to reallocate neurons in ways that make them more efficient." If there is a limit to the number of connections our brains can support, then as we continue to learn more and face new environmental challenges throughout our lives, there must be a neural mechanism that allows us to store more information per synapse. Thus, even though in Greenough's view the brain might be able to form new synapses well into middle age, the ability to change synaptic efficiency in response to new experiences must also be part of the brain's neural toolbox.

The work of Greenough and his colleagues, going back almost thirty years, is a superb example of how neuroscientific research advances our understanding of how the brain works and develops. However, Greenough's 25 percent, as important as it is, is carelessly over- and misinterpreted in the Myth argument. These misinterpretations prompted Greenough's comments that I cited in Chapter 1. As he pointed out in his *APA Monitor* article, based on his research, experience does play a major role in brain development, but claims that it plays a more important role in the first three years than at other times need to be assessed carefully. His research indicates that the brain continues to be plastic—modifiable by experience—throughout later development and into adulthood. Based on the existing neuroscientific and behavioral evidence, he concludes, we should not think that the only, or the most important, time to provide enrichment is the early years.

Yet once again, the Myth persists.

The Plastic Primate Brain

Work like Greenough's shows that experience can cause changes in the adult rodent brain. New synapses form and/or existing synapses become more efficient. The adult rodent brain is *plastic*, as neuroscientists say. Adult brain plasticity is not confined to rats. It also occurs in primates. This brings us, for the first time, to some genuinely new neuroscience.

Until the early 1980s, neuroscientists tended to believe that the adult primate brain was immutable, or "cooked," to use Reiner's colorful expression. Michael Merzenich, Jon Kaas, and their colleagues challenged that belief. The somatosensory cortex allows us to process sensations of touch on our bodies. To do this, the brain contains a map, actually many maps, of our body surface. These maps are highly distorted. Areas of our bodies that are extremely sensitive to touch, like our lips and fingertips, are represented by proportionately larger map areas than are less sensitive, but physically larger, parts of our bodies, like our backs. Using microelectrodes that recorded electrical responses to sensory simulation in the brain, neuroscientists discovered the location, size, and extent of these sensory maps in the brain. They called these maps the cortical somatosensory representation. Researchers could find a map and then find specific areas of the map that received input from the hand, from a finger, and from a particular part of a finger.

Once they discovered the maps in a normal animal, they could also do what Hubel and Wiesel did. They could see what happened to the cortical maps when particular areas of the body were deprived of sensory input. In the initial studies, using various procedures, neuroscientists deprived adult monkey brains of sensory input from a finger. Merzenich, Kaas, and their colleagues found that in less than two months after such deprivation began, the brain's somatosensory map reorganized. Areas of the body that still received sensory input expanded their maps into the deprived finger area of the brain. In these initial studies, scientists saw reorganization over relatively small areas of the brain, areas of one or two square millimeters. Neuroscientists have since documented similar reorganization in auditory, visual, and motor brain maps in a variety of mammals. On the basis of these findings, brain scientists now think that adult brain reorganization is a fundamental feature of mammalian nervous systems. Unlike critical-period changes in development, these changes in adult brains are usually reversible, as long as the altered experience or deprivation is not long-term.

Of course, the same thing Merzenich and Kaas saw in the

monkeys, scientists have also seen (indirectly) in humans. This kind of brain reorganization in adult humans was the exciting, significant finding in the brain-recording study of the string players that we reviewed in the previous chapter. The new and exciting finding in that study was that the brain reorganized in response to experience and practice even in the mature, postpubescent brain.

T. P. Pons and his colleagues found cortical reorganization in the adult monkey cortex over much larger areas, areas up to two centimeters in size. In their experiment, they deprived the monkey's brain of any sensory input from the animal's arm. If one adopted a strict "critical-period" view of an immutable adult cortex, one would expect that the part of the sensory map that received input from the arm would become and would remain totally silent. To see if this was indeed the case, Pons and his colleagues recorded responses from what should have been the "arm" map in the monkeys. Instead of being silent, they found that the brain area had been totally reorganized. The brain area that had been responsive to stimuli on the arm now responded to tactile stimulation of the monkey's chin and jaw.

The same type and scale of change occurs in some human patients following the amputation of a limb. V. S. Ramachandran has reported one of the most interesting and widely publicized such cases. Ramachandran found a patient whose left arm had been amputated just above the elbow. This patient, as do many amputees, reported having sensations in his amputated limb, the *phantom limb* phenomenon. When Ramachandran examined this patient's sensitivity to tactile stimulation of parts of the face known to have their sensory map adjacent to the map for the lower arm, he found that the patient reported sensations in both the face and the phantom limb. The patient's brain was reorganizing so rapidly that within a few weeks after the accident, the cortical representation for the patient's face had expanded into areas that had formerly represented the hand. The happy result for the patient was that when his phantom hand itched, his girlfriend could provide instant relief by scratching the appropriate part of his face. (For some peculiar reason, he obtained no relief from the itching in his phantom if *he* scratched the appropriate part of his face!)

Merzenich and his colleague Greg Recanzone took these findings one step further. It is evident that we have a lifelong ability to learn new skills and to improve our behavioral repertoire, be it typing, hitting a topspin backhand, or learning new vocabulary. Following the critical period bias, many thought that if such learning involved brain reorganization in adults at all, then that reorganization had to occur in the higher, association areas of the brain, areas of the brain that do not receive direct input from the senses. The primary sensory areas, those areas that do receive direct sensory input, neuroscientists assumed, had to be hard-wired after the critical period ended. Merzenich and Recanzone found that if they trained adult monkeys on tactile and auditory discrimination tasks, the training resulted in significant reorganization of even the primary sensory brain areas. Improvements in the monkeys' ability to make sensory discriminations were correlated with changes in the related sensory maps in the brain. As the animal's ability to make fine discriminations among stimuli increased, the brain area devoted to making those discriminations became larger. They also found significant correlations between how well the animals performed discrimination tasks and the magnitude of the brain's response to the stimuli. Merzenich and Recanzone concluded that an individual's perceptual abilities are explained in part by changes in how the brain reorganizes and neurally represents particular features of the learned stimuli. These neural representations in the brain are dynamic. They change as the animal's experiences change and as learning occurs.

Merzenich and Recanzone also found that brain reorganization takes place only when the animal pays attention to the sensory input and to the task. That is to say, this kind of brain reorganization occurs only when the animal is trying to learn or to form a memory.

Greenough and his colleagues reported a similar result for learning and dendritic change in the rat. Training rats to do "acrobatic" tasks changed dendrites in their brains. Running on a treadmill did not. From these studies, it appears that active engagement in a task reorganizes the brain, but passive stimulation does not.

There are similar examples in humans. Some stroke victims who have lost the use of a hand or an arm can regain use of the limb, if their good arm is immobilized and they are forced to use the paralyzed limb. After several weeks of intensive therapy, a hand that has been paralyzed for decades is able to manipulate small objects and make precise, controlled, normal movements. A therapist passively manipulating a stroke patient's hand has no therapeutic effect.

Changes in the environment often demand changes in behavior. Fortunately for us, as our environment changes, new brain representations emerge and neural circuitry reorganizes to support and enable the new behaviors. This is the type of brain plasticity that Greenough called *experience-dependent*. The neural mechanisms underlying experience-dependent brain plasticity allow us to learn and to form memories throughout our lives.

Oldsmobiles and Experience-Dependent Brain Reorganization

What neuroscientists find most interesting about all this research might be captured in the slogan "It's not your father's Oldsmobile." Several years ago, General Motors tried to increase sales to aging baby boomers through an ad campaign that emphasized how the new Oldsmobiles were different from the image we boomers had of them. The new Oldsmobiles were sporty and sleek, in contrast to the staid and stodgy models in which our fathers had driven us to summer camp.

The finding that the adult primate brain remains plastic opened a new perspective on brain development. The brain is not completely hard-wired at birth, or at age 3, or at puberty. On the contrary, experience influences brain structure, clearly and quite rapidly, throughout an animal's lifetime.

Yes, critical periods do exist, but there are other mechanisms for brain development that allow us to adapt to our environment and learn throughout life. For neuroscientists, adult brain plasticity opens a new vista on the brain, one that is in stark contrast to viewing the brain primarily from the vantage point of critical periods. From the new perspective, it is not your father's Oldsmobile.

One consequence of Hubel and Wiesel's important work was that it prompted some scientists (not Hubel and Wiesel) to assume uncritically that the adult brain is immutable. This assumption became neuroscientific dogma. One might say that neuroscientists tended to accept, at least implicitly, the first two tenets of the Myth: the adult brain was hard-wired, and once puberty had passed, the brain was relatively immutable; and that it was only during those critical windows of opportunity that mammalian brains were plastic. From this traditional view, one might tend to think that critical periods govern brain development, and that when those periods end, so does brain development.

The phenomenon of adult brain plasticity overthrew this dogma. Rather than seeing critical periods everywhere and assuming that they were all-determining, the new perspective tends to see the brain as generally plastic. Critical periods, then, are exceptions to this general rule of plasticity. For some brain functions, like binocular vision and functions related to ocular dominance columns, something exceptional happens that renders certain brain structures immutable and no longer plastic. It is from the vantage point of the new Oldsmobile that Floyd Bloom and Charles Nelson, as you read in Chapter 1, remind us that we should question any simple assumptions about the brain being optimally plastic or malleable only during the early years of life.

This new perspective underscores the significance of the distinction Greenough and his colleagues drew between *experience-expectant* and *experience-dependent* brain plasticity, between critical periods and lifelong learning. The neural mechanisms responsible for information storage in adulthood and throughout life are different from those governing critical periods in the development of sensory and motor systems. We must have a way to store information in the brain that arises from our unique life experiences, even though we all pass through species-wide, experience-expectant, critical periods. Binocular vision might only develop during a certain period, but we can learn algebra at any point in our lives. This distinction between lifelong learning and early development is present in many of Greenough's articles, including the articles cited in the early childhood literature. In his own articles, Greenough never discusses complex environments in the context of critical periods, nor critical periods in the context of complex environments. He sees these two bodies of research as addressing very different kinds of brain plasticity. The Myth literature, tending as it does to see only the old Oldsmobile, invariably runs these two bodies of research together. The Myth takes evidence that shows there is a lifelong learning and brain reorganization as evidence for the singular importance of early enrichment during a critical period.

The new Oldsmobile is much more appealing than the old. The new Oldsmobile holds out some exciting possibilities for both children and their parents.

What's Good for Rats Is Good for Rugrats: Early Intervention, Intelligence, and School

Generally, the Myth literature does little else with the complex-environment research other than to cite Greenough's result in support of the claim that early experience, during the critical period, but not later experience, has a unique, permanent impact on brain development. The Myth literature argues that early-enrichment programs can do for children what the Club Meds do for rats. Although, as we saw, it is not straightforward to extrapolate from the rats to children, the real problem is that the Myth literature never carefully considers what the human analogue of the rat Club Med might be.

There are hundreds of examples of early-intervention programs for children. However, the examples of early intervention that appear most frequently in the popular Myth literature are the North Carolina Abecedarian Project, started under the auspices of the Frank Porter Graham Child Development Center at the University of North Carolina and the Infant Health and Development Program, a national collaborative study funded by federal agencies and private foundations. These two examples are prominent because, unlike traditional Head Start, which begins at age 3 years, these two programs worked with infants during the critical period of birth to 3. The Abecedarian Project provided and evaluated an early enrichment program for socially and economically deprived, predominantly African-American children (98 percent of the participants), near Chapel Hill, North Carolina. The Infant Health and Development Program (IHDP) did the same for low-birth-weight premature infants, in enrichment programs provided at multiple sites throughout the United States.

Both of these projects examined the immediate and long-term impact of high-quality, early childcare services for at least the first three years of life (IHDP) and as long as the first eight years of life (Abecedarian Project). Both are important pieces of scientific research, but we should realize that they are behavioral science, not brain science. Neither of these projects involved brain-recording or brain-imaging studies of the children. The two efforts studied how children's measurable behaviors changed over the course of the intervention programs and, in follow-up studies, how their behavior changed after the program ended. The major outcome measures were children's IQ scores and school achievement. This is brain-relevant data only on the assumption that IQ and school achievement, like all our behaviors, are somehow based on what our brains can do and how experience might change our neural circuitry. Remember that neither neuroscientists nor behavioral scientists have the vaguest notion of how differences in brains translate into differences in IQ or how a brain that can pass third grade differs from one that cannot.

The significance, as well as the limitations, of the Abecedarian Project and the IHDP derive from their experimental design and extended follow-up. In both projects, the researchers assigned children randomly to either the experimental group that received an intensive early childcare program, or to a control group that did not receive the program. This allowed the researchers to draw strong conclusions about the effects of the intensive early experience compared to the normal or traditional care that the children in the control group received. The investigators assessed the long-term impact of early childhood enrichment through periodic follow-up studies for several to many years after the special programs ended. The scientists continue to follow the Abecedarian Project graduates, who are now approaching their mid-20s. Although the IHDP program ended when the children were 3 years old, the scientists were able to assess the impact of that program in follow-up studies when children reached 5 and 8 years of age.

The Abecedarian Project and IHDP feature in the popular brain and early childhood literature as evidence for at least three claims that are fundamental to the Myth. First, and here *Starting Points* provides a good example, the Abecedarian results are taken to provide scientific evidence that early environments have a long-lasting impact on brain development. These interventions derive their power, as the *Washington Post* explained, because they provide stimulating environments at the critical time in development, when the brain can be most readily influenced and intellectual ability increased. Second, and here *It Takes a Village* is an example, the Abecedarian Project is viewed as giving us hard evidence to counter the claim, derived from Richard Herrnstein and Charles Murray's book *The Bell Curve,* that children's intelligence is fixed at birth. We can raise children's intelligence, if we give them the appropriate early experience, particularly infant experience. Third, Ron Kotulak emphasizes the special importance of the IHDP study. The IHDP included children and families from all economic classes and racial groups. It included middle-class white and middle-class black children. Thus, according to Kotulak, the IHDP results serve as a basis for making a generalization about the importance of early experience: Early experience is important for the intellectual development not only of socially and environmentally deprived African-American children, but also for middle-class black and white children. Early experience is important for everyone, Kotulak argues. Kotulak believes that the IHDP study proves that we can make all children more intelligent through early intervention.

But, however much we might wish these Mythic claims to be true, neither of these projects supports any of these claims.

The Abecedarian Project's aim was to determine if mental retardation (as they defined it, IQs of less than 70), caused by inadequate, nonstimulating early childhood environments, can be prevented if at-risk children from those environments are given high-quality preschool programs that begin at birth and continue through kindergarten entry.

Craig Ramey and Frances Campbell have reported the results of the Abecedarian Project in a series of research papers beginning in 1984. Intuitively, the case for early interventions seems obvious and attractive, despite, as Ramey and Campbell noted, the lack of scientifically rigorous studies to support that intuition. From the outset, Ramey and Campbell intended that the Abecedarian Project and its ongoing evaluations would generate the evidence to confirm or dispel our intuitions about the positive value of early intervention.

The project, which began in the early 1970s, included 107 high-risk, low-income families whose children were at greatest risk for low IQ and poor school achievement because of familial, economic, and social circumstances. The study included only children who at birth appeared to be without physical handicaps or genetic and physical conditions associated with mental retardation.

As infants, half the children were randomly assigned to an untreated control group. These children received whatever care and stimulation their families happened to provide. The other infants were the "intervention" group. When the study began, there were no significant differences in intelligence, age, or socioeconomic status between the two groups. Starting at around 4 months of age and continuing until they reached kindergarten age, the intervention children attended an all-day, fifty-week child development preschool, which offered a special curriculum developed for the project. The curriculum emphasized language development and preliteracy skills, including prephonics training. During the summer before kindergarten entry, the children in the intervention group attended a six-week preparatory, prekindergarten session.

At school entry, the Abecedarian scientists randomly divided the two groups once again. Half of the children in the intervention group continued to receive additional help through a program in which special-resource teachers developed individualized materials for the parents to use with their children at home. The other half of the intervention group received no further special help after kindergarten entry. Among the children in the original control group, half received the individualized parent-provided help and half received no supplementary program. The parent-provided, school-age assistance continued for three years.

In this way, the Abecedarian Project had four different groups of children that they could subsequently assess and follow. Each group had around twenty-five children in it. One group had received eight years of special help—five years of preschool and three years of school-age, parent-provided assistance. A second group had received five years of special help, the preschool program only. A third group, the original control children who received the school-age program, received three years of special help beginning at age 5. Finally, the fourth group remained the pure control, children who had received no special help whatever.

Ramey and Campbell assessed the impact of these different interventions on IQ score (using age-appropriate standardized tests) and school achievement when the children were 5, 8, 12, and 15 years old. They are currently working on a follow-up assessment at age 21 years.

The first evaluation reported the results of testing done on the children at ages 12, 18, 24, 42, 48, and 54 months. Significant differences in IQ scores first appeared between the treated and untreated children at age 18 months. These differences, favoring the educationally treated group, persisted on all subsequent tests through age 54 months. At these various ages, children in the treatment group had IQs between 10 and 18 points higher than the children in the control group. Other tests indicated that the intervention had a broad-based impact on children's cognitive development, particularly in verbal development, perceptual-motor tasks, and acquiring early quantitative concepts. Also during the first five years of the project, children in the intervention group were much less likely than children in the control group to have IQ scores lower than 85. Even for children in the intervention group, however, their intense educational experience did not produce IQ scores in the superior range. The children who attended the special preschool maintained an IQ of 100, an IQ at or near the national average.

For the eight-year evaluation, Ramey and Campbell reported IQ scores for children in each of the four groups (eight years of the program from infancy, five years of the program from infancy, three years of parent-mediated at-home help, and no special help). Their statistical analysis revealed that the children who had been in the preschool program had higher IQs at ages 5, 6½, and 8 years than did children in the control group. The differences ranged from at most 8 points at age 5 to less than 3 points at age 8, a decrease from the 10-to-18-point differences seen earlier in the study. There was no significant effect on the IQs of the children who had only the three years of help delivered by their parents beginning at age 5.

Of course, at age 8 years the children had been in elementary school for three years. To assess school achievement in reading and mathematics, Ramey and Campbell administered the Woodcock-Johnson Psychoeducational Battery, Part 2: Tests of Achievement, and the California Achievement Test. On both these measures of school performance, the pattern was clear. The amount of time in the program (eight, five, three, or no years) was directly related to children's scores on these tests of school learning. The program also showed some positive improvement on retention rate. Children in the program were less likely to be held back a year in school than were children in the pure control group.

The age 12 evaluation occurred four years after all treatment had ended and after seven years of public schooling. In this evaluation, Campbell and Ramey tested the hypothesis that there might be a direct linear relation between the number of years of early intervention and improved intellectual and academic outcomes. They found that the preschool treatment through age 5 years, but not the school-age program, had a positive impact on children's overall IQ. The largest IQ difference between groups reported in this evaluation was about 6.5 points and was found between the children who had attended the preschool program only (average IQ of 94.23) and children who had received only the school-age program (average IQ of 87.71).

The IQ tests they used on the school-age children gave both Verbal and Performance IQ, which are then combined to compute a full-scale IQ. Verbal IQ assesses things like general knowledge and vocabulary. It measures the knowledge one picks up through daily experience and from exposure to one's culture. Performance IQ measures mental flexibility and the ability to solve novel problems, or what a layman on the street might call "raw brainpower." Ramey and Campbell found that the Verbal IQ scores and the scores on the Woodcock-Johnson achievement tests were highly interrelated. So they treated Verbal IQ and academic achievement as one outcome measure, or factor, in their statistical analysis. They called this factor Verbal Achievement. Performance IQ was the other factor. In their analysis, Verbal Achievement accounted for about 68 percent of the improvement in full-scale IQ and Performance IQ accounted for about 13 percent. They found that the length of time children had spent in the program was significantly associated with improvement in Verbal IQ but not Performance IQ. Participation in the preschool program was also associated with improved scores on the Woodcock-Johnson tests for reading, knowledge, and written language. However, the preschool program did not improve scores on the mathematics test. This is understandable, because the preschool program had emphasized language skills and development, not math and quantitative reasoning. The school-age program added nothing to the scores of children who had also attended the preschool and did nothing for the children who had only participated in the school-age program. This supports a conclusion that, for some reason, the preschool program was effective in improving Verbal IQ and school achievement up to seven years after the program ended, but the school-age program had little effect at all.

The most current published evaluation looks at the effects of the Abecedarian intervention at age 15 years, seven to ten years after the program had ended. At age 15, children who had been in the preschool program had full-scale IQ scores 4.6 points higher than children in the control group. Thus, just as with Head Start, the early gains in IQ that resulted from an early educational intervention decreased over time. A difference of 4.6 IQ points would probably not be evident in a student's classroom performance at age 15. The early intervention program did not contribute to what might be considered an educationally significant improvement in IQ for those who had participated in it. In short, the final effect of this early intervention was not as robust as many people had hoped nor as many still believe.

This 4.6-point change in IQ is, however, the source of another commonly cited Myth "fact." Based on this result, for example, Colorado Governor Roy Roemer recently told the *Rocky Mountain News*, "Brain research showed that early childhood education could increase adult intelligence by a third." First of all, we have seen that there is no brain research at all involved in the Abecedarian Project, and second, we have seen that the project did not result in a 30 percent increase in adult intelligence. IQ scales are constructed so that the mean, or average, score is 100 points and so that one standard deviation is 15 points. This is where the governor made his mistake. On an IQ test, 4.6 points are about one-third of a standard deviation, but an increase of one-third the standard deviation is not a 30 percent increase in intelligence. For these children, a 4.6-point improvement was approximately a 5 percent increase in measured intelligence, an increase hardly noticeable in the classroom or on the job.

However, IQ was not the only outcome measure used in the Abecedarian Project. On the positive side, the Abecedarian results on school achievement tell a more encouraging, and interesting, story. Benefits of the early preschool program were more strongly associated with children's academic test scores than they were with IQ. Both duration of treatment and the preschool program alone contributed to significant improvements in reading and mathematics test scores. Similarly, children in the program were less likely to fail a grade or need special education services through age 15.

On the other hand, in their statistical analyses, Ramey and Campbell also found that the mother's IQ was a more powerful factor in explaining a child's performance than was participation in the program. Maternal IQ could explain about 10 percent of the difference between treatment and control groups on IQ tests and about 25 percent of the difference in academic achievement at age 12. Participation in the early intervention program explained only between 3 to 6 percent of the differences. Maternal characteristics, either genetic or as provided in home environments, had a larger impact at age 12 than did the early intervention program.

The Infant Health and Development Program (IHDP) studied the impact of early education, family support services, and pediatric follow-up for low-birth-weight premature infants, children known to be at risk for developmental delays. The IHDP used the same child development center approach and preschool curriculum that the Abecedarian Project used. The infants attended the child development center at least four hours a day from 12 months adjusted age through 36 months adjusted age. (Adjusted age, often used in premature infant studies, is the child's chronological age less the time premature. An infant with a chronological age of 8 weeks, born three weeks prematurely, has an adjusted age of 5 weeks.) The IHDP also used many of the same assessment tools that the Abecedarian project used. The study included 985 infants at eight clinical sites around the United States. All the infants in the study were born at least three weeks prematurely and weighed less than 2,500 grams (5 pounds 8 ounces). The IHDP also looked separately at results for children weighing between 2,001 and 2,500 grams (4 pounds 9 ounces to 5 pounds 8 ounces, the high-birth-weight group) and children weighing 2,000 grams or less (less than 4 pounds 9 ounces, the low-birth-weight group).

Jeanne Brooks-Gunn was one of the lead investigators on the IHDP. She and her colleagues first saw effects of the program at ages 24 and 36 months, after at least one year in the program. At age 3 years, the children in the intervention group had significantly higher average IQs than children in the control group. For the high-weight babies, IQs were 13.2 points higher than those of children in the control group. For the low-weight babies, IQ scores were 6.6 points higher. At age 3 years, the children in the intervention group also showed fewer behavioral problems. There was only a small, but a significant, increase in minor illnesses for the low-weight group as a result of attending a day care center with other children. The groups did not differ in the incidence of serious medical problems. The program showed less of an effect for children whose mothers were white than for those children whose mothers were black or Hispanic.

They also found that children whose mothers had a high school education or less benefited from the program and attendance at the child development center. However, white children whose mothers had attended college did not show a significant improvement in IQ scores at age 3 years. Children in this group had the highest IQs in the study anyway, 109.9 if they had attended preschool and 107 if they had not. White children whose mothers had attended college were the only group in the study that had IQs over 100. The increase of 2.9 points in IQ for children in this group who had attended the preschool suggested to Brooks-Gunn and her colleagues that a program like the IHDP might provide, at best, negligible practical or clinical benefit for children of highly educated mothers. Although there were too few infants of black mothers who had attended college in the study to draw statistically reliable conclusions, children of these mothers did not seem to benefit from the program either.

The IHDP did follow-up evaluations of their children at 5 and 8 years of age. Overall, at age 5 years, there were no significant differences in IQ scores between children in the treatment group and children in the control group. However, there were differences between the high- and low-birth-weight groups. The high-birth-weight premature infants in the intervention group had significantly higher full-scale IQ scores (4.7 points higher) and Verbal IQ scores (4.2 points higher), but no difference in Performance IQ, compared to infants in the control group. For the low-birth-weight infants, there were no significant differences from infants in the control group on any of the IQ scores. Brooks-Gunn and her colleagues concluded that their findings at age 5 years are consistent with there being no sustained effect of the early intervention program for premature infants. In other words, the magnitude of the effects they found would probably not make much real-world difference for these infants.

The IHDP evaluation at age 8 was no more encouraging. At age 8, there were no differences between the intervention and control children on any of the primary outcome measures used in the study. The high-birth-weight children still had full-scale IQ scores 4.4 points higher (98.5 versus 94.3) than children in the control group. The children who were in the heavier group as infants also had mathematics achievement scores 4.8 points higher and receptive vocabulary scores 6.7 points higher than did children in the control group. However, even in the high-birth-weight group, the substantial early gains seen at age 3 years had largely evaporated by age 8. Using maternal education as an indirect measure of socioeconomic status, they found that children from poor homes showed no special benefit from the program at age 8. They found no differences in the percentage of children who repeated a grade or who needed special education services.

What evidence do these two studies actually provide for the claims that early education programs have long-term effects, that intelligence is highly malleable in early childhood, and that the power of early interventions is universal across all social classes?

I will address the last part of this question first, because it is the easiest to answer. In the paper Ron Kotulak delivered at the June 13, 1996, Chicago meeting, Brain Development in Young Children, he emphasized that the IHDP study was important because it included both middle-class and low-income families. He interpreted the study to show that "these across the board intellectual and behavioral improvements among all socioeconomic levels indicate that early intervention has universal powers." The IHDP results, he suggested, would allow us to go beyond looking at the effects of early intervention on poor and disadvantaged children and to infer that early intervention is powerful for all children. He also reported that the IHDP results remained solid after 5 years and appeared to be holding at 8 years of age.

Based on the published evaluations, this is an inaccurate and misleading interpretation of the IHDP results. As early as age 3, the IHDP reported that the intensive early intervention program had negligible, if any, effect on the scores of children of white mothers who had graduated from or who had attended some college. Maternal education is strongly associated with social class. The reported results thus suggest that as early as age 3 the intervention had little benefit for white middle-class children and possibly that the same was true for black children of college-educated mothers. As for the gains staying solid at age 5 and 8 years, the IHDP in fact reported that even for the high-weight infants there was a substantial drop in the effect of the program on IQ scores between age 3 and age 5. At age 3, the high-birth-weight infants had IQ scores 13.2 points higher than controls. At age 5, this difference decreased to 4.7 points. Contrary to what Kotulak claims, the IHDP study does not show the universal power and the lasting solid effects of early intervention on intelligence.

What do these studies show about the efficacy of the *early* educational interventions that they employed? Note that, in the Myth's view of brain development, what was special about both these programs was that the intervention occurred early, during the supposedly critical first three years. Despite what we read in the Myth literature, neither of these studies can, as a consequence of how they were designed, provide unambiguous evidence that early interventions are particularly powerful and have long-lasting effects.

The Abecedarian Project, specifically the preschool intervention, did have some long-term effects on school achievement, but the study cannot provide clear-cut answers to the question of why those effects occurred. Campbell and Ramey are well aware of this limitation in their study's design: "The design unavoidably confounds duration (8 versus 5 versus 3 years), timing (infancy and early childhood versus the primary school years), and treatment delivery models (attending a child development center versus school-supported but family-provided academic help) . . . such that it is impossible to know for certain what factors were responsible for the stronger influence of preschool treatment on intellectual and academic outcomes." As Campbell and Ramey noted, although their results do provide some evidence that the treatment had an effect, they do not prove that the intervention had these effects *because* the program occurred during the birth-to-3- or the birth-to-5-year period. Based on their data, there is no way to know whether it was the timing—the age at which the program began for the children—and not the duration or the special impact of a school-like program, that was critical in causing whatever positive effects the Abecedarian Project had. For example, we do not know what would happen if children started the special preschool curriculum later, at age 3 or 4, rather than at infancy. To answer this question unequivocally would require a study that provided the same intervention to all children in the study, but where the intervention started at different ages and continued for the same length of time.

In interpreting the IHDP results, Brooks-Gunn mentions the same limitation in their study. The IHDP study does not and cannot tell us what would happen to children if the preschool intervention occurred in a different time frame. We don't know what would have happened if the program had started at 2 or 3 years of age rather than at age 1 year. Brooks-Gunn emphasizes that this remains a highly important, yet unanswered, question. This confounding of age at intervention with duration of intervention in the IHDP study is the same problem psycholinguists encountered when trying to determine if there was a critical period for second-language learning and the same one we encountered in the brain-imaging study of the string players.

Ramey himself often argues that the Abecedarian results support what he calls an *intensity hypothesis*. The project shows that timing *and* duration of the intervention matter. However, we still do not have compelling data from studies that look at the effects of timing and length of intervention independently. We know that interventions that begin earlier *and* last longer seem to be more powerful than interventions that begin later *and* are of shorter duration. All else being equal, however, interventions that begin earlier *can* last longer. We do not have studies of these early childhood interventions that provide data anything like Newport and Johnson's studies of critical periods in second-language learning. As Ramey and his wife, Sharon, wrote recently, "To date, there are no compelling data to support the notion of an absolute critical period such that educational intervention provided after a certain age cannot be beneficial. . . ."

Finally, what do these studies say about our ability to permanently improve children's IQs through intense intervention? Both the projects, after follow-up, resulted in at most 4-to-5-point improvements in full-scale IQ. Brooks-Gunn and her colleagues question whether a 4-point change in IQ would even produce a noticeable difference in classroom performance between an intervention child and a control child. They also questioned the economic costs of the program. At the IHDP site in Miami, the intervention cost $15,146 per year per child. The research team estimated that they could provide that same intervention in a nonresearch context at a cost of $8,806 per year per child. They questioned whether even an investment of this size per child per year could be justified to maintain a 4-point increase in IQ.

In the Abecedarian Project, children in the preschool program had IQs 4 to 5 points higher than children in the control group at ages 12 and 15. Nonetheless, the early enrichment did not result in these children reaching IQ levels comparable to middle-class children in the community, nor did they reach the national average IQ of 100. Children in the intervention group still scored about 15 IQ points lower than did middle-class children living in Chapel Hill. Although children in the program increased their scores on academic achievement tests by around 5 points (mean 100, standard deviation 15), this improvement compensated for only 25 percent of the 20-point difference found on these tests between underprivileged and middle-class children. These data hardly support a claim that early interventions have substantial, long-lasting, and positive effects on lifelong intelligence and school achievement.

A dyed-in-the-wool Myth adherent might make a counterargument like this one: "What would you expect? Whoever would think that three or five or eight years of intervention would bring children who are highly at risk for environmentally induced mental retardation up to normal or superior levels for life? Early intervention may be necessary but it is not sufficient to help these children. After all, they remain in their poor deprived environments, even though they are in preschool eight hours a day for five years. Programs must continue far longer than the first three or five years of life."

Many advocates of early intervention make exactly this argument. It is an eminently reasonable one to make. However, if this is the argument they choose to advance on the basis of studies like the Abecedarian Project and the IHDP, then they are certainly going to have to change what they believe and say about the critical first three years of life. They and we are going to have to abandon the Myth. But, I think, we can abandon it in favor of a more hopeful vision.

We saw in Chapter 2 that Benjamin S. Bloom was among the first who argued that there is a critical period early in a child's life during which an enriched environment could permanently raise a child's intelligence. Brooks-Gunn, in discussing her findings that the IDHP did not result in sustained effects, questioned the continued legitimacy of this idea. Bloom, among others, argued for the extraordinary importance of the first years of life. Sometimes an even more radical claim is made that we can inoculate or protect poor, disadvantaged children from the ravages of their social status by providing appropriate enriched environments during their very early years. In the spirit of critical periods, early enrichment could provide lifelong protection against low intelligence. However, rather than supporting this claim, the Abecedarian and IHDP results undermine it. Early intervention, at least the early interventions offered to children in these projects, provided no long-lasting, permanent boost to their measured intelligence.

One of the greatest abuses to the cause of children is misrepresenting the effects of early-intervention programs. Both *Starting Points* and *Rethinking the Brain* are guilty of this when they say that research shows "the influence of the early environment on brain development is long lasting" and that "substantial evidence amassed by neuroscientists and child development experts over the last decade points to the wisdom and efficacy of early interventions." As we have seen, apart from a few well-documented cases of critical periods in the development of sensory and motor systems, there is no neuroscientific evidence to support either of these assertions.

The relevant behavioral and developmental evidence we do have suggests a more guarded, but ultimately less pessimistic and less dangerous, conclusion. Contrary to what *Rethinking the Brain* concludes, Vanderbilt University's Dale Farran wrote in a recent review of early childhood intervention: "Reviewing work related to intervention for children from disadvantaged backgrounds over this past decade is somewhat disheartening. A great deal of money was spent on programs which have not been shown to be more effective than doing nothing at all. . . ." Enlisting brain science in an offhand way to rally support for our previous inconclusive and disheartening attempts to help disadvantaged children is not doing anyone a favor. We need new, dynamic ways to think about these problems and Farran suggests two.

First, she urges us to think about children's development within a more realistic context of the first twelve to fifteen years of life. Given what we know about learning and development, looking too intently through the prism of birth to 3, as we have seen, yields a highly distorted image of the problem, its underlying causes and mechanisms, and the range of possible solutions and opportunities. Overemphasizing the importance of the first three years, especially at the expense of other age groups, amounts to thinking about and attacking problems in development and learning from an artificially limited perspective and with a limited armamentarium of possible interventions. Taking this limited perspective is comparable to a professional hockey team agreeing to play with two men in the penalty box for an entire season. Other teams in the league would think they were crazy. The team would work very hard, draw a lot of attention, and maybe even build character and team spirit, but there would be no Stanley Cup at the end.

Second, Farran suggests that we think about what it must be like to be a poor parent. We might do more for children if we recognize that parents' socioeconomic status and security are huge factors that influence their children's future. Rather than focusing on changing children's brains, we should think more about changing parents' brains and improving their and their children's lives through job training, adult literacy programs, and appropriate continuing adult education. We might do better by transforming our culture into one that recognizes that anyone, at any age, can benefit from education than by transforming our culture into one based on the notion that children belong to the community or the state, and not to the parents.

Of course, both of Farran's insights assume that we learn and change our behavior in response to new experiences and environments throughout our lives. They assume that the adult brain is plastic and that it is not "cooked" early in childhood. Happily, the new neuroscience—seeing the brain as the new rather than your father's Oldsmobile—is consistent with this assumption. Experience does affect the brain, and it appears to do so profoundly, contrary to the tenets of the Myth, throughout the life span.

Brain Plasticity and Lifelong Learning: The Positive Promise of Neuroscience

For the rest of this chapter, let's put aside the Myth's old Oldsmobile and see what the world might look like from the new Oldsmobile of adult brain plasticity. By doing so, we can draw positive, hopeful conclusions about the brain, complex environments, and learning.

For example, as seen from the new Oldsmobile, there are two interesting patterns in the Abecedarian data. First, at age 8, the amount of time children had spent in the program was directly related to their scores on school achievement tests. More time in the program (eight versus five versus three year versus no years) was directly related to school performance. The longer the exposure to the program, the higher the achievement scores. These children were also less likely to be held back in school. Similarly, in the age 12 evaluation, time in the program was directly related to children's scores on reading, knowledge, and written language tests. At age 15, time in the program was also directly related to improvement in reading and math scores.

One way to look at these results is to say that "time on task" is important. The longer children spent in school or were involved in school-like activities, the better the children did in school. This was also true for children in the control group once they began to attend preschools or started formal schooling.

The children in the Abecedarian intervention, immersed in the culturally enriched environment provided by additional schooling, showed improved performance on school-like tasks, including numeracy, language, and reading skills, compared to children who had received no such additional cultural enrichment. These school skills and knowledge are things that we usually acquire as children, but there are numerous examples and data to show that humans can acquire these skills at any point in their lives. The Oksapmin learned arithmetic and spontaneously invented number strategies as adults, even though most Western children usually acquire these abilities at age 5. Learning school- or culturally based skills like arithmetic requires exposure to the subject matter, considerable practice, and, sometimes, formal instruction. Probably the most powerful factor in the Abecedarian successes was that the intervention provided decidedly non-middle-class children additional exposure to that paradigmatic middle-class environment, the school classroom.

Schools are the institutions we have established to convey mainstream, middle-class culture, skills, and values to our children. Children without preschool exposure to that culture can enter school at a considerable disadvantage. Programs like the Abecedarian Project and Head Start (and possibly Early Head Start, when those data start to come in) show us that we can begin to provide this acculturating experience to children as early as infancy. That is a very good thing to know. And given what our schools and culture value, we should do everything we can to assure that all children receive the acculturating experience they need.

However, this is not to say that early infancy is the only time when we can provide such help. The brain is plastic and we are able to learn throughout our lives. If so, we might want to expend more effort figuring out what specific kinds of enriched environments are most effective in helping which age groups acquire the specific cultural knowledge and skills they lack, rather than worrying exclusively about when enrichment can and cannot be usefully provided.

For the past forty years, developmental and cognitive psychologists have studied learning environments, how students' prior knowledge affects learning, and what skills and knowledge students must acquire to achieve mastery of a subject domain. Using such research, we can begin to understand how we might optimize learning environments to help children and adults learn more efficiently. We saw one excellent example of such research in Chapter 4: Robbie Case and Sharon Griffin applied research in cognitive and developmental psychology to improve learning environments for children who might otherwise fail to learn formal arithmetic in kindergarten and the early elementary grades. Educators are beginning to apply this research in our schools.

The second interesting pattern that we find in both the Abecedarian and the IHDP data is that when early interventions improved children's IQs, most, if not all, of the improvement was in Verbal IQ and none, if any, in Performance IQ. There is some controversy over what exactly it is that Verbal, as opposed to Performance, IQ measures. However, a common assumption has been that Verbal IQ measures the knowledge a person acquires based on his or her life experiences—what words a person knows, what facts a person has acquired about the world—whereas Performance IQ measures reasoning abilities and flexibility in mental functioning. Both these IQ measures can be affected by years of schooling, but generally schooling has a larger effect on verbal than on nonverbal intelligence. So, the kinds of improvement the children in the Abecedarian Project and the IHDP show on IQ scores are the kinds one would expect to see as responding most strongly to schooling.

This pattern also fits with the little we currently know about the relation between lifelong brain plasticity and learning. The brain can adapt to new experiences and store information throughout life. Furthermore, psycholinguists tell us that there is no critical period for vocabulary learning. The limiting factor in vocabulary growth, and presumably for some of the other things Verbal IQ measures, is exposure to new words, facts, and experiences. The brain can benefit from this exposure at almost any time—early childhood, childhood, adolescence, adulthood, and senescence.

Tom Sticht gave me an interesting example relevant to both the IQ and the education issues. During the Vietnam War, at the direction of Secretary of Defense Robert McNamara, the armed forces lowered their intelligence standards for recruits to permit severely disadvantaged youths to enter the services and possibly benefit from training and career opportunities. As a result, some 300,000 low-aptitude men entered military service. McNamara saw this as the military's contribution to the War on Poverty. Those not fond of the program called the recruits "McNamara's Moron Corps." At entry into the military, these recruits had all the traits of "poverty syndrome," grown-up versions of children who had been targeted for help in the Abecedarian Project. Yet, of these recruits, over 80 percent successfully served their enlistment and two-thirds used their GI Bill benefits to continue their education when they returned to civilian life. In civilian life, these special recruits secured better and higher-paying jobs than their peers who never served in the military.

Some of McNamara's special recruits stayed on as careerists, spending up to seventeen years in the military. Sticht and his colleagues found data on 7,200 of these careerists and compared their entry-level intelligence test scores and years of education at entry with test scores achieved and years of education in 1983, twelve to seventeen years after their entry into the military. At entry, only 1 percent of these recruits had AFQTs (Armed Forces Qualifying Tests scores, the military equivalent of an IQ) above the 31st percentile. This is equivalent to an IQ of 92 or above. On the bottom end, 98.4 percent of the recruits had AFQTs below the 20th percentile (equivalent to IQs of 80 and below). By 1983, the careerists had improved their AFQT scores. Over 35 percent scored above the 20th percentile on the AFQT (IQ greater than 80) and 27 percent scored above the 30th percentile (IQ greater than 92). The careerists also improved in years of education completed over this time period. At entry, only 65.9 percent of the future careerists had completed at least twelve years of formal education. By 1983, 96.3 percent of these men had completed twelve or more years of formal education. Data like these provide some evidence that people whom society thinks are lost causes because of early sociocultural deprivation may, in fact, surprise us as adults. If the right opportunities present themselves, victims of the "poverty syndrome" can have successful careers and make substantial improvements in their IQs and educational attainment, even if they start relatively late in life. All is not lost by age 3. As Sticht admits, these are not clean data from a randomized controlled study, but given such enticing results, our prevailing biases in favor of early childhood, and what the new neuroscience seems to be saying about adult brain plasticity, it might be worth our while to invest in acquiring clean data.

Finally, of the Myth's three neurobiological strands, the enriched-environment strand is probably the one that is the most dangerous. Scientists like Greenough use the word "complex" to describe laboratory environments intended to approximate animals' wild or natural environments. In the early childhood literature, research intended to assess the effects of "wild" environments on animals, typically rats, becomes proof for the ef-

fects of "enriched" environments on children. Indeed, Greenough's complex environments are sometimes described as
"Head Start for rats." Advocates of the Myth move too readily
from "complex" as a descriptive term for animal environments
to "enriched" as a prescriptive or normative term for human
environments.

This move is not confined to the popular literature. Psychologists are prone to make the same move. In an obituary for
Austin H. Riesen, one of the pioneers in the field of sensory
deprivation research, published in the American Psychological
Society's *APS Observer,* Riesen's psychologist colleagues wrote:
"Riesen's studies revealed that the brain is not completely struc-
tured genetically but only partly so, and that its structure
changes depending upon experience. This suggests that neuronal development in the brain of a child raised in a sensorially
impoverished environment (deprived, for instance, of toys and
enriching experiences) will not be as mature or complex as is a
child with rich experiences. The work reveals how critical experience in early childhood is to the development of every individual." Here, we go from experiments on monkeys raised in
sensory deprivation chambers to children without toys or enriching experiences, whatever those might be—from monkeys
who have never seen the light of day to children who have
never seen the inside of F. A. O. Schwartz.

In the early childhood literature, "enriched" is very much in
the eye of the beholder. What is enriched, as opposed to what
is deprived, often reflects the writers' cultural and class values.
Rich, complex environments tend to include what the authors
value and exclude what they abhor—*Sesame Street* but no other
television, chess but no video games, trips to the museum,
music lessons, athletics, early math instruction, attending the
right preschool. Complex, enriched environments for humans
tend to have all the features of upper-middle-class urban or
suburban life—late twentieth (soon to be twenty-first) century,
American upper-middle-class living as neurological nirvana.
As we think about enrichment, we must pause to remind our-
selves that we should not make inferences from the existence

of a general neural mechanism—experience-dependent brain plasticity—to what subjects and skills children, or adults, *should* learn and what experiences they *should* have. We may have reasons to prefer Latin to ebonics, Mozart to Buddy Guy, squash to stickball, and suburbs to inner cities, but neuroscience does not provide the reasons.

CHAPTER 6

WHAT'S A MOTHER
(OR THE REST OF US) TO DO?

S usan Fitzpatrick, my neuroscientist colleague, was attending
  a conference at a Southern California resort hotel. During a
break, sitting near the swimming pool, she struck up a conversation with a young couple on holiday. As they talked, the couple
watched and interacted with their infant daughter as she played
in the pool. The conversation turned to early childhood and the
brain. In an anxious tone, the mother said, "We've read all the
articles and bought all the books, but, you know, none of them really tell us what to do."

Those Southern California parents were puzzled by what
they had read, just as I had been when I started to read the newspaper articles and magazine stories on the brain. The parents
were having difficulty reconciling the excitement and urgency
conveyed in the popular brain development articles with the
meager practical take-home message the articles yielded. Now
that we have reviewed the Myth's origin, history, and claims and
the brain science it is supposedly based on, we are ready to think
critically and knowledgeably about how to resolve this discrep-
ancy between the headline and the bottom line.

Based on what we know about early childhood and brain development, what is a mother, father, or caregiver to do? What might we tell those parents Susan met at the pool? What should the rest of us, people who are interested in children, the brain, science, and policy, do?

To the Parents at the Pool

If we were to meet those parents at poolside today, and they were to ask us about early childhood and the brain, we could tell them this:

As parents, if you read the Myth articles thoughtfully, you *should* be puzzled. In many cases, it probably was not at all clear to you how the brain science that you were reading about in those articles supported or informed the advice you were being given. You also no doubt observed some inconsistencies and contradictions among the articles you read, as we saw in Chapter 1. Some articles told you to stimulate your baby as much as possible. Other articles told you to provide developmentally appropriate stimulation and cautioned you not to overstimulate your baby. Some of the articles you read told you that the new developments in brain science have profound, revolutionary implications for child-rearing. The insights were so profound that most parents would need expert advice and instruction on how to provide optimal stimulation and the appropriate brain-nourishing activities to their children. The message seemed to be that as parents you could no longer rely on common sense to negotiate those early, critical years successfully. Yet, when you read other articles, you were told that brain science is merely reconfirming what our parents and grandparents have known for years and that common sense is the best guide. No matter whether you were encouraged to renounce common sense or embrace it, the bottom line seemed to be the same: you should talk, sing, and read to your baby.

As an interested and concerned parent, you might have visited the I Am Your Child Web site or sent for the I Am Your Child information packet in an attempt to learn more about how brain science might improve your parenting practices. For the most part, you probably found nothing new there. There were brief descriptions of brain development, little different from what you had read a year earlier in *Newsweek* and in a whole bibliography of child and infant books by authors such as Berry Brazelton and Penelope Leach that you already had on your bookshelf. You did notice the parenting guidelines for healthy child development. Among the guidelines were: Be attentive to the baby; read, sing, and talk to the baby; be selective about television; choose day care that provides safe, attentive care for your child. Your reaction might have been that the guidelines articulate and endorse solid, commonplace, traditional parenting practices that have been typical of American middle-class homes for at least fifty years. If somehow brain science supports these practices, so much the better, you might have thought.

You could not help but notice that I Am Your Child's fundamental theme seemed to be "the first years last forever." This, too, was intuitive, obvious, and strangely reassuring, but hardly novel. The theme is reassuring exactly because it captures the essence of our cultural beliefs about infants, mothers, and the early years of life. These cultural beliefs about the power of a mother's loving care have also been incorporated into our psychological and psychiatric theories of child development.

As parents, none of us should take our culture's beliefs about early childhood lightly. They have worked fairly well for the past three hundred years, just as different beliefs have worked well for other cultural groups. However, we should not accept them uncritically either. One of the things *Starting Points* attempted to encourage was a *scientific* framework of thinking about parenting and childcare. A science of child development can help us take a critical look at our traditional beliefs about early childhood and parenting. If we have the courage to submit our cherished beliefs to scientific test, we might learn that some of our beliefs are worth maintaining, some should be revised, and others might best be abandoned.

You might not have realized it, but with "the first years last forever" theme, you had already moved from a cultural belief into the realm of developmental theory, in particular attachment theory. On the rather strong interpretation of this theory, as in I Am Your Child, the first years last forever, because the quality of a child's attachment relationship to you, its primary caregiver, depends on the quality and characteristics of the care you provide during the critical first few years of life. On this strong, and popular, interpretation of attachment, there is a further claim, the claim that the quality of the attachment relation influences how your child functions from the preschool years all the way through adolescence and adulthood.

Here, as a parent, you should be aware that the popular message going out about brain development and early childhood experiences is based on a rather extreme position and interpretation of the evidence. The scientific evidence to support a claim that the first years last forever is not all that strong. First, research on attachment has not been able to identify *specific* parental behaviors that lead to secure attachment between infant and caregiver. This lack of specificity is part of the reason why you sense that the brain and early childhood articles do not tell you specifically what to do. You are told to be "sensitive" and "attentive" to your baby. That is no doubt good advice, but just what is sensitive and attentive parenting? Again, the most specific advice you get is to talk, read, and sing to your baby.

The second problem for the strong "first years last forever" interpretation of attachment is that once attachment relationships form they do not necessarily remain stable. In this respect, secure and insecure attachment are a little different from the development of ocular dominance columns. What does seem to be true is that attachment relationships remain stable as long as the childcare situation, and the circumstances of the parents and family, remain stable. Furthermore, early attachment predicts later personality and behavior only to the extent that the childcare situation and circumstances remain stable in the interim. If a child and family's childcare situation and circumstances change—a formerly attentive parent becomes inattentive or an attentive caregiver replaces an inattentive one—the child's subsequent behavior cannot be reliably predicted from her early experiences. If so, it is not the case that as the twig is bent, so grows the tree. Later experience, it seems, can straighten a bent twig or bend a straight one. The first years do not last forever in the strong, formal sense of a critical period.

Finally, as a parent, you should know that there is at present no research that links brain development and attachment theory. On this issue, I Am Your Child, and the related Myth literature, send a highly inaccurate, misleading message to parents and caregivers.

What about the simple, popular understanding of the Myth that we first reviewed in Chapter 1: the period of rapid synapse formation in the early months and years of life is a critical period in brain development during which enriched environments can have a powerful, irreversible impact on brain development. What should you as a parent understand about this claim?

Now that we have teased apart the Myth's three neurobiological strands, you should understand that the Myth oversimplifies, misinterprets, and confuses what we know about early brain development.

As we saw in Chapter 3, there is a period early in childhood, ending at around 3 years of age, based on Huttenlocher's data, when synapses form in the brain much faster than they are eliminated. The net result is an increase in the brain's synaptic density. During childhood, synaptic densities remain at levels far in excess of those found in mature, adult brains. However, based on the best neuroscientific data available, this process is primarily under genetic, not environmental, control. The amount and quality of early stimulation affects neither the timing nor the rate of synapse formation. You can and should read, sing, and talk to your baby. It might make your baby smarter, it might not, but we have little idea what these activities are doing to synapses in your baby's brain. You can be confident, however, that these activities are not causing more synapses to form more quickly.

If we look at how a basic cognitive skill, like representational memory, develops, we see that this skill does not become hardwired when rapid synapse formation ends in the brain's frontal cortex. It is only when the rapid synapse formation peaks that the skill first appears in rudimentary form. This basic learning and memory skill continues to develop, reaching adult levels only after synapse elimination in the frontal cortex is nearly complete. If other basic learning skills are like representational memory, the first three years are not the only time you have to help your child build a better brain.

It is also clear from the brain science that more synapses do not mean more brainpower and that we have no idea how experiences during infancy and childhood affect which and how many synapses are pruned away at puberty. Engaging in a developmental full-court press during the early years to preserve synapses is not a parenting strategy that has any basis in neuroscience. In fact, losing synapses is a normal, healthy part of your child's neural development.

Critical periods do exist in brain development. As a parent, it is helpful to think about critical periods as the results of experience-expectant brain plasticity. Animals with complex nervous systems, humans among them, expect that certain kinds of experiences will occur at specific times in development to fine-tune neural systems. Critical periods and experience-expectant brain plasticity are the solution nature has adopted to achieve this fine-tuning. It is a fail-safe method because the stimuli the brain expects are available in any reasonably normal human environment, from Manhattan condominiums to Mongolian yurts. For this reason, it is unlikely that your child will "miss" a critical period because the required stimuli are not available in its environment. Nature's method of fine-tuning also implies that critical periods are limited to acquiring species-wide skills and behaviors—vision, hearing, movement, language, basic memory, and possibly some species-typical emotional and social behaviors. Critical periods are not limited to the first three years of life, and, given the complexity and duration of critical periods, it makes little sense to speak of *the* critical period in brain development.

Learning culturally transmitted skills—reading, numeracy, chess, music—are not limited to critical periods and are acquired through mechanisms of experience-dependent brain plasticity, mechanisms that function throughout our lives.

The Myth tends to obscure what might be the most important

lesson for parents about critical periods and early brain development. The Myth's treatment of critical periods tends to make you focus on the environment, urging you to be sure that the right kinds of stimulation and experiences are present in your child's environment. As we have seen, the environmental input your child needs to acquire species-wide skills that are subject to critical-period constraints are universally available in any normal human situation. Most often things go wrong during a critical period not because there are problems in the environment but because there are problems in the child. Most developmental problems occur because there are problems with the child's sensory receptors—cataracts, strabismus, chronic ear infections. Even in a normal environment, the kind of environment your child most likely inhabits, your child cannot use that normal, expected input to fine-tune his or her sensory and motor brain circuitry if he or she cannot sense that input or if the input is highly distorted.

The primary message from brain science for you as a parent is the same today as it was thirty years ago when physicians first began to realize what Hubel and Wiesel's blind kittens meant for treating congenital cataracts: Make sure your child's sensory receptors are working normally. Fix vision problems early. Treat hearing problems early. Be sensitive to language problems related to phonology and grammar. Understand, for example, that chronic ear infections can affect hearing and impede language development, learning to read, and subsequent educational success. Know when and where to seek help for possible problems in these developmental areas.

As for the Myth's third strand, enriched environments can influence brain structure via mechanisms of experience-dependent brain plasticity. However, experience-dependent brain changes continue to occur throughout your child's (and your own) life. Although we do not know how the brain does it, children *and* adults who partake of educational opportunities—both disadvantaged children and McNamara's recruits—can improve their intelligence scores and literacy skills. For most learning, particularly learning culturally transmitted skills and knowledge such as reading, mathematics, and music, the windows of experience-dependent opportunity never close. One of the beauties of the neuroscientists' new Oldsmobile is that you and your children can benefit from exposure to complex, enriched environments throughout your lifetimes. Based on the research, earlier is better only because enrichment that starts earlier can—odds are—last longer.

As a parent, then, you can stop being puzzled. There is little that is new in the brain-based parenting advice, and the articles do not give you much specific guidance on what to do, other than to follow traditional middle-class parenting practices. If you were expecting new insights, based on brain science, your conclusion that the articles do not tell you what to do was the correct one. Although science and a science of child development can help all of us parents, we have to realize that we are far from being able to raise scientifically correct children and, in our current science of child development, brain science still plays a relatively small role. As Floyd Bloom, a former president of the Society for Neuroscience and now editor of *Science* magazine, said recently, "I don't think neuroscience has brought childhood development to the level where we can be the Dr. Spocks of the 21st century."

Now that we better understand what neuroscience does know about synapse formation, critical periods, and experience-expectant versus experience-dependent mechanisms of brain organization, there is one reassuring message that we can take away. As Steve Petersen, a neuroscientist at Washington University in St. Louis, told the *New York Times* and participants at the Denver Education Commission of the States meeting, "At a minimum, development really wants to happen. It takes very impoverished environments to interfere with development because the biological system has evolved so that the environment alone stimulates development. What does this mean? Don't raise your children in a closet, starve them, or hit them in the head with a frying pan." Our folk beliefs about children highlight their fragility, and as parents we should never forget how much our children depend on us. However, we also have something going for us that can see us through difficult times. We should never forget that humans are highly adaptive and our children are remarkably resilient.

Furthermore, normal development happens in a wide range of environments and circumstances. As the psychologist Sandra Scarr noted in a recent commentary: "Can it be true that babies must have specific early experiences to become normal adults? Hardly. If our species had evolved to require scarce or unusual experiences for normal development to occur, humans would be extinct. Cultural variations in child-rearing practices around the world demonstrate that normal human development occurs in many different environments. Reading is one way to interact with babies, but it's not the only right way."

What about the question that caused me to start thinking about the Myth? What can neuroscience tell you as a parent about choosing a preschool or childcare? It should be obvious by now that "Absolutely nothing" was the right answer. There is no research on how different kinds of day care or preschool affect a child's brain. However, there is some behavioral research on how early childcare outside the home affects a child's development and learning. You should also find the message based on that research reassuring.

The reassuring message was part of the 1997 White House Conference. One of the speakers at the conference was Dr. Deborah Phillips of the National Research Council. In her eight minutes, Phillips briefly described findings from an $88 million, multiyear study, the National Institute of Child Health and Development (NICHD) Study of Early Child Care.

The NICHD study involved over a thousand families of diverse ethnicity and social class in a longitudinal study. The study included both children who were cared for at home and children whose parents had placed them in various forms of childcare outside the home. The research team followed these children from birth through the first grade. The team collected data on the parents, children, and childcare settings that allowed them to look at how differences in the home, the child's own temperament and personality, and the childcare setting interacted to affect mother-infant attachment.

Their data revealed that there were no significant differences in attachment security that were related to childcare outside the home versus home care. This was true even if childcare outside the home began early in the child's life. It was also true even if childcare outside the home was unstable or was of poor quality, based on the study's quality criteria. The research indicated that the best predictors of secure mother-infant attachment were the characteristics of the mother. Psychologically well-adjusted mothers and sensitive, responsive mothers had the most securely attached infants. Mother-child attachment depends on the interaction between mother and infant, not on features of the childcare setting. As Dr. Marsha Weinraub, one of the principal investigators involved in the NICHD study, testified before the Congressional Caucus for Women's Issues: "Once we took into account variations in the mother's behavior, child care amount, stability, type, or quality did not affect the children's attachment to their mothers."

Similarly, Phillips said at the White House Conference, "We now know, for example, that placing a baby in child care does not interfere with the development of the mother-infant attachment relationship or the father-infant attachment relationship. These bonds are extremely resilient."

The NICHD study did find that children raised in economically disadvantaged homes were more likely to be insecurely attached to their mothers and that high-quality childcare could compensate, to some extent, for poor mothering. However, based on the NICHD study, for most children from ordinary homes, the quality of care does not affect mother-infant attachment. To the extent that such attachment has long-term effects on child development (if it does at all, remember), quantity, duration, and quality of childcare would not be expected to have lasting effects. As Phillips told the White House Conference participants, "Research on child care has affirmed the centrality and durability of the family in the development of young children." The environment that the family provides—genes, home, neighborhood, friends, socioeconomic status—not day care, remains the most powerful influence on a child's development.

The NICHD study also looked at how quality of childcare affects children's cognitive and mental development. These results were first reported in a poster session at the 1997 conference of the Society for Research in Child Development. Again, the study found that the best predictors of a child's cognitive and mental development are the characteristics of the child's mother and family. Here, though, the story is more nuanced and the spin a little different from what the study learned about attachment.

In telling this part of the story at the White House Conference, Phillips said, "Neuroscience tells us that these sub-optimal child care environments should affect early development. Child care research confirms that they do. The quality of the child care environment affects virtually every domain of development that we know how to measure, whether it's problem-solving skills or social interactions or attention span or verbal development. . . . Children show significantly better cognitive and language development when they are cared for by adults who engage with them in frequent affectionate responsive interactions. . . ."

In response to a question from Hillary Clinton, Phillips elaborated on the significance of this finding: "The other message is that if you can place your child in high quality child care, you can actually supplement what you're giving them as a parent and that's why the value of making high quality child care affordable for more families cannot be undervalued."

However, this message to you as a parent is not necessarily all that clear cut. The NICHD study did find that the quality of childcare did make a *statistically significant* contribution to explaining differences in early cognitive and language development during the first three years of life, even after maternal characteristics were taken into account. However, the impact of quality care on cognitive and mental development was very small, accounting for between 1 percent and 4 percent of the differences in children's scores on tests of cognitive and mental development. High-quality day care makes a difference and a statistically significant difference, but in fact a rather small difference.

Before you as a parent can make a reasonable judgment about the added value of high-quality over quality or average care, there are two things you would have to know. Do these statistically significant differences at age 3 years translate into an educationally or developmentally significant difference, either in the short term or the long term? Or, do these differences, like the few-percentage-point improvements in IQ found in the IHDP study, not contribute to noticeable changes in classroom performance?

You as a parent would also have to know how much the 1 percent to 4 percent improvement would cost. We cannot assume that we can buy a few percentage points more for a few dollars more. A few percentage points may in fact cost a fistful of dollars. These are difficult question for parents to think about and become even more problematic when we try to think about the broad policy implications.

Ideally, as a parent you would like to do everything you can for your children, and as a nation we would like to do everything we can for all children. However, given economic realities for families and fiscal and political realities for national policies, most of us must make compromises. High-quality and highly regulated childcare centers may have a small incremental impact on development, but how much does that incremental impact cost? How many families who need childcare could afford to purchase the increment? Would most low-income working parents and families be able to afford it? Currently, it is these parents and families who face the most difficult decisions. Upper- and middle-income families are able and willing to pay for high-quality care, and families at the poverty level can receive government assistance and subsidies that allow them to opt for higher-quality care.

Questions about reasonable trade-offs between quality and cost are fundamental to childcare policy. Given the small incremental impact of high-quality care versus good to mediocre care, what is the preferable way to invest the resources that we are likely to have at our disposal? Should we invest in fewer but higher-quality childcare slots or in more but less-expensive slots? Which and how many people would be best served by one choice or another? These are the difficult policy questions.

It is always emotionally difficult, at least initially, to leave your young child in someone else's care, and as a parent you cannot help worrying about your child's safety. However, for you, as for most parents, what the research we do have says about the effects of early childcare outside the home are reassuring: "Within a broad range of safe environments, quality variations in child care have only small and temporary effects on most children's development. . . . Quality variation within the range of centers studied does not have a major impact on the development of children from ordinary homes."

As for the Rest of Us

For the rest of us, the Myth of the First Three Years can serve as an interesting case study for how science is used and abused in policy debates.

The Sunday, May 17, 1998, *New York Times* "Week in Review" published a Don Wright political cartoon that provides an instructive, final perspective on the Myth.

The cartoon showed two Washington policy wonks in conversation:

"In Washington the search for truth is a creative process. First, you create a premise. Next, you create a statistic to back it up. Then you create an audience by repeating it over and over again, until the media pick it up. That's when you know you've done it."

"Done what?"

"Created a fact!"

Our particular Washington-style search for truth, the Myth, began with an appealing premise, created a neuroscientific statistic to back it up, and created an audience by repeating it till the media finally picked it up. The Myth then became a fact to guide parenting, policy, and legislation.

As a nation, we are aware that children from economically disadvantaged homes, particularly poor inner-city homes, are at greater risk for school, career, and life failure than are children from upper- and middle-income homes. Apart from addressing this problem for reasons of social justice, some believe that the situation is so perilous that it poses a threat to civil society. Government officials, policy advocates, and researchers are continually involved in finding and implementing politically acceptable solutions to this acknowledged problem.

Starting Points was an attempt to formulate and advance a solution. That report was intended to create the political resolve to engage in a national crusade on behalf of disadvantaged children. It claimed to provide a science-based agenda as a basis for that crusade. The crusade's fundamental premise was: "How individuals function from the preschool years all the way through adolescence and even adulthood hinges, to a significant extent, on their experiences before the age of three. . . . A good start in life can do more to promote learning and prevent damage than we ever imagined."

I Am Your Child stated the premise even more concisely, "The early years last forever."

This is a powerful premise. It resonates with our centuries-old cultural intuitions and folk theories about children, childhood, motherhood, and parenting, intuitions and theories tied to infant determinism. Because the premise also appears as a basic assumption in our most popular scientific theories of child development, it allows childcare advocates to identify and introduce a body of research that promises a scientific framework for a program of action to help young, disadvantaged children. The premise links the solution of a pressing social problem with both our commonsense cultural beliefs about early childhood and our science. Scientists agree with it. Congressmen like it. Parents understand it.

The premise, then, is hardly something new. It has a long history and has been invoked numerous times before, but with only limited success and limited public interest. The immediate and subsequent response to *Starting Points* was, as David Hamburg noted, unprecedented in the field of childcare. The difference this time was the two-page, brain-science rhetorical flourish at the beginning of *Starting Points*. We can think of this flourish as the creation of the "statistic" in the creative search for truth. The flourish did not introduce a percentage or a rate; rather, it introduced an image that allowed us to think about child and brain development in quantitative, hard-science terms and to think about our success as parents in terms of neural accounting and synaptic reckoning: billions and billions of synapses form during the critical period from birth to 3, synapses that are desperate to be enriched before they are pruned away.

Rhetorically, this was the perfect statistic to introduce, as the authors of *Starting Points* subsequently realized. We are fascinated by the mysteries of the brain and by what modern neuroscience seems to be revealing about them. Adding brain science to the mix gives the premise and its agenda a significant, novel boost. As one observer close to the issue told me, "*Starting Points* . . . and other major efforts have documented the need for more attention to the early years. But none of these projects has had the clout that white-coated researchers command." As the organizers of I Am Your Child realized early on, the mechanical image of brain wiring and zapping circuits could make issues of child development appealing to men as well as to women, a big plus if the premise and agenda were to result in action and legislation. In the current policy battles about early childhood, education, and welfare reform, it is better to have synapses than even God on your side. Damaged brains are more compelling than damaged lives or insecure attachments.

Having synapses on your side is also a powerful persuasive tool for parent educators and caregivers working on the front lines. Remember that the problem is disadvantaged children, children who are at the greatest risk for unfavorable developmental outcomes. One thing we do know from research on attachment is that mothers who behave in acceptable American middle-class fashion tend to have securely attached children. The challenge is to get more noncomplying, mostly minority and disadvantaged, mothers to act in this way. How do we accomplish this without alienating the mothers and without feeling overly guilty about discouraging the traditional, but possibly nonconforming, practices of minority social and cultural groups? As Jerome Kagan, in his critique of infant determinism and the developmental science based on it, observed, "A preferred, and more benign, approach acknowledges that poor mothers love their children but do not know the basic facts of human development. If they were aware of the importance of playing with, talking to, and reading to their children, they would implement these rituals at once." If one adds to this that mothers who do not implement these rituals are damaging their children's brains, one has an even more compelling message.

With the premise and statistic in hand, repeating them was not left to chance. The Myth did not spread by casual word of mouth. Already in 1994, plans were underway for a national awareness campaign that would propagate it. I Am Your Child took shape in 1996 and, as we have seen, its organizers did an excellent job. By spring 1997, the message had indeed been re-peated, and repeated in the right places: Hillary Clinton's book, a national governors' conference, a State of the Union address, and the White House Conference.

Media coverage before, during, and subsequent to these major events brought the Myth to the attention of mainstream America and millions of people around the world. Fantasy be-came fact as stories appeared on the front pages and in the sci-ence sections of major newspapers and weeklies. And then, another change occurred in the story. The articles, while some-times mentioning the "quiet crisis" confronting young disad-vantaged children, no longer limited their message to what happened to the brains of poor, abused, or neglected children. If there was a brain science of early child development, then that science had implications for all children, not just for the disad-vantaged. Middle-class parents had better worry about synapses, critical periods, and enriched environments, too, and not squan-der the few years they had available to build better brains in their children. By age 10, if not before, the "brain is cooked," as Reiner told the governors. Neuroscience proves it. Parents had better talk, sing, and read to their babies with a single-minded devo-tion; start those piano, ballet, and tennis lessons; and build the logical mathematical brain before the windows closed for good. Educators should realize that by the time a child enters first grade the most important learning years are over. Legislators had better get their act together to fund early childhood programs that would avert the crisis. The Myth had become the national and international gospel of parenting and early childhood policy. To question the gospel became heresy.

No one in particular, if anyone at all, is responsible for transforming the Myth into fact. Yet, to a certain extent, we all helped. A premise and a statistic tend to be repeated and to be the subject of cover stories when they convey a message that many of us want to hear.

We all like "hard data" to help answer questions and solve problems that are important to us. We read articles and books on diet and nutrition that appear to give us "hard," but often contradictory, "research-based" advice, because our health and appearance are important to us. Some of us read and follow silly, but "research-based," advice published in golf, tennis, or running magazines, because those activities are important to us. For parents, nothing is more important than their children. Parents want to know if and how they can make their children more intelligent, better adjusted, and more successful. They want to know when and where to start the music, second-language, and athletic lessons. Parents want to know what toys, what lessons, and what schools they might best choose. Parents are ready and willing to believe that brain science may provide the answers and that there are hard data that confirm, rationalize, and justify our prior beliefs about who parents are, what they can do, and what they should do. In such circumstances it is surprisingly easy for us to suspend our critical judgment and to overlook or ignore data and facts that are inconsistent with our prior beliefs.

Policy advocates want to believe the Myth because it nicely melds our folk and behavioral theories about childhood and parenting with selected strands of hard brain science, which obviously can help advance particular agendas. As Matthew Melmed, executive director of Zero to Three, commented in the February 3, 1997, *Time* magazine, neuroscience provides hard quantifiable evidence to support beliefs and policies previously supported only by anecdote. "Because you can see the results under a microscope or in a PET scan," he observes, "it becomes that much more convincing."

Childhood researchers want to believe the Myth because it is based on, and is consistent with, their prevailing theories that emphasize the importance of the early years. Childhood researchers are happy to bolster their case by pointing to and speculating about hard neuroscientific and biological data that appear to support their behavioral findings, findings that are often viewed by "hard" scientists and the general public as "soft" science. As Ed Zigler, director of the Bush Center in Child Development and Social Policy at Yale, said to *Education Week*, "If you tell decision makers or parents, 'Your child will have a better brain if you do this or that,' then that seems to have a more seductive appeal than anything we educators can say." Most behavioral scientists and even psychiatrists working in the field of child development do not know much about synapses in rat, kitten, or human brains. Nonetheless they are happy to speculate that what happens to rat synapses explains the success or failure of Head Start.

Neuroscience is a young science that has undergone astounding growth over the past thirty years. Neuroscientists are just beginning to find widespread applications of their basic science to clinical problems. They hope, too, that one day their science will contribute to our understanding of learning, intelligence, and personality. When a journalist asks a brain scientist about the relevance of his or her research to issues in child development, it is the rare neuroscientist who would say the work has no relevance at all. Generally, neuroscientists offer some response, but do tend to be rather cautious and guarded in their speculations. Nonetheless, they do speculate, even though they know no more about early childhood and education than the childhood experts know about synapses.

Journalists' stories are as good as their sources. Science journalists are hardly expert or familiar with all of the scientific fields that are relevant to mind, brain, and child development. If most people journalists interview want to believe the Myth, that is what the stories will reflect. To the extent that journalists follow leads from the policy reports, the public education campaigns, and the accompanying press releases and contact lists, coverage will reflect the message the reports, campaigns, and releases intend to convey. Furthermore, neuroscientists who are willing to speculate about what critical periods mean for learning math, and behavioral scientists who are willing to speculate about what rat synapses mean for Head Start, often can provide better copy than scientists who might want to stick to their data. It would help science, journalism, and policy if scientists avoided saying things to journalists that they would not say to an audience of their professional peers.

All these factors conspired to transform the Myth rapidly and easily into fact, and contributed to its aggressive spread.

Some Rules of Thumb

One way for us to avoid being blinded by science in the popular news and in policy discussions it to maintain our critical judgment. As a case study of how science is used in policy debates, the Myth suggests some rules of thumb we might all use to make informed, critical judgments about science and its relevance to policy recommendations.

One rule of thumb is to be wary of absolute, categorical statements. Science, particularly biological science, is rarely definite and clear-cut. Here, critical periods are an excellent example. They are not windows that slam shut. They are complex. They pass through stages. As we saw in Chapter 4, they are more like reservoirs that evaporate and reservoirs that we can sometimes replenish, if we know enough about the brain areas involved and the kinds of experiences to provide. Similarly, the first three years are not the *only* years we have to build better brains. The brain is not "cooked" by age 3 or age 10. Our brains remain remarkably plastic and we retain the ability to learn throughout our lives. Generally, anytime you read such absolute statements and are told that science supports them, the warning flags should go up. Chances are the science is being overly simplified to make a dramatic or rhetorical point.

Second, always be aware of and sensitive to possible overgeneralizations. We have seen a number of instances of overgeneralization in the development of the Myth. The blind kittens do present a compelling image. However, it is a massive overgeneralization to infer from Hubel and Wiesel's blind kittens that unless are children are stimulated as much as possible, they are somehow deprived and irreversibly damaged.

Just because some critical periods occur early in development, as they happen to with vision, we should not generalize that all or even most critical periods occur early in development. Nor should we infer that because there are critical periods for species-typical abilities like vision and language that there are critical periods involved in all kinds of learning. We should also be cautious of overgeneralizations about the neural mechanisms that underlie brain plasticity. For example, we should be cautious of statements like "a mechanism that works fine for wiring vision is not likely to be abandoned when it comes to circuits for music," unless we are told considerably more about the specific mechanism and given some explanation of why being able to see is at all like learning to play the violin. The brain may indeed be frugal, relying on some form of activity-dependent competition to reorganize itself, but that does not mean that all activity-dependent competition is time-limited.

We should be careful not to overgeneralize from rats to children and from complex, "wildlike" rodent environments to what Head Start should be like. We should be cautious when the descriptive term "complex environment" is replaced in an argument by the highly normative term "enriched environment." We should be particularly alert to descriptions of "enriched environments" that sound like descriptions of our own preferred cultural niche, or an author's own personal, idealized neurological nirvana.

Also, in trying to determine what science might contribute to policy, we should be wary of placing too much weight on single, isolated studies. There are several examples where this rule of thumb is violated in the Myth literature.

The best example is the research on the effects of music on spatial-temporal reasoning. One study on the effects of listening to Mozart on college students' reasoning skills and one study on the effect of piano lessons on preschool children's reasoning skills

are interpreted as showing that music is good for brain development. There is no data on brain development presented in these
studies, despite their popularity in the Myth literature and with
music teachers. The result may hold up after further research and
may one day prove to be important, but these few studies are
hardly sufficient to support recommendations about CDs for infants and music instruction in schools.

There is a popular fact in the Myth literature that is based on
only a single, preliminary study: children who do not receive ad-
equate stimulation have brains that are 20 to 30 percent smaller
than those found in normal children. This fact is cited in
Newsweek, Time, and on the Ounce of Prevention Web site, a
source of information on brain development intended for parents
and caregivers. It is also cited as one of the brain-relevant findings in the Early Childhood Development Act of 1997 (S.756) as
published in the *Congressional Record.*

The popular articles credit Bruce Perry, one of Reiner's cop-
resenters at the National Governors' Association Conference, for
this work. I could not find the published scientific article that presented the result. When I contacted Perry, he kindly faxed me an
abstract and the materials he had used to present the work in a
poster session at the 1997 Society for Neuroscience meeting, "Altered Brain Development Following Global Neglect in Early
Childhood." He found that twenty-eight children, categorized as
"globally neglected," had head circumferences that were in the
8th percentile for normal development. These children had suffered profound social isolation during their first three years of life,
receiving only minimal exposure to linguistic, emotional, tactile,
and cognitive stimuli. Some of these children, Perry suggests, had
been raised in near–deprivation chamber conditions. Another
twenty-six children were classified as "neglected," because they
had been raised in "chaotic settings" and their medical histories
were consistent with physical, emotional, social, or cognitive neglect. The neglected children had normal head circumferences
that fell in the 56th percentile for normal development. These percentile differences translate into the 20-to-30-percent-smaller-
than-normal brains for the *globally* neglected children.

Perry's finding is at best a preliminary result that, no doubt, he and his colleagues will build on and elaborate when they eventually do publish it in a scientific journal. Such a finding, even a preliminary one, should not be taken lightly. However, it should strike us as odd that such an isolated, obscure result appears so widely and prominently in the Myth literature and is cited as *the* brain-relevant fact in federal legislation. It suggests that the fact's appeal is due more to the image it conveys than to the scientific and evidentiary weight it carries.

As a final rule of thumb, we should be wary of policy arguments and recommendations that rely on unpublished scientific data. This also occurs in the Myth literature.

The special *Newsweek* issue published some stunning PET images of a normal child's brain beside an image of a severely neglected child's brain. These images were picked up and published by newspapers around the country. Child advocacy groups distributed them in their press kits and in information packets for parents and childcare providers. Berry Brazelton, in his *Boston Globe* op-ed piece on smoking, referred to the brain images that we have all seen in newspapers and on television that show a normal brain juxtaposed with a neglected brain. (See Chapter 2.) In *Inside the Brain*, Ron Kotulak described the benefits of an early childhood education program, the North Carolina Abecedarian Project. (See Chapter 5.) Apparently referring to these images (which were not images of the Abecedarian children's brains), he concluded his discussion: "PET scans, which measure brain activity, showed that the brains of the children exposed to stimulating environments were perking along at a more efficient rate than those of normal control children."

When I called one national early-childhood organization that was distributing these PET images in their press kits and asked the public relations officer where the images had been originally published, she told me, "In *Newsweek*."

I eventually learned that the *Newsweek* brain scans had come from Dr. Harry Chugani's laboratory at Wayne State University in Detroit. I contacted Dr. Chugani by e-mail in early 1998 to find out where the brain images had been published in the scientific literature so that I could read his study. He told me that they had not yet been published, but when the manuscript was accepted for publication, he would be happy to send me a copy of the paper. The images that appeared in *Newsweek* have not yet been published in a scientific journal (as of May 1999).

Why should we care?

As I said in Chapter 3, PET images are not Polaroids of the brain. Images are difficult to obtain and difficult to interpret. Images that show "pictures" of healthy versus neglected brains, like those published in *Newsweek,* can be particularly persuasive, allowing us to see, we might think, the permanent effects of bad childhood experiences on young brains. But before we are persuaded, we should be sure of exactly what it is we are seeing.

It is next to impossible to understand what you are seeing, given the way most brain-imaging studies are presented and described in the popular media. Sometimes it is possible to figure out what the images do and do not portray, if you can read the original paper in a scientific journal. The standards of scientific publishing require that the authors make clear what it was they did to whom and what happened, in sufficient detail to allow other interested scientists to repeat the experiment if they wished to do so. The report of what was done and what happened also constrains the interpretation that the author can justifiably give his data. When we cannot consult the original paper, or when there is no paper to consult, we are standing on shaky ground.

We are on shaky ground indeed with the *Newsweek* images of healthy versus neglected brains. Based on the *Newsweek* story, we do not know who the experimental subjects were or what was done in the experiment. I learned later from Dr. Chugani that the neglected brains were those of Romanian orphans. What does "neglected" mean here? Currently, PET scans are not tools that could be used to support a psychiatrist's or social worker's diagnosis of "neglect." Are these images of "resting" brains, brains engaged in the same cognitive task, or two brains engaged in two different cognitive tasks? What are we to make of the brain labeled "normal" in these images, against which the "neglected" brain is compared? Because PET scans require the injection of radioactive substances, researchers can only scan children for clinical and diagnostic reasons. They cannot do scans on normal healthy children. Thus, there had to be something wrong with the "normal" child if he or she had a PET scan done.

The pictures are nice, but we still need the thousand words (at least) if we are to be able to separate fact from fiction, science from PR. Preferably the thousand words should appear in a peer-reviewed scientific journal before they appear in *Newsweek* or are sent out in information and press kits to concerned parents and interested journalists and before we decide what the implications of a scientific study might be for policy and practice.

In the case of the Chugani-*Newsweek* PET scans, we have not seen the thousand words. What is more, we never will. At a May 22, 1999, scientific meeting on early brain development, sponsored by the Sackler Institute for Developmental Psychobiology, Chugani presented his PET images of neglected versus normal brains. He told the meeting participants that subsequent statistical analysis of his data revealed no significant differences between the brains of the neglected children and the brains of children in his "normal" comparison group. He has no plans to write up the data for publication in a scientific journal. It is a nonresult. No scientific journal would publish it. Unfortunately, it is also unlikely that *Newsweek, The Boston Globe,* or Kotulak's *Chicago Tribune* will ever report the final outcome of Chugani's neglected- versus normal-brain PET study.

When any of these four rules of thumb are violated in a science-based policy argument, you should suspect that the science is neither being treated appropriately nor being taken seriously. You can suspect that as far as that argument is concerned, serious science has not had a seat at the policy table.

Will the Circle Be Unbroken?

On the surface, the Myth of the First Three Years appears to be every early childhood advocate's dream. It seems to present a coherent, compelling argument that appeals to behavioral and biological science and that supports deeply held beliefs about early childhood. The Myth tells a coherent, compelling, easy-to-believe story, because it was constructed—hand-wired—to do just that. It presents a tight circle of mutually supporting beliefs, selected facts, and crafted interpretations that lead directly to the desired conclusion that the early years last forever. *Starting Points* set the tone. The report's starting assumption was that the first three years of life are critically important. According to the report, neuroscience tells us that the brain grows rapidly during those years. The time of rapid growth is *the* critical period in brain development. Enrichment is most effective and deprivation most damaging during the critical first three years of life.

This Myth tends to overlook or downplay any findings from behavioral or biological science or any interpretations of those findings that might complicate the story line. Developmental research that questions the causes, stability, and long-term consequences of early childhood experience is overlooked, as is the gaping chasm that exists between our theories of child development and brain science. The brain science used in the story is hardly new. And the genuinely new insight from brain science— that the brain remains highly plastic throughout life—is rarely mentioned. The Myth has more the quality of a legal defense or a forensic argument in the affirmative than of a scientific framework for an early childhood agenda. This renders the Myth dangerous in the policy realm and counterproductive in our attempts to develop a comprehensive scientific framework for understanding child and human development.

It is no accident that the chapter in Hillary Clinton's book *It Takes a Village* in which she reviews brain science and child development is entitled "The Bell Curve Is a Curve Ball." The Myth is intended to be an argument, based on neuroscience, that settles the nature-versus-nurture debate firmly on the side of nurture and that provides a scientific response to genetic determinism. In her Chapter 4, Mrs. Clinton wrote: "It has become fashionable in some quarters to assert that intelligence is fixed at birth, part of our genetic makeup that is invulnerable to change, a claim promoted by Charles Murray and the late Richard Herrnstein in their 1994 book, *The Bell Curve*. This view is politically convenient: if nothing can alter their intellectual potential, nothing need be offered to those who begin life with fewer resources or in less favorable environments. But research provides us with plenty of evidence that this perspective is not only unscientific but insidious." As one conservative critic pointed out, what is new in this liberal response to the unscientific *Bell Curve* argument is that familiar claims about the importance of early childhood education for cognitive development "are now being treated as a neuroanatomical fact."

As a policy argument, the greatest danger with the Myth is not that its political and ideological opponents will reject it; rather, the greatest danger is that they will embrace it. Remember, the Myth's basic premise is "How individuals function from the preschool years all the way through adolescence and even adulthood hinges, to a significant extent, on their experiences before age three." This is the basic infant-determinist premise that the Myth now attempts to present as a "neuroanatomical fact." The Myth rejects strong *genetic* determinism in favor of strong *early neural-environmental* determinism. The danger is that this enlightened response is still heavily deterministic. In fact, the Myth argument is but one rhetorical move away from an early-environmental version of the *Bell Curve*.

A critic could readily agree that the early years last forever and even willingly accept that this is a neuroanatomical fact. But the critic could then proceed to point out that federal early childhood programs like Head Start and Even Start, and most probably Early Head Start, are costly and that there is far from unanimous agreement on whether they are effective. The critic would not have a hard time finding some support for this premise, even among thoughtful, enlightened critics of early childhood programs. For example, recall Dale Farran's review of early childhood intervention programs that I mentioned in the previous chapter. Her conclusions were that the results were disappointing and that we had squandered resources on ineffective programs. So, the critic might argue, given our past track record, we should not be too optimistic about our chances of building better brains on a national scale. There might not, in fact, be much

we can do for disadvantaged children. They are not born genetically deficient, but the effects of their early environments are
quickly overwhelming. Given what we are likely to be able to do,
lost at birth or lost at 3 years old, it comes to the same unfortu-
nate end.

There is a second dangerous policy consequence that can follow if we take the Myth to heart. It can weaken our willingness
and resolve to aid older citizens. From a policy perspective, as
Ann Hulbert wrote in a *New Republic* article, "If children become
neurologically unresilient at an early age, then only intrusive and
expensive remedial efforts seem equal to the job. But if—or, let's
face it, when—these don't materialize, the case for subsequent
help is bound to seem weaker."

If we take the Myth to heart, it seems to follow that if we can't
help children by age 3, then we can't help them at all. Critical periods, windows slamming shut, loss of neural plasticity, and
cooked brains draw attention to the quiet crisis, but they do so
at a price. A strong and beguiling neural-environmental determinist argument for the critical importance of the first three years
weakens the policy case for supporting programs and interventions to assist older children and citizens. Why provide literacy
and education programs in prisons? Why recruit individuals
with low intelligence into the armed forces? It's too late to
help them.

Such a policy outcome is not a mere logical and theoretical
possibility. It is already happening. State legislatures are considering bills that would decrease or eliminate support for later
childhood interventions to invest those funds in birth-to-3 programs on the belief that this age range, when children are still
neurologically resilient, is the only time we have to build better
brains. These legislators believe the Myth, but are they friends
or foes of child and human development?

In her article, Hulbert zeroed in on the Myth's greatest weak-
ness: "alarmism risks being self-defeating." The danger is that
the Mythmakers may get what they ask for and more (in fact,
less) besides. In the final analysis, the Myth seems to be as unscientific and insidious as *The Bell Curve*. To move ahead posi-

tively, we have to abandon the Myth and break out of its tight circle of mutually supporting ideas.

I suggested earlier that the rest of us might best think critically about the Myth in terms of its premise—the early years last forever—and its statistic—neuro-anatomical "facts" about what happen to synapses early in development. As we have seen, the Myth's three neuro-biological strands do not provide neuroscientific support for its premise. We cannot currently bridge the gap between our theories of child development and developmental neurobiology. If anything, what we see in current neuroscience is the recognition that the brain is more plastic and malleable than brain scientists thought even ten years ago. Based on the neuroscience, we should give up the idea that children become neurologically unresilient at an early age. We should give up the statistic.

However, if we abandon the statistic, we move only from a strong neural-environmental determinist position to a strong environmental determinist position. If we still uncritically accept the Myth's premise, if we insist on continuing to view the world through the prism of birth to three, the unhappy consequences of the Myth still follow minus the neural accounting and synaptic reckoning.

Maybe the best way to escape the Myth's dangerous consequences is not only to reject its contrived neuroscientific trappings but also to critically question its basic deterministic premise. As comfortable as we find the premise, it may just not be the case that how we function throughout our lives is determined by the experiences we had during the first three years of life. We have encountered numerous reasons to be skeptical about this premise. *Starting Point* did not make a strong case for the permanent long-term effects of early experience on brain function. The evidence supporting the stability and predictive value of early attachment is not as strong as popular views suggest and as some scientists maintain. Thoughtful developmental scientists, like Sam Meisels, recognize that although the early years are interesting and important, what they are studying are not critical periods in the strict sense of time-limited learning, irreversible effects, and permanently bent twigs. We have seen how looking through the prism of the first three years tends to distort rather than enhance our view of children, brains, and social problems. What we know about the brain, childhood, and human development all suggest that the world is likely much more complicated than the Myth's premise allows.

Questioning the premise can help us break out of a conceptual web that weaves together so tightly our beliefs about the unique importance of the early years and our scientific theories of child development. Questioning the premise, even though some might think it heretical, can help us envision new possibilities and help us formulate questions, do research, and interpret its results in ways that would be difficult as long as we remain within the web.

As Ross Thompson wrote recently, "Developmental theorists have for so long regarded early experience as foundational for later development that the emergence of voices questioning the formative significance of infancy for later sociopersonality functioning sound jarring." But maybe there is more progress to be made, not by denying that infancy is important, but by realizing, like Jake, that a lot happens between birth and adulthood. We would no longer be burdened by determinism. And we might be able to develop new theories, perspectives, and notions about children and how to help them that would be more appropriate for twenty-first-century life. Appealing to neuroscience in attempts to transform a folk theory and cultural artifact into a biologically privileged worldview will do little to help children or parents.

The parents at the poolside, and other parents, who have been bewitched by the Myth, can relax. Those parents were doing exactly what they should have been doing. They were interacting with their child as she played. Brain science and the Myth have nothing new to say. Parents can talk, sing, and read to their babies. It can't and doesn't hurt. Brain science, even if we add in behavioral science, cannot tell us how to raise a scientifically correct child. Parents should realize that children thrive in a wide variety of physical and cultural environments and learn and benefit from experiences throughout their lives. Being highly critical and skeptical of any claims to the contrary is one of the best things parents could do for their children.

Being highly critical and skeptical of any claims to the contrary is also the best thing researchers, policymakers, and advocates could do for children. We would all do well to abandon the Myth.

NOTES

Chapter 1. Through the Prism of the First Three Years

page

1   She was doing: *Years of Promise: A Comprehensive Learning Strategy for America's Children* (New York: Carnegie Corporation of New York, 1996).

2   In spring 1996: Ibid.

2   About that time: "The IQ Gap Begins at Birth for the Poor," *Chicago Tribune*, April 28, 1996, Commentary sec. A, p. 19.

5   It was Hamburg: *Starting Points: Meeting the Needs of Our Youngest Children* (New York: Carnegie Corporation of New York, 1994).

9   "A child born today": J. E. Kyle, "First Three Years Critical to Children's Healthy Development," *Nation's Cities Weekly*, April 1997.

10   He told them, "Whether": M. A. Barton, "Reiner: Justice Starts in High Chair Not Electric Chair," *County News On-Line* 30(15) (1998), www.naco.org/pubs/cnews.

10   The source of the message: *Starting Points*; R. Shore, *Rethinking the Brain: New Insights into Early Development* (New York: Families and Work Institute, 1997).

11   As *Rethinking* put it: Shore, *Rethinking the Brain*, p. 20.

12   And I have, a bit: Ounce of Prevention Fund, "Starting Smart: How Early Experiences Affect Brain Development," 1996, www.bcm.tmc.edu/civitas/links/ounce.html.

13   "There is an urgent need": J. M. Nash, "Fertile Minds," *Time*, February 3, 1997, pp. 48–56.

13   Because, as some early: Ounce of Prevention Fund, "Starting Smart."

14   Children enter Head Start: *Starting Points;* J. Beck, "For Kids, Learning Doesn't Start in School," *Chicago Tribune,* May 3, 1997, p. 2; S. Begley, "Your Child's Brain," *Newsweek,* February 19, 1996, pp. 55–62; C. Russell, "Early Help Improves Learning Ability: Study Finds Long-Term Benefits in Educational Programs for Very Young Children," *Washington Post,* February 13, 1996, p. 7.

14   In *Inside the Brain:* R. Kotulak, *Inside the Brain: Revolutionary Discoveries of How the Mind Works* (Kansas City, Mo.: Andrews McMeel, 1996), pp. ix–x.

15   Kotulak explains why: Ibid., p. 186.

15   Too few synapses in the parents: "It Begins at Birth," *Chicago Tribune,* November 3, 1994, editorial, p. 2.

15   Children *belong* to the community: B. D. Perry, "Incubated in Terror: Neurobiological Factors in the 'Cycle of Violence,'" in J. D. Osofsky, ed., *Children in a Violent Society* (New York: Guilford Press, 1997), pp. 124–147.

16   Now research in brain development: F. Newman, "Brain Research Has Implications for Education," *State Education Leader* 15(1) (1997).

16   As one widely circulated: Kotulak, *Inside the Brain.*

16   Early, but not later: *Better Beginnings* (Pittsburgh; University of Pittsburgh, Office of Child Development, 1997); J. Barry, "Building a Better Brain: A Child's First Three Years Provide Parents Once-In-Lifetime Opportunity to Dramatically Increase Intelligence," *Miami Herald,* November 4, 1994, Living sec., p. F1; D. Viadero, "Brain Trust," *Education Week,* September 18, 1996, pp. 31–33.

16   Parents should make: Viadero, "Brain Trust," pp. 31–33.

17   "if they, or their baby sitter": M. Leonard, "A Guilt-Edged Occasion: It Would Seem that Today's Moms Have Much to Celebrate. Instead, Many Are Feeling Insecure and Torn," *Boston Globe,* May 11, 1997, Focus sec., p. E1.

17   Because we now know: S. Begley and P. Wingert, "Teach Your Parents Well: As Research Unlocks the Secrets of Babies' Brains, Families Have a Hard Time Learning the Lessons," *Newsweek,* April 28, 1997, p. 72.

17   Chugani, a pediatric neurologist: C. Leroux and C. Schreuder, "The Minds of Babes: A Lifetime of Problems Can Result If Newborns Lack Parental Support," *Chicago Tribune*, October 31, 1994, p. 1.

18   "Only 20 to 30 percent": Begley and Wingert, "Teach Your Parents Well."

18   Parents are told: J. Beck, "Smarter Children: The Earlier Kids Get Cognitive Attention, the Better," *Detroit Free Press*, April 16, 1997, p. 11A.

18   In Sandra Blakeslee's: S. Blakeslee, "Studies Show Talking with Infants Shapes Basis of Ability to Think," *New York Times*, April 17, 1997, p. D21.

21   According to the brain: H. R. Clinton, "Comfort and Joy," *Time*, February 13, 1997, p. 63; J. Healy, "Brainpower! You Can Make Smarter Babies," *Parents' Magazine*, December 1986, pp. 100–105. I Am Your Child, 1997, www.iamyourchild.org/start.html; C. Jabs, "Your Baby's Brainpower," *Working Mother*, November 1996, pp. 24–28; B. Kantrowitz, "Off to a Good Start: Why the First Three Years Are So Crucial to a Child's Development," *Newsweek*, Spring/Summer 1997, pp. 7–9; D. Rosenberg and L. Reibstein, "Pots, Blocks, and Socks," *Newsweek*, Spring/Summer 1997, pp. 34–35; R. Louv, "The Good Enough Parent: How Parents and Community Can Best Help Their Children's Brains Grow," 1997, www.kidscampaigns.org/Hot/Early/issues.html.

22   Much research remains: C. J. Shatz, "The Developing Brain," *Scientific American*, September 1992, p. 61.

22   From that time until: H. R. Clinton, *It Takes a Village* (New York: Touchstone Books, 1996), p. 57.

22   There is this shaping process: R. Kotulak, "Unlocking the Mind: Research Unraveling Mysteries of the Brain," *Chicago Tribune*, April 11, 1993, www.bcm.tmc.edu/civitas/new.html.

23   Although clearly much: C. A. Nelson and F. E. Bloom, "Child Development and Neuroscience," *Child Development* 68(5): 983 (1997).

23   But I believe this is: A. Scheibel, "Thinking About Thinking," *American School Board Journal* 184(2): 22 (1997).

24   "Research bears out": Shore, *Rethinking the Brain*, p. 37.

24   "In an environment rich": A. Barnet and R. Barnet, "Childcare Brain Drain?" *Nation* 264(18): 6 (1997).

24   In 1997, William Greenough: W. T. Greenough, "We Can't Just Focus on Ages Zero to Three," *Monitor* 28: 19 (1997).

Chapter 2. The Starting Points
page
29   According to Kagan: J. Kagan, *Three Seductive Ideas* (Cambridge, Mass.: Harvard University Press, 1998.)

31   According to Freud: S. Freud, *An Outline of Psychoanalysis* (New York: Norton, 1940), p. 45.

31   John Bowlby and Erik Erikson: J. Bowlby, *Attachment and Loss*, vol. 1 (New York: Basic Books, 1969); E. Erikson, *Childhood and Society* (New York: Norton, 1963).

31   Bowlby's theory: M. Ainsworth, "The Development of Infant-Mother Attachment," in B. Caldwell and H. Ricciuti, eds., *Review of Child Development Research* (Chicago: University of Chicago Press, 1973), pp. 31–94.; M. Ainsworth et al., *Patterns of Attachment* (Hillsdale, N.J.: Erlbaum Associations, 1978).

31   Harlow's experiments: H. F. Harlow, "The Nature of Love," *American Psychiatry* 13: 673–685 (1958); H. F. Harlow, "Love in Infant Monkeys," *Scientific American* 200(6): 68–74 (1959).

32   During these periods: B. Bloom, *Stablity and Change in Human Characteristics* (New York: Wiley, 1964).

34   All of the themes: S. Greenspan, *Infants in Multirisk Families: Case Studies in Preventive Intervention* (New York: International Universities Press, 1987).

34   The volume's introductory: J. S. Chall and A. F. Mirsky, "The Implications for Education," in J. S. Chall and A. F. Mirsky, eds., *Education and the Brain* (Chicago: University of Chicago Press, 1978), pp. 371–378.

35   As a working hypothesis: T. J. Teyler, "The Brain Sciences: An Introduction," in Chall and Mirsky, ed., *Education and the Brain*, p. 27.

35   He also used his theory: H. T. Epstein, "Growth Spurts During Brain Development: Implications for Educational Policy and Practice," in Chall and Mirsky, eds., *Education and the Brain*, p. 362.

35   Based on his theory: Ibid., p. 359.

35   The editors of *Education and the Brain:* Ibid., p. 360.

35   It persists in the popular: Chall and Mirsky, "The Implications for Education"; J. Levy, "Right Brain, Left Brain: Fact and Fiction," *Psychology Today* 19: 38 (1985).

36   The first popular: M. Ibuka, *Kindergarten Is Too Late!* (New York: Simon & Schuster, 1977).

37   Goldman-Rakic summarized research: P. S. Goldman-Rakic, "Setting the Stage: Neural Development Before Birth," in S. Friedman, K. Klivington, and R. Peterson, eds., *The Brain, Cognition, and Education* (Orlando, Fla.: Academic Press, 1986), p. 245.

37   Mark Rosenzweig from the University: M. R. Rosenzweig, "Multiple Models of Memory," in Friedman, Klivington, and Peterson, eds., *The Brain, Cognition, and Education*, pp. 347–372.

38   "At a time when": S. F. Chipman, "Integrating Three Perspectives on Learning," in Friedman, Klivington, and Peterson, eds., *The Brain, Cognition, and Education*, p. 226.

38   William Greenough, James Black, and Christopher Wallace's: W. T. Greenough, J. E. Black, and C. S. Wallace, "Experience and Brain Development," *Child Development* 58(3): 539–559 (1987).

38   Patricia Goldman Rakic's: P. S. Goldman-Rakic, "Development of Cortical Circuitry and Cognitive Function," *Child Development* 58: 601–622 (1987).

38   A 1985 *Children Today* article: "The Infant: Ready and Able to Learn," *Children Today* 14: 19 (1985).

39   In a 1986 article for *Parents' Magazine:* J. Healy, "Brainpower! You Can Make Smarter Babies," *Parents' Magazine*, December 1986, p. 100.

39   Healy discussed Marian Diamond's: M. Diamond, *Enriching Heredity* (New York: Free Press, 1988).

39   She elaborated on these ideas: J. Healy, *Your Child's Growing Mind: A Parent's Guide to Learning from Birth to Early Adolescence* (Garden City, N.Y.: Doubleday, 1987).

40   A May 31, 1985, editorial: "Investing in Early Learning Breaking the Chain," *Chicago Tribune,* May 31, 1985, editorial, p. 22.

40   The 1985 *Tribune* recommendation: J. Beck, "A Meeting of

Minds Between Neuroscientists and Educators Is First Step in Improving America's Schools," *Chicago Tribune,* October 17, 1997, p. 23.

40   According to the report: Heart Start: The Emotional Foundations of School Readiness, Arlington, Va.: Zero to Three: National Center for Clinical Infant Programs, 1992, p. 13.

40   In 1996, Kotulak's Pulitzer Prize: R. Kotulak, *Inside the Brain: Revolutionary Discoveries of How the Mind Works* (Kansas City, Mo.: Andrews McMeel, 1996).

41   As he says, "Society": Ibid., pp. ix–x.

43   In April 1994: *Starting Points: Meeting the Needs of Our Youngest Children* (New York: Carnegie Corporation of New York, 1994).

44   According to the report, the gap: Ibid., p. 6.

44   When *Starting Points:* "Nature and Nurture," *Boston Globe,* April 13, 1994, sec. 3, p. 16; M. A. Lev, "Youngest Kids Need Help, U.S. Told: Federal Government Urged to Focus on Their 1st 3 Years," *Chicago Tribune,* April 12, 1994, News sec., p. 1; J. Beck, "How Should We Care for All the Children Whose Parents Can't?" *Chicago Tribune,* April 24, 1994, Perspectives sec., p. 3; George Johnson, "Building a Better Brain for Baby," *New York Times,* Ideas and Trends sec., April 17, 1997; Judy Mann, "Children in Peril," *Washington Post,* April 15, 1994, p. E3; B. Vobejda, "6 Million of Nation's Youngest Children Face Developmental Risks," *Washington Post,* April 13, 1994, p. A3.

45   However, a *New York Times:* Johnson, "Building a Better Brain for Baby."

45   As a review of *Starting Points:* D. R. Neuspiel, "Starting Points: Meeting the Needs of Our Youngest Children" (book review), *Journal of the American Medical Association* 272(16): 1301 (1994).

45   Hamburg hoped that the report: Lev, "Youngest Kids Need Help, U.S. Told."

45   In an age of cynicism: D. Hamburg, "National Governors' Association," 1997, www.nga.org/HotTopics/ECIssuesPlenary.htm.

46   The story of how: J. Klein, "Clintons on the Brain," *New Yorker,* March 17, 1997, pp. 59–63; M. B. Tabor, "Actor-Director Focusing on Children," *New York Times,* August 6, 1997, sec. 1,

p. 8; R. Reiner, "National Governers' Association," 1997, www.nga.org/HotTopics/ECIssuesPlenary.htm.

47   He discovered *Starting Points:* R. Reiner, "National Governers' Association," 1997.

47   While the campaign was: S. Begley, "Your Child's Brain," *Newsweek,* Spring/Summer 1996, pp. 55–62.

48   Her article states, "Children": Ibid., p. 62.

49   It resulted in the publication: R. Shore, *Rethinking the Brain: New Insights into Early Development* (New York: Families and Work Institute, 1997).

49   The experts advised Galinsky: R. A. Thompson, "Brain Development Is Headline News," *Family Futures,* in press.

50   The organizer's chose: Ibid.

50   Also in 1996: H. R. Clinton, *It Takes a Village* (New York: Touchstone Books), 1996.

50   "But by age 10": Reiner, "National Governers' Association," 1997.

52   We have reached a point: S. S. Hall, "Test-Tube Moms," *New York Times Magazine,* April 5, 1998, pp. 22–28.

53   According to the survey: Zero to Three, "Public Awareness Campaign," 1997, p. 20, www.zerotothree.org/parent.html.

53   A famous study of Jerome Kagan's: J. Kagan, "The Infant: Ready and Able to Learn," *Children Today* 14: 19 (1985).

54   Yet by adolescence: J. Kagan, "Resilience in Cognitive Development," *Ethos* 3(2): 231–247 (1975).

54   Deborah Blum in *Sex on the Brain:* D. Blum, *Sex on the Brain* (New York: Viking, 1997); Robert E. Pool, *Eve's Rib: The Biological Roots of Sex Differences* (New York: Crown Publishers, 1994).

54   If we look more carefully: M. E. Lamb et al., "Security of Infantile Attachment as Assessed in the 'Strange Situation': Its Study and Biological Interpretation," *Behavioral and Brain Sciences* 7: 127–171 (1984); R. A. Thompson, "Early Sociopersonality Development," in W. Damon, ed., *Handbook of Child Psychology,* 5th ed. (New York: Wiley, 1998), pp. 25–104.

55   Some attachment theorists: L. A. Sroufe, "The Coherence of Individual Development," *American Psychologist* 38: 834–841 (1979).

55   In the late 1960s: M. D. Ainsworth and B. A. Wittig, "Attachment and Exploratory Behavior in One Year Olds in a Strange Situa-

tion," B. M. Foss, ed., *Determinants of Infant Behavior*, vol. 4 (London: Methuen, 1969), pp. 111–136.

56   There is considerable variation: Thompson, "Early Socioperson-ality Development."

56   At least two major research reviews: Ibid.; Lamb et al., "Security of Infantile Attachment as Assessed in the 'Strange Situation.'"

58   A 1984 review concluded: Lamb et al., "Security of Infantile Attachment as Assessed in the 'Strange Situation.'"

58   In a 1998 review: Thompson, "Early Sociopersonality Development."

61   In the November 15, 1998: T. Oliphant, "Tobacco Tax's Surprise Win," *Boston Sunday Globe*, November 15, 1998, p. D7.

61   The discovery that: S. Groginsky, S. Christian, and L. McConnell, "Early Childhood Initiatives in the States: Translating Research into Policy," *State Legislative Report* 23(14) (1998), www.ncsl.org/programs/cyf/ccslr.htm.

62   Contrary to the governor's: F. H. Rauscher, G. L. Shaw, and K. N. Ky, "Music and Spatial Task Performance," *Nature* 365 (6447): 611 (1993); F. H. Rauscher, G. L. Shaw, and K. N. Ky, "Listening to Mozart Enhances Spatial-Temporal Reasoning: Towards a Neurophysiological Basis," *Neuroscience Letters* 185(1): 44–47 (1995); F. H. Rauscher et al., "Music Training Causes Long-Term Enhancement of Preschool Children's Spatial-Temporal Reasoning," *Neurological Research* 19(1): 2–8 (1997).

63   Rauscher pointed out that: C. Holden, "Mozart for Georgia Newborns," *Science*, January 30, 1998, p. 663.

63   The pediatrician T. Berry Brazelton: T. B. Brazelton, *Boston Globe*, May 21, 1998, p. A19.

Chapter 3. Neural Connections: Some You Use, Some You Lose

page

66   The *Newsweek* Special Edition: B. Kantrowitz, "Off to a Good Start: Why the First Three Years Are So Crucial to a Child's Development," *Newsweek*, Spring/Summer 1997, p. 7.

66   You gently touch: S. Begley, "Your Child's Brain," *Newsweek*, February 19, 1996, p. 55.

66   Parents, educators, the babies' early experiences: D. Viadero, "Brain Trust," *Education Week*, September 18, 1996, p. 31.

67   Which keys are typed: Begley, "Your Child's Brain," p. 55.

67   As one prominent textbook: E. Kandel and J. Schwartz, *Principles of Neural Science*, 2nd ed. (New York: Elsevier, 1985), p. 743.

67   Or as Patricia Goldman-Rakic: P. S. Goldman-Rakic, J.-P. Bourgeois, and P. Rakic, "Synaptic Substrate of Cognitive Development: Synaptogenesis in the Prefrontal Cortex of the Nonhuman Primate," in N. A. Krasnegor, G. R. Lyon, and P. S. Goldman-Rakic, eds., *Development of the Prefrontal Cortex: Evolution, Neurobiology and Behavior* (Baltimore: Paul H. Brooks Publishing Co., 1997), p. 27.

71   Counting synapses in studies: P. Rakic et al., "Concurrent Overproduction of Synapses in Diverse Regions of the Primate Cerebral Cortex," *Science* 232: 232–235 (1986); P. Rakic, J.-P. Bourgeois, and P. S. Goldman-Rakic, "Synaptic Development of the Cerebral Cortex: Implications for Learning, Memory, and Mental Illness," in J. van Pelt et al., eds., *Progress in Brain Research*, 102: 227–243 (1994).

72   In 1975, Brian Cragg: B. G. Cragg, "The Density of Synapses and Neurons in Normal, Mentally Defective, and Ageing Human Brains," *Brain* 98: 81–90 (1975).

72   Two years later: J. S. Lund, R. G. Boothe, and R. D. Lund, "Development of Neurons in the Visual Cortex (Area 17) of the Monkey (*Macaca nemestrina*): A Golgi Study from Fetal Day 127 to Postnatal Maturity," *Journal of Comparative Neurology* 176: 149–188 (1977).

73   "It is perhaps important": Lund et al., "Development of Neurons in the Visual Cortex (Area 17) of the Monkey," p. 159.

73   Some of the best work: P. S. Goldman-Rakic, "Setting the Stage: Neural Development Before Birth," in S. Friedman, K. Klivington, and R. Peterson, eds., *The Brain, Cognition, and Education* (Orlando, Fla.: Academic Press, 1986), pp. 233–258; P. Rakic et al., "Concurrent Overproduction of Synapses in Diverse Regions of the Primate Cerbral Cortex," *Science* 232: 232–235 (1986); Rakic, Bourgeois, and Goldman-Rakic, "Synaptic Development of the Cerebral Cortex."

74   In the monkey: J-P. Bourgeois and P. Rakic, "Changing of Synaptic Density in the Primary Visual Cortex of the Rhesus Monkey from Fetal to Adult Stage," *Journal of Neuroscience* 13: 2801–2820 (1993).

74   Huttenlocher has reported results: P. R. Huttenlocher, "Synaptic Density in Human Frontal Cortex—Developmental Changes of Ageing," *Brain Research* 163: 195–205 (1979); P. R. Huttenlocher et al., "Synaptogenesis in Human Visual Cortex—Evidence for Synapse Elimination During Normal Development," *Neuroscience Letters* 33: 247–252 (1982); P. R. Huttenlocher and Ch. de Courten, "The Development of Synapses in Striate Cortex of Man," *Human Neurobiology* 6: 1–9 (1987); P. R. Huttenlocher and A. S. Dabholkar, "Regional Differences in Synaptogenesis in Human Cerebral Cortex," *Journal of Comparative Neurology* 387: 167–178 (1997).

75   He concluded: "This": Huttenlocher, "Synaptic Density in Human Frontal Cortex," p. 201.

77   A 1987 positron emission: H. T. Chugani, M. E. Phelps, and J. C. Mazziota, "Positron Emission Tomography Study of Human Brain Function Development," *Annals of Neurology* 22: 487–497 (1987).

81   According to *Starting Points: Starting Points: Meeting the Needs of Our Youngest Children* (New York: Carnegie Corportion of New York, 1994).

81   This part of the brain: R. Shore, *Rethinking the Brain: New Insights into Early Development* (New York: Families and Work Institute, 1997), p. 39.

82   In their original paper: Chugani, Phelps, and Mazziota, "Positron Emission Tomography Study of Human Brain Function Development," p. 496.

82   For Chugani, however: H. T. Chugani, "Positron Emission Tomography Scanning: Applications in Newborns," *Clinics in Perinatology* 20(2): 399 (1993).

83   "The evidence indicates": R. Kotulak, *Inside the Brain: Revolutionary Discoveries of How the Mind Works* (Kansas City, Mo.: Andrews McMeel, 1996), p. 20; *Better Beginnings* (Pittsburgh: University of Pittsburgh, Office of Child Development, 1997);

"The Latest on How the Brain Works," *NEA Today* 20(16): 9 (1997); "1997 Education Agenda/Priorities," Education Commission of the States, 1997, www.ecs.org/ECS/231e.htm.

83　"brain connections develop": "Neuroscience Research Has Impact for Education Policy," *Policy Brief*, Education Commission of the States, 1996, www.ecs.org/ECS/240e.htm.

83　In *It Takes a Village:* H. R. Clinton, *It Takes a Village* (New York: Touchstone Books, 1996), p. 58.

83　According to *Inside the Brain:* Kotulak, *Inside the Brain*, p. 186.

84　Another article tells us: "1997 Education Agenda/Priorities."

84　What happens, she concludes: J. Beck, "How Should We Care for All the Children Whose Parents Can't?" *Chicago Tribune*, April 24, 1994, Perspective sec. p. 3; J. Beck, "Bring Up Baby: Worthwhile Programs, Not Welfare Checks, Should Be Used to Help a Child Through Its First Three Years," *Chicago Tribune*, August 27, 1995, Perspective sec., p. 3; J. Beck, "A Meeting of Minds Between Neuroscientists and Educators Is First Step in Improving America's Schools," *Chicago Tribune*, October 17, 1997, p. 23; J. Beck, "Low Dosage of Mental Stimulation Crippling Our Kids," *Chicago Tribune*, November 3, 1994, Perspective sec., p. 31; J. Beck, "Smarter Children: The Earlier Kids Get Cognitive Attention, the Better," *Detroit Free Press*, April 16, 1997, p. A11; B. Kantrowitz, "Off to a Good Start: Why the First Three Years Are So Crucial to a Child's Development," *Newsweek*, Spring/Summer 1997, pp. 7–9; J. Barry, "Building Better Brain: A Child's First Three Years Provide Parents Once-in-Lifetime Opportunity to Dramatically Increase Intelligence," *Miami Herald*, November 4, 1994, Living sec., p. F1.

85　As early as 1975: B. G. Cragg, "The Density of Synapses and Neurons in Normal, Mentally Defective, and Aging Human Brains," *Brain* 98: 81–90 (1975).

85　Huttenlocher reported a case: Huttenlocher and Dabholkar, "Regional Differences in Synaptogenesis in Human Cerebral Cortex," p. 204.

85　It tends to conceal: T. L. Jernigan et al., "Maturation of Human Cerebrum Observed in Vivo During Adolescence," *Brain* 114: 2037–2049 (1991).

86 With fragile-X: T. A. Comery et al., "Abnormal Dendritic Spines in Fragile X Knockout Mice: Maturation and Pruning Deficits," *Proceedings of the National Academy of Sciences* 94(10): 5401–5404 (1997).

86 "From the time a child enters 1st grade": *Bridging the Gap Between Neuroscience and Education: Summary of a Workshop Cosponsored by the Education Commission of the States and the Charles A. Dana Foundation* (Denver: Education Commission of the States, 1996), p. 11.

87 In a 1986 article, Goldman-Rakic wrote: Goldman-Rakic, "Setting the Stage," p. 234.

88 In one experiment: M. Carlson, "Development of Tactile Discrimination Capacity in Macaca Mulatta. I. Normal Infants," *Developmental Brain Research* 16: 69–82 (1984).

89 The rate and extent of synapse formation: J-P. Bourgeois and P. Rakic, "Distribution, Density and Ultrastructure of Synapses in the Visual Cortex in Monkeys Devoid of Retinal Input from Early Embryonic Stages," *Abstracts of the Society for Neuroscience* 13: 1044 (1987).

89 In the increased sensory: J-P. Bourgeois, P. Jastreboff, and P. Rakic, "Synaptogenesis in the Visual Cortex of Normal and Preterm Monkeys: Evidence of the Intrinsic Regulation of Synaptic Overproduction," *Proceedings of the National Academy of Science USA* 86: 4297–4301 (1989).

89 This was clearly stated: Goldman-Rakic et al., "Synaptic Substrate of Cognitive Development," p. 38.

90 These studies examined: A. Diamond and P. S. Goldman-Rakic, "Comparison of Human Infants and Rhesus Monkeys on Piagets A-Not-B Task: Evidence for Dependence on Dorsolateral Prefrontal Cortex," *Experimental Brain Research* 74: 24–40 (1989); A. Diamond, "The Development and Neural Bases of Memory Functions as Indexed by the A-Not-B and Delayed Response Tasks in Human Infants and Infant Monkeys," in A. Diamond, ed., *The Development and Neural Bases of Higher Cognitive Functions* (New York: New York Academy of Sciences, 1990), pp. 267–317 (vol. 608 of the *Annals of the New York Academy of Science*).

90 Representational memory is: P. S. Goldman-Rakic, "Develop-

ment of Cortical Circuitry and Cognitive Function," *Child Development* 58: 604 (1987).

93   However, when he recomputed: Huttenlocher and Dabholkar, "Regional Differences in Synaptogenesis in Human Cerebral Cortex."

93   In their first study: Diamond and Goldman-Rakic, "Comparison of Human Infants and Rhesus Monkeys on Piagets A-Not-B Task."

94   However, she also found: Diamond, "The Development and Neural Bases of Memory Functions as Indexed by the A-Not-B and Delayed Response Tasks in Human Infants and Infant Monkeys."

94   Together these findings suggest: Diamond and Goldman-Rakic, "Comparison of Human Infants and Rhesus Monkeys on Piagets A-Not-B Task."

95   Chugani has both offered: A. DiCresce, "Brain Surges" (1997), www.med.wayne.edu/wmp97/brain.htm.

95   In an academic review: H. T. Chugani, "Neuroimaging of Developmental Nonlinearity and Developmental Pathologies," in R. W. Thatcher et al., eds., *Developmental Neuroimaging* (San Diego: Academic Press, 1996), p. 187.

96   *Rethinking the Brain* makes the same argument: Shore, *Rethinking the Brain*, p. 20.

96   They do not know: Goldman-Rakic et al., "Synaptic Substrate of Cognitive Development."

97   The prefrontal cortex contains: D. A. Lewis, "Development of the Prefrontal Cortex During Adolescence: Insights in Vulnerable Neural Circuits in Schizophrenia," *Neuropsychopharmacology* 16(6): 385–395 (1997); M. S. Keshavan, S. Aderson, and J. W. Pettegrew, "Is Schizophrenia Due to Excessive Pruning in the Prefrontal Cortex? The Feinberg Hypothesis Revisited," *Journal of Psychiatric Research* 28(3): 239–265 (1994); T. U. Woo et al., "Peripubertal Refinement of the Instrinsic and Associational Circuitry in Monkey Prefrontal Cortex," *Neuroscience* 80(4): 1149–1158 (1997).

98   Answers to these questions: Huttenlocher and de Courten, "The Development of Synapses in Striate Cortex of Man," p. 8.

98 And as Pasko Rakic states: P. Rakic, "Introduction," M. Gazzaniga, ed., *The Cognitive Neurosciences* (Cambridge, Mass.: MIT
Press, 1994), p. 123.

99 Goldman-Rakic cautions that: Goldman-Rakic, "Setting the
Stage, Neural Development Before Birth."

Chapter 4. Be All That You Can Be: Critical Periods
page

102 Are critical periods: S. Begley, "Your Child's Brain," *Newsweek*,
February 19, 1996, p. 58.

102 On the down side: S. Begley, "How to Build a Baby's Brain,"
Newsweek, Spring/Summer 1997, pp. 28–32.

103 One parent was quoted: C. Jabs, "Your Baby's Brainpower,"
Working Mother, November 1996, pp. 24–28.

105 For the zebra finch: M. Konishi, "A Sensitive Period for Birdsong
Learning," in B. Julesz and I. Kovacs, eds., *Maturational Windows
and Adult Cortical Plasticity* (Reading, Mass.: Addison-Wesley,
1995).

105 In contrast, Isabelle: S. Pinker, *The Language Instinct* (New York:
Morrow, 1994), p. 291.

106 These observations have led: R. A. Spitz, "Hospitalism: An Inquiry into the Genesis of Psychiatric Conditions in Early Childhood," *Psychoanalytic Studies of the Child* 1: 53–74 (1945).

106 Harry Harlow's research: H. F. Harlow, "Love in Infant Monkeys," *Scientific American* 200(6): 68–74 (1959); H. F. Harlow,
"The Nature of Love," *American Psychiatry* 13: 673–685 (1958).

106 Such long-term problems: James Tobin, "Is It Ever Too Late for
a Child's Brain to Grow?" *Parents' Magazine*, September 1997,
p. 54.

108 Greenough calls this kind: W. T. Greenough, J. E. Black, and
C. S. Wallace, "Experience and Brain Development," *Child Development* 58(3): 539–559 (1987).

111 For example, *Rethinking the Brain*: R. Shore, *Rethinking the
Brain: New Insights into Early Development* (New York: Families
and Work Institute, 1997), p. 20; R. Kotulak, *Inside the Brain:
Revolutionary Discoveries of How the Mind Works* (Kansas City,
Mo.: Andrews McMeel, 1996).

111   Children in the cities: Shore, *Rethinking the Brain*, p. 20.

112   Among these students: A. S. Palincsar and A. L. Brown, "Reciprocal Teaching of Comprehension Fostering and Comprehension-Monitoring Activities," *Cognition and Instruction* 1(2): 117–175 (1983); A. S. Palincsar, K. Ransom, and S. Derber, "Collaborative Research and the Development of Reciprocal Teaching," *Educational Leadership* 46: 37–40 (1988).

113   With continuing opportunities: T. Sticht, *The Military Experience and Workplace Literacy* (San Diego: Applied Behavioral and Cognitive Sciences, 1992).

113   After one year: S. A. Griffin, R. Case, and R. S. Siegler, "Rightstart: Providing the Central Conceptual Prerequisites for First Formal Learning of Arithmetic to Students at Risk for School Failure," K. McGilly, ed., *Classroom Lessons: Integrating Cognitive Theory and Classroom Practice* (Cambridge, Mass.: MIT Press, 1994), pp. 25–50.

114   Cognitive psychologist Geoffrey Saxe documented: G. B. Saxe, "Culture and the Development of Numerical Cognition: Studies Among the Oksapmin of Papua New Guinea," C. J. Brainerd, ed., *Children's Logical and Mathematical Cognition* (New York: Springer Verlag, 1982), pp. 157–176.

115   One important neuroscientific study: T. Elbert et al., "Increased Cortical Representation of the Fingers of the Left Hand in String Players," *Science* 270: 305–307 (1995).

118   Although the blind kittens: D. H. Hubel and T. N. Wiesel, "Functional Architecture of Macaque Monkey Visual Cortex," *Proceedings of the Royal Society of London B* 198: 1–59 (1977); D. H. Hubel, T. N. Wiesel, and S. LeVay, "Plasticity of Ocular Dominance Columns in Monkey Striate Cortex," *Philosophical Transactions of the Royal Society of London B* 278: 307–409 (1977); S. Levay, T. N. Wiesel, and D. H. Hubel, "The Development of Ocular Dominance Columns in Normal and Visually Deprived Monkeys," *Journal of Comparative Neurology* 19: 11–51 (1980).

119   This means, as more recent studies: J. C. Horton and D. R. Hocking, "An Adult-Like Pattern of Ocular Dominance Columns in Striate Cortex of Newborn Monkeys Prior to Visual Experience," *Journal of Neuroscience* 15(5): 1791–1807, 1996.

120   In monkeys, spontaneous: M. P. Stryker and W. A. Harris, "Binocular Impulse Blockade Prevents the Formation of Ocular Dominance Columns in Cat Visual Cortex," *Journal of Neuroscience* 6: 2117–2133 (1986).

120   Taken together, Hubel: D. Purves and J. W. Lichtman, "Elimination of Synapses in the Developing Nervous System," *Science* 210: 153–157 (1980); D. Purves and J. Lichtman, *Principles of Neural Development* (Sunderland, Mass.: Sinauer Associates, 1985).

121   Children with congenital: N. Daw, *Visual Development* (New York: Plenum Press, 1995), p. 127.

122   How best to use: R. S. Harweth et al., "The Effects of Reverse Monocular Deprivation in Monkeys. I. Psychophysical Experiments," *Experimental Brain Research* 74: 327–337 (1989).

122   when it comes to critical periods: E. Kandel and J. Schwartz, *Principles of Neural Science,* 2nd ed. (New York: Elsevier, 1985), pp. 292, 295.

124   This experiment tells us: J. C. Horton and D. R. Hocking, "Timing of the Critical Period for Plasticity of Ocular Dominance Columns in Macaque Striate Cortex," *Journal of Neuroscience* 17(10): 3684–3709 (1997).

124   Finally, reverse closure: Harweth et al., "The Effects of Reverse Monocular Deprivation in Monkeys. I. Pscyhophysical Experiments"; M. L. Crawford et al., "The Effects of Reverse Monocular Deprivation in Monkeys. II. Electophysiological and Anatomical Studies," *Experimental Brain Research* 74(2): 338–347 (1989).

125   So, like the monkeys: N. Daw, "Critical Periods and Strabismus: What Questions Remain?" *Optometry and Vision Science* 74(9): 690–694, (1997).

125   These studies show that: Ibid.; M. H. Birnbaum, K. Koslowe, and R. Sanet, "Success in Amblyopia Therapy as a Function of Age: A Literature Survey," *American Journal of Optometry and Physiological Optics* 54(5): 269–275 (1977); M. Oliver et al., "Compliance and Results of Treatment for Amblyopia in Children More Than 8 Years Old," *American Journal of Ophthalmology* 102(3): 340–345 (1986); B. Wick et al., "Anisotropic Amblyopia: Is the Patient Ever Too Old to Treat?" *Optometry and Visual Science*

69(11): 866–979 (1992); G. Woodruff et al., "Factors Affecting the Outcome of Children Treated for Amblyopia," *Eye* 8(pt. 6): 627–631 (1994).

127   Rob Reiner and the authors: R. Reiner, "National Governers' Association," 1997, www.nga.org/HotTopics/ECIssuesPlenary.htm.

128   He argued that a person: E. Lenneberg, *Biological Foundations of Language* (New York: Wiley, 1967).

129   Forty years ago, based on: W. Penfield and L. Roberts, *Speech and Brain Mechanisms* (Princeton, N.J.: Princeton University Press, 1959), p. 255.

129   Parents in other cultures: S. Pinker, *The Language Instinct* (New York: Morrow, 1994).

130   Kuhl and her colleagues: P. K. Kuhl et al., "Linguistic Experience Alters Phonetic Perception in Infants by 6 Months of Age," *Science* 255: 606–608 (1992); P. K. Kuhl, "Learning and Representation in Speech and Language," *Current Opinion in Neurobiology* 4(6): 812–822 (1994); P. K. Kuhl et al., "Cross-Language Analysis of Phonetic Units in Language Addressed to Infants," *Science* 277: 684–686 (1997).

131   James Flege has recently published: J. E. Flege, M. J. Munro, and I. R. A. MacKay, "Effects of Age of Second-Language Learning on the Production of English Consonants," *Speech Communication* 16(1): 1–26 (1995).

133   She found that native learners: E. L. Newport, "Maturational Constraints on Language Learning," *Cognitive Science* 14(1): 11–28 (1990).

133   Newport, along with Jacqueline Johnson: J. S. Johnson and E. L. Newport, "Critical Period Effects in Second Language Learning," *Cognitive Psychology* 21(1): 60–99 (1989).

134   Recent research has caused: E. Bialystok and K. Hakuta, *In Other Words: The Science and Psychology of Second-Language Acquisition* (New York: Basic Books, 1994); J. E. Flege, G.H. Yeni-Komshian, and S. Liu, "Age Constraint on Second-Language Acquisition" to appear in *Journal of Memory and Language*.

134   As adults, we continue: Pinker, *The Language Instinct*.

135   Betty Hart and Todd Risley found: B. Hart and T. Risley, *Meaningful Differences in the Everyday Experience of Young*

American Children (Baltimore: Paul H. Brookes Publishing Co., 1995).

135 They use a brain-recording technology: H. J. Neville, "Developmental Specificity in Neurocognitive Development in Humans," in M. Gazzaniga, ed., *The Cognitive Neurosciences* (Cambridge, Mass.: MIT Press, 1995), pp. 219–231.

136 Brain-imaging studies in normal humans: T. L. Jernigan et al., "Maturation of Human Cerebrum Observed in Vivo During Adolescence," *Brain* 114: 2037–2049 (1991).

140 Merzenich and Tallal ran experiments: M. M. Merzenich et al., "Temporal Processing Deficits of Language-Learning Impaired Children Ameliorated by Training," *Science* 271: 77–81 (1996); P. Tallal et al., "Language Comprehension in Language-Learning Impaired Children Improved with Acoustically Modified Speech," *Science* 271: 81–84 (1996).

140 Jay McClelland and his colleagues: J. L. McClelland, "Failures to Learn and Their Remediation: A Competitive Hebbian Account," in J. L. McClelland and R. S. Siegler, eds., *Mechanisms of Cognitive Development: Behavioral and Neural Approaches* (Mahwah, N.J.: Erlbaum, in press); B. D. McCandliss et al., "Eliciting Adult Plasticity: Both Adaptive and Non-Adaptive Training Improves Japanese Adults' Identification of English /r/ and /l/," *Society for Neuroscience Abstracts* 24 (1998).

142 One of Harry Chugani's: *State Education Leader* 15(1): 7 (1997); S. Begley, "Your Child's Brain," *Newsweek*, February 19, 1996, pp. 55–62; R. Kotulak, *Inside the Brain: Revolutionary Discoveries of How the Mind Works* (Kansas City: Andrews McMeel, 1996), p. 32.

Chapter 5. Club Med or Solitary: The Importance of Enriched Environments

page

144 Because, as we read: Ounce of Prevention Fund, "Starting Smart: How Early Experiences Affect Brain Development," 1996, www.bcm.tmc.edu/civitas/links/ounce.html.

145 In 1868, Charles Darwin noted: C. Darwin, *The Variation of Animals and Plants Under Domestication* (New York: O. Judd & Company, 1868).

145   Fifty years ago, Donald Hebb: D. O. Hebb, "The Effects of Early
       Experience on Problem Solving at Maturity," *American Psychol-*
       ogist 2: 737–745 (1947).

147   In the early 1970s: F. R. Volkmar and W. T. Greenough, "Rearing
       Complexity Affects Branching of Dendrites in the Visual Cortex
       of the Rat," *Science* 176: 1445–1447 (1972); W. T. Greenough,
       F. R. Volkmar, and J. M. Juraska, "Effects of Rearing Complexity
       on Dendritic Branching in Frontolateral and Temporal Cortex of
       the Rat," *Experimental Neurology* 41: 371–378 (1973).

147   Like Hebb's rats: J. M. Juraska, C. Henderson, and J. Muller,
       "Differential Rearing Experiences, Gender, and Radial Maze
       Performance," *Developmental Psychobiology* 17(3): 209–215
       (1984).

148   They found that: A. M. Turner and W. T. Greenough, "Differen-
       tial Rearing Effects on Rat Visual Cortex Synapses. I. Synaptic
       and Neuronal Density and Synapses per Neuron," *Brain Research*
       329: 195–203 (1985).

148   There are various views: J-P. Changeux and A. Danchin, "Selec-
       tive Stabilisation of Developing Synapses as a Mechanism for
       the Specification of Neuronal Networks," *Nature* 264: 705–712
       (1976).

148   Others believe the primary: P. S. Goldman-Rakic, J-P. Bourgeois,
       and P. Rakic, "Synaptic Substrate of Cognitive Development:
       Synaptogenesis in the Prefrontal Cortex of the Nonhuman Pri-
       mate," in N. A. Krasnegor, G. R. Lyon, and P. S. Goldman-Rakic,
       eds., *Development of the Prefrontal Cortex: Evolution, Neurobiology*
       and Behavior (Baltimore: Paul H. Brooks Publishing Co., 1997),
       pp. 27–47; P. Rakic, J-P. Bourgeois, and P. S. Goldman-Rakic,
       "Synaptic Development of the Cerebral Cortex: Implications for
       Learning, Memory, and Mental Illness," in J. van Pelt et al., eds.,
       Progress in Brain Research, 102: 227–243 (1994).

148   Greenough and his colleagues: W. T. Greenough and J. E. Black,
       "Induction of Brain Structure by Experience: Substrates for Cog-
       nitive Development," in M. Gunnar and C. A. Nelson, eds., *De-*
       velopmental Behavioral Neuroscience (Hillsdale, N.J.: Erlbaum
       Associates, 1992), pp. 155–200.

149   However, the increases they saw: Greenough et al., "Effects of

Rearing Complexity on Dendritic Branching in Frontolateral and Temporal Cortex of the Rat."

150 One-year-old rats that spent: W. H. Riege, "Environmental Influences on Brain and Behavior of Year-Old Rats," *Developmental Psychobiology* 4(2): 157–167 (1971).

150 In the late 1970s, scientists: H. B. Uylings et al., "Effects of Differential Environments on Plasticity of Dendrites in Cortical Pyramidal Neurons in Adult Rats," *Experimental Neurology* 62(3): 658–677 (1978); J. M. Juraska et al., "Plasticity in Adult Rat Visual Cortex: An Examination of Several Cell Populations After Differential Rearing," *Behavioral and Neural Biology* 29: 157–167 (1980); J. R. Connor et al., "Dendritic Length in Aged Rats' Occipital Cortex: An Environmentally Induced Response," *Experimental Neurology* 73: 827–830 (1981).

150 Running mazes increased: W. T. Greenough, J. M. Juraska, and F. R. Volkmar, "Maze Training Effects on Dendritic Branching in Occipital Cortex of Adult Rats," *Behavioral and Neural Biology* 26: 287–297 (1979).

150 In 1983, Greenough's group: E. J. Green, W. T. Greenough, and B. E. Schlumpf, "Effects of Complex or Isolated Environments on Cortical Dendrites of Middle-Aged Rats," *Brain Research* 264(2): 233–240 (1983).

150 In 1986, Greenough and Hwa-Min Hwang: H-M. F. Hwang and W. T. Greenough, "Synaptic Plasticity in Adult Rat Occipital Cortex Following Short-Term, Long-Term, and Reversal of, Differential Housing Environment Complexity," *Society for Neuroscience Abstracts* 12: 1579 (1986); W. T. Greenough and J. E. Black, "Induction of Brain Structure by Experience: Substrates for Cognitive Development."

150 Furthermore, the changes: W. T. Greenough, G. S. Withers, and B. J. Anderson, "Experience-Dependent Synaptogenesis as a Plausible Memory Mechanism," in I. Gormezano and E. A. Wasserman, eds., *Learning and Memory: The Behavioral and Biological Substrates* (Hillsdale, N.J.: Erlbaum Associates, 1992), pp. 209–229.

153 In these initial studies: M. M. Merzenich et al., "Somatosensory Cortical Map Changes Following Digit Amputation in Adult

Monkeys," *Journal of Comparative Neurology* 224: 591–605 (1984).

153   On the basis of these findings: J. H. Kaas, "The Reorganization of Sensory and Motor Maps in Adult Mammals," in M. Gazzaniga, ed., *The Cognitive Neurosciences* (Cambridge, Mass.: MIT Press, 1995), pp. 51–71.

154   T. P. Pons and his colleagues: T. P. Pons, "Abstract: Lesion-Induced Cortical Plasticity," in B. Julesz and I. Kovacs, eds., *Maturational Windows and Adult Cortical Plasticity* (Reading, Mass.: Addison-Wesley, 1995), pp. 175–178.

154   The happy result for the patient: V. S. Ramachandran, "Plasticity in the Adult Human Brain: Is There Reason for Optimism?" in B. Julesz and I. Kovacs, eds., *Maturational Windows and Adult Cortical Plasticity* (Reading, Mass.: Addison-Wesley, 1995), pp. 179–197.

155   Merzenich and his colleague: G. H. Recanzone and M. M. Merzenich, "Functional Plasticity in the Cerebral Cortex: Mechanisms of Improved Perceptual Abilities and Skill Acquisition," *Concepts in Neuroscience* 4(1): 1–23 (1993).

157   This new perspective: W. T. Greenough, J. E. Black, and C. S. Wallace, "Experience and Brain Development," *Child Development* 58(3): 539–559 (1987).

160   These interventions derive: C. Russell, "Early Help Improves Learning Ability: Study Finds Long-Term Benefits in Educational Programs for Very Young Children," *Washington Post,* February 13, 1996, p. 7.

160   We can raise children's intelligence: H. R. Clinton, *It Takes a Village,* (New York: Touchstone Books), 1996.

160   Third, Ron Kotulak emphasizes: R. Kotulak, *Inside the Brain: Revolutionary Discoveries of How the Mind Works* (Kansas City, Mo.: Andrews McMeel, 1996).

162   The first evaluation reported: C. T. Ramey and F. A. Campbell, "Preventive Education for High-Risk Children: Cognitive Consequences of the Carolina Abecedarian Project," *American Journal of Mental Deficiency* 88(5): 515–523 (1984).

163   The age 12 evaluation: F. A. Campbell and C. T. Ramey, "Effects of Early Intervention on Intellectual and Academic Achieve-

ment: A Follow-Up Study of Children from Low-Income Families," *Child Development* 65: 684–698 (1994).

165   The most current published evaluation: F. A. Campbell and C. T. Ramey, "Cognitive and School Outcomes for High-Risk African-American Students at Middle Adolescence: Positive Effects of Early Intervention," *American Educational Research Journal* 32(4): 742–772 (1995).

165   Based on this result: L. Seebach, "'Brain Research' May Lead Education Astray," *Rocky Mountain News,* April 15, 1998, p. B2.

167   Jeanne Brooks-Gunn was one: J. Brooks-Gunn et al., "Enhancing the Cognitive Outcomes of Low Birth Weight Premature Infants: For Whom Is the Intervention Most Effective?" *Pediatrics* 89(6): 1209–1215 (1992); J. Brooks-Gunn, F. Liaw, and P. K. Klebanov, "Effects of Early Intervention on Cognitive Function of Low Birth Weight Preterm Infancts," *Journal of Pediatrics* 120: 350–359 (1992); J. Brooks-Gunn et al., "Enhancing the Development of Low-Birthweight, Premature Infants: Changes in Cognition and Behavior over the First Three Years," *Child Development* 64: 736–753 (1993).

170   Campbell and Ramey are well aware: Campbell and Ramey, "Cognitive and School Outcomes for High-Risk African-American Students at Middle Adolescence."

170   As Campbell and Ramey noted: Campbell and Ramey, "Effects of Early Intervention on Intellectual and Academic Achievement."

170   In interpreting the IHDP results: J. Brooks-Gunn et al., "Enhancing the Development of Low-Birthweight, Premature Infants."

171   As Ramey and his wife: C. T. Ramey and S. L. Ramey, "Early Intervention and Early Experience," *American Psychologist* 53(2): 109–120 (1998).

173   Both *Starting Points* and *Rethinking: Starting Points: Meeting the Needs of Our Youngest Children* (New York: Carnegie Corporation of New York, 1994), p. 8; R. Shore, *Rethinking the Brain: New Insights into Early Development* (New York: Families and Work Institute, 1997).

173   A great deal of money: D. C. Farran, "Another Decade of Intervention for Children Who Are Low Income or Disabled: What Do We Know Now?" in J. Shonkoff and S. Miesels, eds., *Hand-*

book of Early Childhood Intervention, 2nd ed. (New York: Cambridge University Press, in press), p. 32.

176   We saw one excellent example: J. T. Bruer, *Schools for Thought: A Science of Learning in the Classroom* (Cambridge, Mass.: MIT Press, 1993); K. McGilly, ed., *Classroom Lessons: Integrating Cognitive Theory and Classroom Practice* (Cambridge, Mass.: MIT Press, 1994), pp. 25–50.

177   Both these IQ measures: S. Cahan and N. Cohen, "Age Versus Schooling Effects on Intelligence Development," *Child Development* 60: 1239–1249 (1989); S. J. Ceci and W. M. Williams, "Schooling, Intelligence, and Income," *American Psychologist* 52(10): 1051–1058 (1997).

177   Tom Sticht gave me: T. G. Sticht et al., *Cast-Off Youth: Policy and Training Methods from the Military Experience* (New York: Praeger, 1987), pp. 57–59.

178   In the early childhood literature: W. Herbert, "Politics of Biology," *U.S. News and World Report*, April 21, 1997, pp. 72–80.

179   In an obituary: D. H. Warren, "Austin H. Riesen (1913–1996) Sensory Deprivation Pioneer," *APS Observer* 9(6): 29,31 (1966).

Chapter 6. What's a Mother (or the Rest of Us) to Do?
page

188   As Floyd Bloom, a former president: S. S. Hall, "Test-Tube Moms," *New York Times Magazine*, April 5, 1998, pp. 22–28.

189   Reading is one way: S. Scarr, "New Research on Day Care Should Spur Scholars to Reconsider Old Ideas," *Chronicle of Higher Education*, August 8, 1997, p. A48.

189   The study, which included: NICHD Early Child Care Research Network, "The Effects of Infant Child Care on Infant-Mother Attachment Security: Results of the NICHD Study of Early Child Care," *Child Development* 68(5): 860–879 (1997).

190   "Once we took into account": M. Weinraub, "Testimony by Marsha Weinraub, Ph.D., on the NICHD Study of Early Child Care," *APA Science Advocacy*, 1997, www.apa.org/ppo/weinraub.html.

190   The NICHD study also looked: NICHD Early Child Care Research Network, "Mother-Child Interaction and Cognitive Outcomes Associated with Early Child Care: Results of the

NICHD Study," *Biennnial Meeting of the Society for Research on Child Development, Washington, D.C.,* 1997, www.sfchild net.org/data/nichd.htm.

192   Upper- and middle-income families: Weinraub, "Testimony by Marsha Weinraub, Ph.D., on the NICHD Study of Early Child Care."

192   However, for you, as for most: S. Scarr, "Why Child Care Has Little Impact on Most Children's Development," *Current Directions in Psychological Science* 6(5): 147 (1997).

194   The crusade's fundamental premise: *Starting Points: Meeting the Needs of Our Youngest Children* (New York: Carnegie Corporation of New York, 1994), p. 3.

196   If they were aware: J. Kagan, *Three Seductive Ideas* (Cambridge, Mass.: Harvard University Press, 1998).

197   "Because you can see": J. M. Nash, "Fertile Minds," *Time,* February 3, 1997, p. 56.

198   As Ed Zigler, director: D. Viadero, "Brain Trust," *Education Week,* September 18, 1996, pp. 31–33.

200   For example, we should be: S. Begley, "Your Child's Brain," *Newsweek,* February 19, 1996, pp. 55–62.

200   One study on the effects: F. H. Rauscher, G. L. Shaw, and K. N. Ky, "Music and Spatial Task Performance," *Nature* 365(6447): 611 (1993); F. H. Rauscher, G. L. Shaw, and K. N. Ky, "Listening to Mozart Enhances Spatial-Temporal Reasoning: Towards a Neurophysiological Basis," *Neuroscience Letters* 185(1): 44–47 (1995); F. H. Rauscher et al., "Music Training Causes Long-Term Enhancement of Preschool Children's Spatial-Temporal Reasoning," *Neurological Research* 19(1): 2–8, 1997.

201   This fact is cited in: J. M. Nash, "Fertile Minds," *Time,* February 3, 1997, p. 51; Ounce of Prevention Fund, "Starting Smart: How Early Experiences Affect Brain Development," 1996, www.bcm.tmc.edu/civitas/links/ounce.html.

202   The special *Newsweek* issue: S. Begley, "How to Build a Baby's Brain," *Newsweek,* Spring/Summer 1997, p. 30.

202   Apparently referring to these images: R. Kotulak, *Inside the Brain: Revolutionary Discoveries of How the Mind Works* (Kansas City, Mo: Andrews McMeel, 1996), p. 47.

206   But research provides us: H. R. Clinton, *It Takes a Village* (New York: Touchstone Books, 1996), p. 59.

206   As one conservative critic: R. Ponnuru, "Child's Play," *National Review*, May 19, 1997, p. 26.

206   For example, recall: D. C. Farran, "Another Decade of Intervention for Children Who Are Low Income or Disabled: What Do We Know Now?" in J. Shonkoff and S. Miesels, eds., *Handbook of Early Childhood Intervention*, 2nd ed. (New York: Cambridge University Press, in press), p. 32.

207   From a policy perspective: A. Hulbert, "Brainstorms (New Portrayals of Childhood, Parenting, and Kids' Neurobiology)," *New Republic* 216(21): 46 (1997).

209   As Ross Thompson wrote recently: R. A. Thompson, "Early Sociopersonality Development," in W. Damon, ed., *Handbook of Child Psychology*, 5th ed. (New York: Wiley, 1998), p. 26.

INDEX